SPIRAL FORECASTING

NATURE'S INSIDE TRACK
TO FUTURE SUCCESS

NAHU LANHAM

NATURE SURVIVES BY PREDICTION

Living matter thrives by forecasting, i.e. predicting the feasibility of its own probable future order and survival. The holographic self-generating observer, feedback loop from micro to macrocosm implies self-determination through information assimilation. As such, this process of forecasting, enigmatically, has its flower in the past and its roots deeply entrenched in the future. Indeed, it is a self-regulating, oscillatory principle governing the Whole and its Parts.

Nahu 2015

CONTENTS

INTRODUCTION

The natural world around us is full of wonder and mystery, from the vast expanse of the universe to the smallest particles of matter. As humans, we have long been fascinated by the patterns and rhythms that underlie our world and have dedicated centuries to understanding them. Despite this relentless pursuit of knowledge, there are still many secrets that remain hidden from our view.

However, what if we told you that there is a way to unlock the secrets of the universe, and use them to predict the future with an almost mystical accuracy? What if we could tap into a code hidden within the very fabric of nature itself, one that holds the key to unlocking insights and foresight into the world around us?

This is the groundbreaking premise of "Spiral Forecasting - Nature's Inside Track to Future Success", authored by the intuitively gifted mind of a professional psychic for over forty years. In this book, readers embark on a journey of discovery into the hidden patterns and rhythms of the natural world. Drawing on years of investigation and research into the cosmic order that governs everything from the far-flung galaxies to the double helix within our genetic code, the book presents a compelling case for harnessing these patterns to make better decisions and navigate the complex challenges of our modern world.

By examining the principles of spiral forecasting, the author shows readers how they can tap into the power of nature to gain an edge in all areas of life. With examples drawn from the worlds of science, business, and everyday life, the book provides practical tools and insights for anyone seeking to unlock the secrets of the universe and gain an inside track to future success.

Through "Spiral Forecasting", readers will learn how to tap into the power of natural patterns and rhythms to create a brighter future for themselves and those around them. They will gain a deeper understanding of the interconnectedness of all things and the ways in which we can harness the power of nature to achieve our dreams and goals.

In conclusion, "Spiral Forecasting" is a must-read for anyone seeking to unlock the secrets of the universe and gain an inside track to future success. It is a book that will inspire, enlighten, and empower readers to tap into the power of nature and create a better future for themselves and the world around them. So, join us on this incredible journey of discovery and let the secrets of the universe reveal themselves to you.

UNCERTAINTY AND THE QUEST TO KNOW THE FUTURE

"The essence of life is suffering," said Buddha, implying that the work of Buddhism is to relieve that suffering through right mindfulness and the pursuit of enlightenment." Author's interpretation of the essence of Buddha's Teachings

Chance and the Dirty Low Down

Sir Arthur Eddington once wrote, "If I let my fingers wander idly over the keys of a typewriter, it might happen that my screed will make an intelligible sentence. If an army of monkeys were strumming on typewriters, they might write all the books in the British Museum." The statement, in its implied content, clearly casts doubt that random chance or happenstance could produce all the wonders that we see about us, suggesting, albeit indirectly, that order must arise according to some kind of intelligent design.

Not by coincidence, both intelligent design and chance or 'accidental order' by their descriptions, reflect two perspectives: one positive and the other negative concerning the nature of the process and its meaning in the creation of the universe. Creationism is at its roots positive, since it allows for intentional design of a higher order, although it doesn't accept a spontaneous creative process whereby order comes about through the evolutionary necessitates of the system. Chance, or accidental order, which science seems to believe to be the basis of life in the universe, on the other hand, apparently is negative in that it asserts that all order comes about by chance design or guidance of any sort from a premeditated plan.

Dwelling on the probability of accidental order without plan, Sir Arthur Eddington unconsciously presented some of my own unspoken queries. In short, that the two foregoing perspectives can best be understood in the metaphor of a half empty or half full glass. For example, both represent positive or negative beliefs about the meaning or lack of meaning one might place on the nature of life and the origin of order in the universe. In essence, these two perspectives question whether we are to believe that a) life is the purposeless byproduct of random probabilities in a chance-bound chaotic universe, (this is the half empty view) or b) that it was premeditated, i.e., a carefully planned, albeit *calculated* risk, perhaps better understood at some unknown 'bigger picture' level by some presumably higher consciousness. Of course, the latter view presents the half full perspective.

In short, everyone would like to know once and for all - is there an intelligent though unseen pattern leading to order rather than the current view of chance presented by scientists; many who openly admit to being biased skeptics? Most assuredly, one cannot help but wonder, as did Eddington, would we be here even if there wasn't a grand plan by which order and biogenic life came about? If it is a predetermined and predictable plan, therefore, would it not also necessitate the presence of some unseen grand designer who conceived that design or at least some guiding principle by which it was implemented?

Indeed, it is hard to imagine such precise and complex order arising without a thinker who created what appears to be a well thought out, orchestrated pattern. Should the scientific assumption prove wrong, it would establish without question that both the existence of a thinker or at least a 'pattern-behind-matter' gave birth to a plan - which is unquestionably a logical probability. This concept of creation was embraced by no less than one of the greatest philosophers in history, better known as Plato. Thus, this concept deserves some consideration, does it not?

But whether we believe in a planner or a mute principle, more importantly: if there is an orchestrated innate design with a purpose, the next question one might ask would be: can we avail ourselves to that plan and thereby exercise a greater modicum of control over both our collective as well as individual fate? If so, how much control and by what method? Impatient to put this innate wisdom to use, the thought would thusly drive us forward to seek proof of its source, nature, and clockwork mechanic.

For the author, one central question stood out clearly: during change, how did life maintain order and overcome dissolution and chaos? Not surprisingly, the answer pointed in the direction of the *accumulation of mass via the storage of information*. In my own search I have become more certain that order does indeed triumph through cumulative replication, i.e., the recycling of information into progressively greater and greater adaptive units of wholeness. In fact, that is what the DNA process is all about. Information stored in this way produces incremental mass-accumulating growth via calculated spurts of energy or data-waves, which perpetuates life beyond any temporary stasis point. Moreover, it does all this according to a plan with a predetermined goal somewhere at a future point that ensures that life persists through the present and beyond.

What is even more startling is that this process begins quite early in the development of the cosmos via the interstellar spiral galaxies and the compounding accumulation of mass. Over time this process is transferred into ongoing units of molecular, chemical and biological accumulations we know as biogenic growth. Moreover, the process doesn't stop there, it continues through social evolution as tribes becomes nations and transform into countries and finally, into complex global communities. What we are witnessing is local order with a global purpose or consciousness. Put simply: Part with an awareness of a greater Whole, although that Greater Whole may not be conscious to the Part.

If we look deeper, we discover that the principle of accumulation and replication between Whole and Part through evolution has its roots in an over-arching, dualistic cosmic spiral principle. In its essence the creative impulse came to be associated with Eros or love, the drive to survive, or *life*, that which triumphs over Thanatos; the tendency toward dissolution and *death*. Indeed, in this pulsating, revolving loop of wholeness the dual poles of existence and non-existence can be seen as two parts of one process. Now here's the kicker: how well we comprehend this *process of duality* as a species can be seen as our durability through time and this is true both individually and collectively. In an ongoing manner each singular effort to survive eventually compounds as a triumph for the human species over the rigors and uncertainty of change in a mysterious universe of infinitely changing probabilities.

In short, any serious efforts to reconcile this uncertainty reveal society's successful efforts to perfect the best stress-reducing answers. For example, intellectually, the best philosophical examples could be seen in the various attempts both religion and science use to convince us of their verbose claims to reduce uncertainty and bring about certainty. On one pole, religion strives to achieve this through prayerful communication to Source while on the other, science proudly displays its success through logic and repeatable mathematical principles and scientific experimentation. In a battle of wits, each hotly remains at odds to deliver the final answer to these issues.

For instance: on the scientific side we all are familiar with the local weather report presented by a meteorologist who tells us that there is a 30% chance of rain, which seems to suggest that there is a greater chance it will not rain than that it will. This is an exercise in the half empty analogy. If it does rain the next day, we curse him because we got soaked for placing our faith in his predictive wizardry. Relegating our future to the hands of a trained meteorologist we are trusting science and technology to anticipate what we cannot, that is, look out for us as we move onward through changing, future weather conditions. In doing so, we defer to their *predictive acumen*, shall we say, and confidently leave our umbrella behind on our daily walk. Returning home soaked and dismayed, we complain that the new gods of science are no better at predicting our future for us than the old.

Strangely, we have returned to the ancient worldview of the gods shared by the Greco-Romans. For them the immortals on Mt. Olympus actually were not so omniscient either, but in reality, shared our limitations. Human-like in their perspectives, they appeared unfortunately myopic in their prognostication of the future yet, curiously, still occupied a lofty status over other earthly denizen. Now skeptical, one would speculate that if the new gods of science cannot accurately predict the weather from one day to another, perhaps that explains why they can't seem to determine something as small and supposedly simple as the simultaneous position and momentum of an individual particle.

Disenchanted we turn to our scryers for certainty through prediction, searching for some indication of perceptual omniscience if not divine intervention. Yet we are left to discover, in most cases, spiritual leaders who present a dire picture of the future, and reality in general. In fact, most simply suggest suffering is to remain our lot while here on earth. For example, even Gautama Buddha was known to insist that life is basically all about continuous suffering, thereby predicating in this statement that's what we're to anticipate from now on.

However, he did go on to say that the only way to escape this inevitable end is by giving up our materialistic human ego's thereby transcending the Maya of suffering by way of the meditative path. Seen from one perspective, Buddha's reasoning appears optimistic, proposing freedom from the stress of existence. Yet, on the other hand, his teaching also evinces pessimistic overtones. For example, it implies that without liberation from the struggle of existence, life will remain interminably intolerable; suggesting life is inexorably bound to a future of struggling *unless we are willing let go and give up on it,* so to speak.

The end result of this perceptual winnowing of the spiritual wheat from the material chafe, so to speak, is the ostensive attainment of liberation from the attendant stress of investing in the illusion; a contemporary term for suffering. Hence, enlightenment leads to the acquisition of a positive new world view. This change in perspective requires detachment from the material illusion of the old-world view and the reorientation to a new one free of analytical fragmentation. In short, the apparent unspoken goal of dharma as implied by the Eight Jhana's or Pali Canons, (similar to the Ten Commandments in Christianity) is a total immersion into the Buddhist way of being in the world. In this view one must wholly divest themselves of all the former beliefs and habits that lead to the establishment of the illusion. Suggesting that without adopting the Buddhist process of disassociation, we will be trapped forever in the suffering that comes with the illusion.

Spiritual paths not withstanding - frustrated by what seems to be a pessimistic alternative, many reach a point where they feel that the only way out of the torment is to suck it up and admit they're incarcerated in a fixed reality, changeable only by first relinquishing the most prized possession – the subjective epitome of our presence here – our Selves. Once the Self is relinquished along with the thinking process, we are to devote our life to selflessness less we continue to be vainly driven by the illusion that physical happiness comes through the attachment and acquisition of material things. What we are left with in this final analysis are the choices that determine our direction through the material maze. Instead of a selfish path leading inexorably toward misery, we must adopt the selfless –

perhaps fancifully hoping that someone in the position of leadership will make the right decisions for the good of the group, since there is always an outside chance that our individual perception of what lies ahead is wrong.

In this unconscious act of giving up on the illusion, as it is termed, we unwittingly adopt a belief that suggests life is like a negatively stacked deck of cards with a predictably bad outcome. A certain catch-22 -- once adopting this interpretation, we are stuck with living our life according to its rules. But the question remains, does this have to be the only offer available on the table of prediction? Why can't we take the best of what a philosophical principle has to offer and let the rest fall by the way? Like the old saying goes, buying the milk doesn't always mean that we must also buy the cow, nor the whole farm, for that matter. There are, of course, some meditation practitioners who inform us that meditation is enough…if we are willing to practice for interminably long hours to achieve the discipline leading to total self-awareness.

THE UPSHOT OF THIS LOW DOWN

Meanwhile, in the urban apartment of our average individual, Joe Schmo is facing mid-week and still out of a job. He sits at home in his shorts and undershirt on the couch hoping those papers he filled out for government assistance and food stamps will pan out, and possibly unemployment compensation, if the latter doesn't come through and if he's eligible. When the mailman comes and goes, his anxiety heightens and he thinks of selling that old Chevy from his youth still parked out there in the garage. With anticipation boiling up in his gut, he contemplates going down to the Employment Office for the third time this week, knowing he'll probably sit there for hours and when his turn comes up, find out that the only job available are crappy fast-food service, car wash attendant or a dish washing job no one can live on let alone feed a family. Plus, they're all on the other side of town and already ten people were sent out hours before him. Oh, well, he couldn't afford the gas anyways!

Some people worry about how they're going to feed and care for that little baby boy, and if they're extra unlucky, bitterly recall that spending grandfather's inheritance money on a new home, car and that 'must do' trip to the Caribbean, (because he deserved it) when mama warned him it was time to put those bucks into higher schooling. But somehow, he thought, with the current state of the employment market, he'd have no trouble landing a job in a Coca

Cola bottling factory nearby. With grim regrets he remembers that was last year and this year they had to lay off people because sales had fallen and there was a surplus of young people looking for jobs. Now he's flat broke, drunk and pissed to boot. In his befuddled state of mind, he regretfully wishes he could have predicted the future. But for all the gusto placed into reading books borrowed from the library on beginner's luck, precognition and the secret formula for success, regardless of how hard he studied and tried to apply the magic formula - nothing seemed to work.

Undaunted, he continues his fantasy, secretly planning to win the Power Ball Lottery, but gets a head's up from a pal that the odds of winning are about 1 out of 146,000,000. Chest fallen but unbowed he decides to blow his secret stash in one big wad on numbers 3 14 19 18 and 13 straight across board in bingo (cause that's what your grandma did and she won) with money hustled from good old uncle Chester; you know the one on disability. Before he play's he tosses a neatly folded Benjamin hidden in his shoe to a lady in a scarf who makes mystical guesses under a pyramid based on the magic of his Sun sign – yeah, that arcane data was garnered down at the market on Saturday. After all, she looked like the real McCoy in her tent reeking with the smell of Rajneesh incense and something curiously smelling of opium. Turns out that regardless whether he was the seventh of a lucky seventh son born in Pisces on the auspicious cusp of Aquarius in a numerically perfect year on a particularly magical day, with all his planetary houses in perfect alignment with that odd cross in the middle of his hand, he didn't win and now he's flat broke. What make's matter's even worse is his extra secret wish didn't transpire – you know that one he never told anyone about but his dog – that money was going to fall out of the sky from a plane if he believed it strong enough – nope that didn't happen either.

Outside of selling dope and stealing he realizes with near suicidal rancor that there's no way he can reliably discern what's going to happen tomorrow. Bitterly he concedes that he'll just have to wing it and trust the universe that God at some point will be coming through for him. Maybe, just maybe if he spends a little time on his knees praying and doesn't forget to do 40 Hail Mary's and prays to St. Christopher regularly, god will give him the break in life he deserves

Success and the Probability of Obtaining It

Looking at some of Joe Schmo's cold, hard but questionable *facts* you admit that you find yourself befuddled with the chaos about you but reluctant to give up on the possibility of predicting your future with certainty. Reflecting, you realize you're obsessed with getting ahead but furtively searching for an answer to relieving the stress of an unpredictable future. Disgusted with your lot you look for something you can believe in, definitely an alternative to cold, hard chance and random probabilities. Wishing for something to arise, you pick up a copy of the Wall Street Journal. Spilling through the articles you find yourself searching for a company or idea that can predict the stock market trends.

Pondering the slew of data, you read how one company after another swears, they know exactly why stocks rose or fell the week before. Considering each interpretation, you're left shaking your head. Essentially, you're left feeling unsatisfied with the assurances and wistfully mutter to yourself that if these guys could accurately tell us exactly why stocks rose and fell last week, then how come they can't come up with a dependable method that predicts the market with certainty? Now that would be something, because if they did we'd all be rich! Hoping the universe might have heard you and finally is willing to give you the break of a life time, the next week with bated breath, you again search for the results of these brilliant prognostication methods and discover with deepening dismay that not one proves accurate. It seems they all do a bang-up job of predicting through hindsight, it's their foresight that lacks!

Another thing that dismays you is that the journal features a mathematician who offers advice on the odds of winning based on the statistics of probability theory. You're back to square one. Like the others, he speculates there are no simple criteria for determining failure or success; statistically speaking. Something like trying to determine an electron's position and momentum at the same time; nearly impossible. But it is feasible if you know some the parameters. For example, again, it's all about big figures, or Large Number Theory. LNT is a statistical probability law which, when reduced to bare essentials, seems to suggest that if you gamble enough, you're bound to inevitably win sometime - or at least that's your interpretation for now - and you're sticking to it.

Well, hello! Isn't this the gist of addiction - the idea that somehow, you're bound to win *sometime*, so why not continue every day because chances are, you're going to win! Resisting further cynicism yet curious, you pause to consider the implications. Let's see, the law tells us that the odds against losing increase with the number of attempts. If that true, and it seems that it is, than the chances of winning could simply increase if we enlist a greater number of players. That's easy, so all a person has to do is find enough idealistic people with money and time to invest and, butta bing, butta boom - everyone's a winner. Your mind races and you begin thinking that if you're smart, you'd get all your friends together – but then you remember most of them are out of work too!

However, on the plus side of this statistic, employees in some companies have been winning more lotteries by enlisting larger numbers of investors and being careful to bet on numerical variability, which means using different large number combinations and buying a great many tickets; thus, the chances of winning exponentially increases and the odds against losing reduced. Nonetheless, though the proceeds for each individual were more certain and impressive compared to their singular chances of winning, one problem did arise – like the old adage warns - too many chefs spoil the porridge. Disputes broke out over dispensation of monies and in some cases, lottery sharks swam among them and downright theft occurred, not to mention the actual cash won is comparatively reduced.

With plenty of time on your hands to think things through, gradually, a new vision begins to unfold in your mind. In its misty outlines you see the vestiges of a larger number principle emerging. It tells you that you can increase the certainty by reducing the odds, and this is a **REALLY IMPORTANT POINT**. Something about the spiral going into this 'bigger picture' implies that 'cubing' up the probabilities in a batch, so to speak, is more apt to snowball into quick positive results than others. Even LNT dashes the doubts in an average poker game, where odds of getting a winning hand, such as a royal spade flush compared to five random non-winning cards is exactly the same – 1 out of 2, 588, 960, if you're playing with a standard deck of 52 playing cards! That kind of talk can kill the urge to gamble. One fact remains: *someone wins and someone loses in every game that much is true regardless of the odds, and the odds get better the more you tune into the larger number*. It's like winning on exponentials. You feel you're getting closer to an answer. The larger (perhaps prime) numbers hold the key to sudden success which amounts to reducing the odds to increase the chances of winning.

However vague that might seem at this point, despite the uncertainty, you sense a law which states that prediction is about combinatory numbers. Thus, you realize that the math of statistics is the closest you've come to a so-called pure science of prediction. In fact, the hidden purpose of any basic course in mathematics turns out to be a method for accurately predicting the future outcome of something from random probabilities -- within a curve. Granted you know all the variables. And I added the curve to remind you, that the large number reflects a hidden field of certainty among the forest of probabilities.

Listening to an excellent course on mathematics the other day, it occurred to me that one of the central features that really turned this particular instructor on was that mathematics *increases the probability of certainty*. By the way, this seems to be a central figure of any successful movement toward order. Based on this view, the essence of life and all worldly processes can best be viewed as the outcome of the gradual increase of larger numbers to reduce the probability of the odds of randomness found in the minimum. Or put in another way, expanding one's perspective gradually reduces the probability of uncertainty. Because of the presence of random uncertainty in life, over the last two centuries, certain types of predictive methods have crept into all forms of planning. To achieve this aim, risk analysts have become preoccupied with determining the probabilistic components of a proposed system.

For instance, in physics, thermodynamics calculations are based on the movement of millions of random molecules. Incased within a container, such chaotic randomly moving molecules can quickly get out of control, causing volatile explosions to suddenly occur. To deal with so many component probabilities in a great number of sciences, which are for the most part beyond our present computations, analysts are forced to determine the proposed *aggregate* outcome of these forces; something like The Large Number Theory. Included in these calculations for gas, for instance, is its probable combustibility based on a time table according to its expansiveness under pressure and the proposed interactive outcome of contributory forces. Not surprisingly, even biology, genetics and evolution are actually based on random genetic traits and their probable outcomes, as is the statistical outcome of social self-organization, expansion and growth within a known parameter or area.

However, myriad factors of randomness still continue to haunt our every footfall into the future, thus necessitating a system of prediction that can deal with the reduction of probabilities to do-able future aggregates.

Certainty, the Individual and the Bigger Picture

The foregoing pages presented the idea that life and order grew out of the reduction of probabilities to emerge as LNT or Large Number Theory. In terms of organic life, this theory emphasizes that while personal reality tends to continue, it constantly hovers at or near the cutting edge of chaos until it reaches a certain satiation point – then something causes it to reassemble into order. This point is a place just before a Black Swan or chaos-engendering event. My purpose in describing reality this way was to acquaint you with the statistics presented by two systems of reasoning. On the one hand science presents a theory of life which suggests that existence rests on a quivering uncertainty which originates in the quantum substrate of the universe. A place that even the genius of Louis DeBroglie that seems to be totally unpredictable according to quantum science.

In contrast to its uncertainty of random probabilities, you also discovered that mathematics seeks to provide a predictive or quantitative answer which states that the possibility of certainty increases with higher numbers. This means that regardless of the fact that life rests on a quantum uncertainty, over time improbabilities narrow toward greater certainty. Quantitative numbers appear to self-organize into grand figures, sums hidden in a shadowy, twilight parameter that can be thought of as the 'bigger picture.' The *bigger picture* increases with the decrease in random probabilities contrasted by the individual picture. That's exactly what the left brain strives to do, i.e., reduce the probability of uncertainty by eliminating as much of the random fluctuations in the statistics as possible.

Let's put the big picture into mundane terms: from the position of the everyday man struggling to survive in a shaky and unstable economy such as the one that prevailed at the end of the George W. Bush administration, one would suspect there would be little chance of getting sufficient help from the 'big guys' at the top of the economic heap. However, the Federal Government managed, despite the odds of those at the bottom, to issue subsidy checks to help improve a flagging economy. The government also made an effort to continue shelling out Food Stamp relief and welfare funds to the needy and to reduce taxes to large corporations and make loans more readily available to the small business man. In time, the bigger picture which emerged was one of growth and stability through conscientious recycling of the excess. Thus, regardless of the input of the uncertainty in the smaller picture during that incremental time period, the persistence of stability in the bigger picture was progressively improved. The key was conscientious interaction between Part and Whole.

Consider this thought: in essence if we had a 'psychic viewfinder' that operated like your cars GPS – that is, from a position above and outside our narrow range of perception, it could give us astounding information about what is coming about, even though from where we were in the 'present' there would be little data available on it. In short, it would provide that 'bigger picture' we needed to make a better decision about what we must do to reach our goal amicably.

To make this bigger picture more comprehensive, imagine it this way. From the perspective of the individual versus the collective the context in appearances between chaos and order can be compared to a group of cars speeding down a highway and converging. Suddenly, from a riot of individual speeds and separate destinations, the cars mysteriously appear to assemble under the auspices of a shadowy 'bigger picture' which (when seen from above) is a sudden narrowing of the highway miles ahead so that all the vehicles are forced to gradually converge into a concentrated mass. Now, as a group, all the vehicles are headed together toward a general, central target. So far as the perspective of the drivers other than those in front, or at the top of the pyramid, that view is obstructed by the cars in front of them as they converge.

In a nutshell, though we don't have a genie to consult who can magically wrinkle their noses and our proposed dreams materialize, we can be assured that certain outcomes will prevail as we reduce the odds contributing to the growth of a concentrated whole. This means, in a general sense, scientists believe that regardless of the randomness in the behavior of life's various systems during change, certain probable outcomes can be determined and are predictable in terms of a probable aggregate, if we control the variables. Therefore, any hypothetically exact scientific analysis of the aggregate outcome requires careful probabilistic calculations both in terms of whole and part. Determining the aggregate, in this analysis of probabilities is exciting because it increases the probability of certainty. Remember how Raymond, A.K.A. Dustin Hoffmann, the lightning fast, autistic calculator in the movie Rain Man was able to inform Tom Cruise, quite *definitely*, in seconds, the exact large number sum of random matches scattered on a floor? That was possible because the probabilities of each scattered match could be reduced to a near instantaneous grand aggregate. He did it through a larger consciousness that was not altogether focused on the means by which the process worked. Hence, Raymond knew nothing of what he was doing; he just did it. Let us say, therefore, that he simply contacted his psychic GPS and got a leg up on the outcome from a higher source connected to a bigger picture.

This is the kind of unshakable certainty I'm referring to that can intuitively be relied upon to make certain determinations about the future regardless of how little is known about it in the so-called present.

Importantly, the idea of reducing the randomness to near instantaneous certainty is subtle. Granted, though most of the outcomes of these random events are relatively unknown – again – the aggregate or net sum of a given number can be known; like the best 4 out of 4, for instance. It's similar to knowing the whole number by applying the square root to a laundry list of numbers. Summing probabilities in this way reduces the One to the Many. By reducing the One to the Many the probability of determining and/or predicting, shall we say, the aggregate outcome is accelerated. To make these kinds of determinations some general rule of thumb a heuristic must be maintained. Determining the aggregate can be viewed as a holistic sum of probabilities because it provides number analysts seeking to determine the future, an immediate idea of the probable outcome within a given parameter or range of probabilities.

It's like rolling dice on a curve. For example, there are six sides to the dice, in a fair die throw we can presume that after rolling the die, any one of the sides is as likely to arise as any other. To give a numerical probability of a fair die throw coming up with the number five, for instance, we note that there are six equally likely outcomes; a five is one of these outcomes, so chances of the probability of a 5 arising is 1 out of 6 or one sixth that a random throw will produce a specifically designated outcome. Here the aggregate number is than the probability of the five to appear within a specific number of throws instead of the six possible other numbers.

Of course, hypothetically, that probability can change constantly. For instance, you could instead roll six – six times and never get a five hence, the numerical probability is only a hypothetical or idealized outcome, yet for the most part, when thrown a certain number of times its chances to come up within 5 out of six times is the heuristic to bet on – if you're a betting person. However, regardless of the chances, you have to take a chance on everything or you'll never go anywhere. So, in that sense just walking out the door is a probable chance you take with hypothetically predictable odds that you'll make it to your car without dropping dead of a heart attack or getting hit by a frozen halibut falling out of a Fortean sky.

There are always hidden factors associated with an individual's participation in every process. The hidden factor can be any number of outside interferences, including the subconscious influences of the person who rolls the dice. Yes, your participation counts, simply because you can influence the outcome based on your expectations, and there are many levels of influence. Some of these influences also exist on invisible levels where subtlety rules and the outcome cannot be known unless you have a clear profile of the person who rolls the dice.

Therefore, from a subjective level, regardless of any outside hypothetical probabilities, if you believe that life is a gamble, then that belief forms the basis of your influence and thus interferes with your expectations. Hence, your predictions will be primarily framed from a subjective level in the shadow of the half-empty glass. On the other hand, if you expect everything will probably turn out positive, the glass will be hypothetically half full. The trick is giving up the beliefs in expectations and getting to the principles underlying the interactive mechanisms behind what you see and your method of observation. This means learning to step out of the limiting perspective of the individual into the bigger picture.

I say this because, eventually, all odds boil down to a given range of probabilities that on a statistical graph describe a pattern that is outlined by the number of times you execute certain negative or positive decisions. In that sense, each of these times represents a choice descriptive of an unconscious tendency to focus your attention within a given range of probabilities. Like a fingerprint, your choices reveal much about the bigger, unconscious emotional-intellectual picture, plus it unveils your strengths and weaknesses in the construction of good and bad habits. For example, a lefty tends to lean toward the left, so if they walk into a room they will invariably move toward the chairs on the left side. The same can be said of right-handed people, they will tend to move toward the right side of the room. In fact, you can trace a person's movements the more you know about their habitual patterns. The FBI and other law enforcement agencies when looking for a wanted criminal will simply develop a statistical print-out of the perpetuator's patterns of behavior and follow it closely to nail down the exact whereabouts of the fugitive.

Now, as to where this leads us is toward the understanding that regardless of the number of probabilities that rule our lives, certain statistical larger number outcomes tend to prevail. These probabilities represent in sum, the net subjective picture of the person, process or system that perpetuates them, just as footprints, smell, shape and behavior instantly form an emergent pattern that distinguishes each animal from the other. In fact, it is these patterns which determine the perpetuation of the species, that is, its ability to attract and reproduce with others of its kind. The end result is a statistical curve of collective probabilities that acts as a modifying lens around which energy builds mass or structure just as gases corralled by the curvature of a galaxy tend to form into orbs, we call stars and planetary bodies. The structure evolved from the presence of the invisible gravitational field is similar to the magnetic filings around a magnet. It illumines and/or reveals the presence of a non-visible process existing in what must be considered as another dimension.

Due to the non-visible presence of the field, like the opaque dark matter behind galaxies, form and mass emerges within areas that are apparently empty and void. The image that emerges out of this invisible but attractive field reveals a deep, intimate picture of its source etched within the visible mass's curvature. Think of this underlying and invisible field as the larger sum spoken above earlier, a maximum probability number (s) which tends to prevail after continuous repetitions over time (for the mathematician see: Richard Feynman's Sum Over History). This picture can be altered, enlarged or reduced or changed in any degree if the input source undergoes any alterations in data. Thus, repetitious or dependable probabilities that tend to snowball into cumulative wholes can be thought as collective data fields.

The cumulative nature of the field is something we will be discussing in the next two chapters. The following chapter specifically will address the process by which any given order comes about. Think of the whole-producing process this way: the form and appearance of any given sum (or anybody of order for that matter) reflects the net data accumulated. In terms of the growth of an organism, this data can be collected over time as well as space through a myriad of processed probabilities. These probabilities are like streams running across a given landscape into a central body of water. From this sum a bio-system emerges into a pattern of wholeness; which is another way of saying that it evolved. For instance, where we are at this point in our evolution is the net result of the space-time encounters and the way the data was processed. One might think of the organism as being under stress, so to speak, the shaping portion of evolution affected by the landscape through which the data flows.

Data processing over time moves and/or snowballs (accumulates) via the spatial landscape which channels its eventual form in time. Therefore, any alterations in the landscape that effect the input data immediately tends to change the momentum of the snowball process, that is, the creation or accumulation of mass and the shaping of form. Evolution, in this description, is how information forms a loop in the space-time elements bent by the process of the mass in its field. In this description time and space must be considered vital entities contributing to the accumulation and propagation of the snowball. For example, time factors at different points in history vary greatly such as during the period in which Buddha's lived and taught. Compared to our high-paced world of today, Buddha's world was an easy-going reality with plenty of time for meditation and self-development. Thus, the Eight Pali Canon's and the rigors of long hours of meditation fitted quite well into its time-space landscape.

However, in today's world people are on the go and have little time to spend on long explanations about how to get from A to Z. So, to facilitate the demands on time constraints, people access the internet and immediately get the data rather than go through a lengthy process to accumulate it. Seen from that perspective, they have little time for an in-depth study of Buddhism, so they spend short periods applying what reduces to the essentials, the nuggets of the important rules. This rule of thumb applies to meditation and its applications. Sum-Over-history or the 'bigger picture' story than, tell us that what people want today is wheat without the worry of removing the chafe. In fact, they want their 'reality-in-a-box' expedited, like Sugar Corn Pops, for quick consumption which means preferably palatable and stress-free as possible. Let the nutritionists worry about the ingredients. Create your item for mass consumption with that heuristic in mind, and you've got the greasy rail to roll your invention to its proposed monetary destination in the shortest amount of time.

Put in a socio-economic framework: the value of any trend, whether it be in stock, sales, imports or commodities depends upon timeliness in terms of both the viability of its consumption and/or its immediate usefulness. Out with the old and in with the new than, equates, in terms of the product's immediate usefulness to its going value. For example, long, complex, boring books with tortuously detailed chapters with thousands of pages were all the rage with Tolstoy's contemporaries where time was cheap and television had not yet been born. But in today's modern high speed internet environment, what sells best is that which appeals to the quick-fix, cortical-steroid loop between visual impact and pure visceral satiation. Therefore, the terms potential energy (or viability of a product) is actually a measure of its ability to meet the parameters of the time and space in which it is born so far as its longevity is concerned. The appeal of the product, its satisfaction ratio, reduces to the net innate potential energy reflected by its current, collective consumption. The net ratio of this consumption emerges as the large number, in terms of its probable salability, over history. This large number, a byproduct of individual consumption in relationship to the times, amounts to the curve which differentiates a salable product and sends a sundry item toward record sales.

Like a rock rolling down a hillside, a products course toward probable success is determined by the collective, space-time landscape of its consumers. If that input parameter is continuous, the item remains popular which means it adapts nicely to the space-time parameters which tipped it into motion. Collectively, such a propitious outcome is particularly auspicious for its longevity. This is true of all timely processes even that of biogenic life itself. If the transmissions of genetic traits are timely, the eventual probability of their replication is auspicious in so far as the future of the organism is concerned. Should its flow through the space-time course reduce its motion and create alternate detours, then the probability of certain traits or characteristics will suffer a significant disruption in that particular pattern leading to a trait summation. When I say 'trait summation,' I am, of course, referring to its longevity over time and through space. However, detoured the flow, it can and will in time emerge minus certain distinct traits or qualities causing the organism to branch and/or transform into an alternate system. This is a natural outcome to the preserving quality of the first law of thermodynamics, the conservation of energy.

Seen from a socio-economic level, for example, if a struggling capitalistic or individual enterprise system collapses that is dependent upon rigid profit and loss margins, it may be forced to rectify this imbalance by reassembling into a different pattern or system. This switch in systems to rectify imbalances is a central feature of nature's organic tendency to conserve by forking or branching to insure the survival of burgeoning, yet important traits or qualities. In terms of a social system such as capitalism, if it cannot adjust to the parameters of the space-time field, then a conservative, socialistic system must arise to make optimum use of the remaining resources. In this way it survives the radical changes in the structure of the system as a whole. Thus, it is able to reduce the effects of instability and overcome the tendency toward entropic dissipation. Disastrous entropic effects reflect the tendency of a system under repeated reductions of input data to dissipate rather than branch, that is, to spiral downward into anarchy – which by the way is akin to chaos.

Put simply: a system is merely a temporary conveyance for the equal distribution of energy between Whole and Part. Hence, a capitalistic system or Whole, in order to survive must distribute its energy equally to its Parts or it may have to morph into an energy-conserving system to survive. This morphing to conserve and redistribute energy between Whole and Part reveals the thermodynamic nature of a system's effort to control its future to survive change. However, in time, should the input energy and/or data stabilize again, the additional cash flow changes the inter-exchange between resources, reassuring its value to the system, thus the Whole experiences a growth spurt. This spurt or branching can lead to either the renewal of the former system with some new features or the development of a new Whole with altered features and a facile appearance of its former order.

Essentially, this ability to change and grow in response to the dictates of time-space necessitates that nature protect its creations by a system of prediction that is frugal and inventive. Thus, prediction aligned with frugality and inventiveness is an ongoing feature of successful evolutionary traits. In the long run this amounts to a system's ability to constantly seek to predict its path through chaos while maintaining vestiges of its original Wholeness while adapting to the process of change. Keeping this idea in mind, one can sense that during change, regardless though the nature of the order one seeks to attain, the cumulative effect of information is necessary to maintain a whole. As such it depends upon the contributory input of its energy streams through space-time and all the while remain as close as possible to the original model.

The interesting and most important feature of a model is its persistence through time. For instance, life is centralized around a nucleus of basic prime characteristics such as the emotions that is common to every living thing. Appeal to the satisfaction of any these primal emotions and you automatically draw attention to your new product, especially if it makes that emotion more accessible or in some cases bearable. A good example is the emotion of fear. Everyone knows what fear is like and can instantly relate to it as a primary emotion, though subjective reactions to its impact varies according to its impact within each individual time-space landscape. Organic life is a model and as such faithfully reflects the rigors of the landscape that shaped it. Thus, anything that persists, in terms of inventions and consumer product success, faithfully reflects within its structural geometry, some special appeal to a primal emotion.

The Fast-Food Parable

What the foregoing section of this chapter seeks to teach in a nutshell, is that, granted, life is in some ways a struggle which both religion and science seek to overcome in their individual way. Religion strives to do it by replacing the process with a transcended path that is meant to alleviate the suffering and thenceforth to bring peace and well-being to each practitioner. Science on the other hand, strives to achieve a similar goal by primarily demonstrating to us through technology and data dissemination, that many of the problems of predicting the most stress-free future can be achieved best by applying scientific methodology to the problem-solving process. However, over all, what transpires is that both seem to be striving to essentially achieve the same end result, i.e., that of extracting the aggravation from the attainment of well-being with the least effort. This reduces to hooking up to the Whole while detouring the probability route as much as possible.

This idea can be explained very clearly by an analogy based on a famous fast-food company, and here I'm referring to McDonald's. McDonald's came up with something no one else had thought of achieving before when they discovered that by removing the chicken bone from the meat, they could provide a hand on and hassle free tasty, readily edible, cheap chicken meal euphemistically known as McDonald's Chicken McNugget. For a society wrapped up in chin-to-chin schedules that keep them frantically on the go, they could care less about the bone removal process, the big plus is that it was tasty, safe and easy to consume on the spot. Thus, freed of the aggravation of removing the bone, the meal fitted ideally into life on the QT. Thus it became an instant hit; a food fit for a time-strapped consumer.

Getting down to brass tacks, the moral of the story implies that instead of trying to make society bend to our demands, we must learn how to bend and/or adapt to its field. It's a social wave and if you're a quick study in a fast-paced world you'll realize that we swim best when we learn to swim with the current than against it. Ideally, the story teaches us that what you have to offer, in terms of inventions, creative material, ideas or philosophy must dovetail with the demands of life, therein is the *key to the bigger picture*. As far as the consumer is concerned, preferably what you offer also reduces stress, thus making life more palatable to ingest. This is what science and religion has striven to do for a long time. That is, they strive to connect to a holistic principle that enables them to move less consciously, to survive - shall we say, the stress of life.

Perhaps this is why Karl Marx often referred to religion as "the opiate of the masses.' Like the drug-users preoccupation with the quest for self-sedation, anything which takes some of the 'stress' out of survival automatically is a winner. The plus factor that emerges from this insight is that a simple modification in the way we do things can suddenly trigger our connection to an expanded panorama. For example, the legalization of marijuana in a lot of states rides the coattails of medication, hence even the most conservative and resistant John Q. Citizen looking at it in that light, have given up viewing it as an evil.

Down deep in the physics of life, the idea of social sedation, shall we say, plays well into the whole principle of the conservation of energy simply because anything that reduces the effort to reach our goals, in the long run preserves it. This is hard-wired in our genes. It is an essential factor which promotes the prediction of a product's longevity simply because it adds to its preservative connotations. Thus, anything that heightens our consciousness and sense of responsibility is instantly resisted or frowned upon by the collective whole even though it may by its nature provide long term energy-conserving elements. It's the sedation of the present aggravations that people are worried about, not the chance of pain associated with the acute headache in a struggle toward long term goals. Ostensibly, if they have to add another problem, they'd more often than not, would prefer to ingest it honey-coated.

Omniscient Mothering

The good that comes out of all this is that long before the world came into manifestation, some form of innate consciousness appears to be looking out for its progeny. For example, it took care of the problem of thinking about large scale solutions to the innumerous small-scale problems by producing a unifying principle that was essentially applicable at all levels of creation. Hence, tuning into its dynamics, so to speak, automatically relieves many of the aggravations and insures the expediency of the process. This is why 'inventions mother' was such a good care-giver, i.e. she was always on the watch for clever solutions that take as much stress out of life as possible to quickly deliver the maximum desired results. So we arrive at expediency, which when applied to survival, tells us that that which gets us through difficulties, and/or stress, is the prime factor desired by nature in the maximum number of situations. Most business people seeking an edge are concerned with location, location, location – well, Mother Nature was on the lookout for energy-conserving Reductions – Reductions – Reductions! Thus, the good old pop-up toaster readily caught on because it served to not only save that last piece of bread from being burnt, but it relieved mom of the worries of watching it, immersed as she was with the worries of a screaming household preoccupied with their own dwindling time limitations.

So, we learn that the 'bigger picture' that resolves the probability problems, lies in win-win for both the puzzle and pieces and where you, the puzzle-solver, exists I this emergent Whole.

Moving forward with that thought, the snowball principle in the chapter ahead will introduce you to the real Mother Jones of creation - the evolution of order from the very womb of the heaven.

MEDITATIONS

1. Start making it a habit right now to look out for connections between your past and future.
2. Strive to sense the future in the present.
3. Forget about what scientists are saying about ESP and make a daily ritual to check your dreams for precognitive data.
4. Make a list of any unusual phenomena or associations that you come by.
5. Study reality with an eye to how she predicts herself, guarantees the future.
6. Get a feel for sensing your own future. Let it happen spontaneously.
7. Strive to listen into the thoughts of others.
8. Look for the bigger picture and stop accepting that you live in a box.
9. Open up to the bigger YOU that are one with all things.
10. Check your personal reality out: what are you expecting? Is your cup half full or half empty?

2

IS PREDICTION BUILT INTO THE FABRIC OF THE UNIVERSE?

"There's no such place as far away." Richard Bach

Predictive Forecasting and Nature's Quest

We will begin this chapter with the exciting idea that suggests life seems to have been able to predict its future survival. To quote the comic genius of Robin Williams: "Reality - what a concept!" Clearly, if it were not so we would not be here at this point looking back through the dusty reaches of time. Most certainly, the idea that life can anticipate its own future is not an idle hypothesis, but a reliable fact built into its longevity these last 3.4 billion years. Indeed, life is ongoing order built upon predictable factors. Let's examine this wonderful premise.

Firstly, the question of knowing the future, and/or predictive forecasting, revolves around, if anything, its valid place and use within the scheme of how things come together. If predicative forecasting in nature is to be recognized as a law, constant or process its function should not only be mathematically certain, but by all accounts, reliable. Therefore, evidence of its presence should be readily viewable firstly within natural events.

Of all the most predictable mathematical processes governing time in a cyclic manner with unerring accuracy, several examples stand out; namely the Fibonacci numbers and the Golden Mean. These two recurring patterns always accompany measurements of time as a series of wave spiral patterns. Scientists intrigued with these predictably repeating numbers find evidence of their reliability as a recurring pattern in all sorts of natural settings, such as pine cones, pineapples, leaves, stems and in floret distributions, nautilus seashells, and many other sources.

The amazing thing that stands out in these spiral patterns is their regular distribution in reliable sequences over space and time. For instance, the displacement of the spirals on stems follows the same numerical sequence every time at the angle of 137.5°. This critical limit point marks a growth of new leaves and stems in a numerically predictable 630 steps arrangement. These botanical facts in themselves are amazing when we stop to consider all the potentially disastrous variables that fragile life sources face in ascertaining longevity in a hostile universe. In essence, the structure and scope of these repeating wave processes preserve an ongoing struggle for order amidst disorder.

Currently there is a big hubbub over what system theorists call self-organization, which is the so-called spontaneous emergence of order out of supposedly random associations or events. In search for understanding of this process, many theories have been presented. The question remains as to how and why meaningful order emerges in so many diverse processes. For instance, primordial organisms, the growth of multicellular complexity, symbiosis, homeostasis and its regulatory balance of complex organisms, the neurological network and its holographic unity in the brain; the cosmological order in the universe, the growth and development of society in general. This list could also include cultural archetypes that contribute to the health and longevity of an economic system and many other forms of order that seem spontaneous but were, in fact, predictable long before they manifested.

Suffice it to say, scientific sources consider it a random process, which is far from the truth and reflects only the limits of their awareness. We have already seen how at some level even random probability eventually converges into order. It just takes time for certain kinds of order to emerge, and the key is spiral formation at certain angles where it automatically bifurcates into new Wholes.

Predictability despite Change

The foregoing fact then, teaches us that predictability is inherently built into the universe with purposeful intent. To demonstrate, the highlight of a living system can be seen as its ability to maintain a stable boundary, to achieve this it must maintain its border during change while always remaining aware of where it is going. Ideally, this system must remain functionally both 'open and closed' so as to convert energy into matter efficiently and still survive the rigors that come during this change. Primarily, it must be open to maintain a stable boundary yet organizationally closed to dissipation. To do this it must have a *holistic* sense of space and time that includes constant feedback between past and future.

To get an idea of how this works a simple, useful physical example of a self-regulating Whole or stable system is the vortex of a whirlpool. It draws in fluids as water flows out the other end while maintaining a stable, spiral shape. On a larger scale, the stability of a self-perpetuating spiral vortex can be found on Jupiter. This one has been there, according to astronomers, for over 300 years. Of course, the best example of a self-maintaining system is our body. An organism operates according to a standard set of rules in the form of a holistic encode which governs the interaction between each part. This system has been in operation for billions of years!

This book will endeavor to introduce you to a natural, structure-maintaining principle in nature that has its origin in the primal creation of our universe. It will demonstrate how it works and give you meditations that will help you apply that principle to your personal life to guarantee its enrichment. In short, this manual will disclose to you the secrets by which it predicts its course through time long in advance by constantly sending back reliable data from the future that can be re-integrated into the evolving new picture. I consider this a 'psychic' function, one that is a powerfully creative, organizational principle - the spiral force. In the pages ahead you will learn to recognize this principle in action and understand how its incredible presence affects all life and insures the efficiency of every organizational process.

To get acquainted with some of the spiral force's qualities, you no doubt were introduced to the spiral shape in geometry classes and learned to recognize the differences between the logarithmic and the mathematician's equiangular spiral in their application to math problems. They represent a few samples of its nature, but there are so many more facts about the spiral process I'm sure your professor might have overlooked. For instance, did he/she also tell you that the spiral shape is commonplace throughout the handiwork of nature; from the mighty galaxies to the swirling dance of phyllotaxis cycles seen in pine cones, flowers, trees, nautilus seashells, or the DNA and RNA helices, as well as everyday social trends and the rise and fall of the stock market?

Spirals on Purpose

It may come as a surprise, but spirals are readily observable in nearly all forms of creation, and if you study them carefully you will note that they look and behave like turbines that accompany and provide powerful, rotating fields of force. What is most exciting about these natural energy-producing dynamos is that they are the powerhouses for generating growth in many systems, including all biogenic processes. The biggest surprise of all is that spiral processes have their cosmic counterparts in the dynamic creative cauldron's astronomers call galaxies, meaning 'island universes.' Such structures form the very foundation of life and order in the universe.

Astoundingly, there are over 100 billion of these energy-generating dynamos in our nearby universe, of which 60% are spiral-shaped. The turbine-like shape does not come by chance but by design. Like the paddle-wheels of ancient mills, rotary engines and interlocking gears, it is the perfect shape for transferring generated energy. Universal powerhouses of creation, galaxies contain approximately over 400 billion energy-radiating stars just like our own sun. A titanic panorama of luminescence in the stillness of space, our Milky Way is 90 to 100,000 light years across and a mere 2000 light years thick. Having the appearance of a disk or cell on edge, our own Milky Way galaxy is a barred, spiral-shaped dynamo.

Astrophysicists inform us that the formation of a galaxies rapidly turning, far-flung spiral arms, gather gases and dust together where it cooks up the hot soup of young stars. In these huge cauldrons of creation, galaxies concoct the *'building blocks'* of matter that later comprise the elemental components of life. What is fascinating about these molecular factories is that the innate design is 'gravitationally contractive' as if designed to purposely preserve the precious stuff of existence. Creating life where nothingness dominates the blackness, these energetic, spiral-manufacturing plants are located in areas of empty space, filling the bleak void with meaning and purpose.

According to Alex Filippenko Ph.D. an astrophysicist from the University of California at Berkeley, galaxies undergo a patterned evolutionary process whereby random bits of matter, gases and dust clouds, coalesce into island, spiral, globular clusters; Harlow Shapley (1917). Forming from clusters that cluster together into mega-clusters or spirals within spirals, these giant systems appear like creatures in space around a nucleus or central hub called a black hole. One is reminded of how microorganisms grow from single cells around a central nucleus and evolve into multicellular complex clusters. The process appears to be indigenous to order of all kinds. The concentric circling is similar to the cymatics process, or energy wave ripples emanating from vibrating substances to form unique patterns of order. Like these cymatics mandalas of order, galactic patterns are thought to be created from density waves which almost lovingly, shall we say, embrace and support the development of the precious stuff of life.

Interestingly, in his lectures on the origins of these cosmic giants, Professor Filippenko mentions that the going hypothesis suggests that spiral galaxies form over points of dark matter accumulations. From the void order and life explodes, shall we say, and it appears to follow a predetermined pattern. We can't see its invisible and non-material origins so we speculate that it has hidden counterparts which provide the framework from which matter and life springs. For instance, we know that the invisible, untouchable mass which astronomers call dark matter exists. It is *theorized* to be the invisible counterpart of visible or *illumined* matter. However, its nature is theoretical even though its presence is palpable. Scientists ask, what is its nature, and why does its presence create the over-arching spiral shape? Based on theoretical speculations as to its nature, dark matter has been described as everything from black holes, brown dwarfs, neutron stars, white dwarfs, WIMPS (weakly acting massive particles), and even planets the size of Jupiter, ad infinitum! Possessing both mass and asserting a gravitational influence, dark matter appears to be an ideal source for housing an information template or foundation by which the spiral dynamo comes into manifestation to bring about mass and order in the cosmos.

For example, astrophysicists know that dark matter (sometimes called the missing mass) exists, because it exerts a gravitational force that cannot be accounted for by standard mass and gravitation measurements. However, Filippenko informs us that the mass *actually isn't missing*, its presence is palpable – it's just simply (like God) not visible. Posing a major enigma for astronomers, the galaxies missing mass, makes-up a whopping 90 % of the known matter attributed to spiral galaxies. That's the predominant whole of the mass and yet – (think on this) it's totally opaque to human senses. This fact isn't new, decades ago astronomer Fritz Zwicky was the first to point out flaws in calculations based on the clustering of galaxies and noted that they could not remain *gravitationally bound* in their far-flung rotations by the pure mass of visible matter. He sensed that some unknown quantity seemed to be responsible for the spiral stabilization in spacetime. Remaining an enigma for object-bound scientists, it meant that an *unknown, (dare we say mystical factor)*, was responsible for the formation of physical worlds and that it was interfering with observations.

So, what we encounter is the presence of an unknown force that provides the foundation of galactic cauldrons that, quite mysteriously, can't be seen, is invisible yet ever-present and responsible for matter and in the end result – the propagation of life. How fascinating and profoundly mystical! Think of it – the mass of our cosmos pivots on an unknown quantity that engenders the production of gravitational mass and the evolution of all-natural order. We ponder on this mystery and it becomes clear, that we are encountering a propagating medium that gives birth to the physical world. For wont of a better explanation by science we are driven by its supportive framework, to see it as an underlying template. Let us examine that supposition.

The Spiral Force

The spiral takes shape from an underlying template which is essentially an information pattern, a guide like any design shall we say, by which order comes about. Like the cookie cutter that presses out gingerbread men, it is the algorithm behind the program. In that sense, the creation process can be viewed as a derivative of an innate data-pattern. Its coextension into physical space, as we know it, asserts a palpable gravitational tug upon all matter, drawing itinerant gases about it. Like the neutrinos or other exotic particles theorized to be its source, an information template in the form of an intermediary field gives rise to the presence of unexpected mass. If this proves to be true, in the not-too-distant future, the underlying template could account for the intra-dimensional source which aids in the construction of galactic spirals, mass and the natural order of all life.

Hypothetically, if ever there were a case for an intelligently driven process from innate design, it is the *divine* way dark matter gives birth to the galaxies which in turn create the stuff by which life evolves out of the *inky void* of interstellar space. Hence, there appears to be a direct corollary between the evolution of galaxies from dark voids in space and Gaia's birth place of life in the inky depths of our primordial seas. Without doubt, for those wishing to plume the mystery of emergent order from a mysterious, invisible underlying template – spiral galaxies provide worthy meditative scrutiny as the way by which this pattern evolves.

Historically, around the globe, spirals have not gone unrecognized in terms of their divine nature. As if with intuitive, nearly every culture is rift with reverence for the mysterious spiral and its presence is *always* associated with what human's term God or the creative force. Artistic relics, pictographs and frescos depict the spiral symbol found in mystic Celtic monoliths, crumbling labyrinthine ruins left behind by the Druids, the spiral-shaped ziggurats of ancient Persia or the serpentine mounds cultures built by Neolithic Native Americans. With intuitive reverence, the universality of this geometric form prompted Zoroaster to declare that "*God is a Spiral Force.*"

Undoubtedly the spiral has played an important part in the creative order of the universe. This realization prompted my own personal spiritual and intellectual journey to understand the intricate link it plays in the union between all-that-is and the origin of living order within the physical world. Contemplation on this dynamic process led me to what I sense to be the principle of creation. This principal links two processes: the dynamo of the spiral form and the snowball effect. Deep inside the quantum field a numerical codifying process furnishes the information or instructions that activate the creative engine; thus, propagating the snowball effect to move into its creative cycle. Together the two processes, dynamo and snowball effect, produce the creative transformation of energy or information into self-sustaining order and the ongoing complexity of life.

To acquaint you with the background of the word dynamo, it originates from the Greek word for power. A dynamo is a force or energy-generating device for inducing power to flow between two points in the form of high-voltage electrical current. Thus, a dynamo converts latent potential into active or kinetic energy. In that sense the spiral productively channels an invisible force to take on meaningful form – and this is very important. This means the source of power-generating force that animates the process of natural form in the universe finds its origin in a mysterious template from beyond the veil. Think on this: often we think of power as the energy needed to achieve something like lifting heavy weights, or simply, the effort to make things happen. Force can also refer to the presence of subtle energies, like gravitational waves that propagate the tides of our massive oceans or electrical forces that energize our children's toy cars. Forces are also those generative waves that move the titanic bulk of the galaxies or the tiny but unbelievably powerful forces in the atom as well as the massive planetary spheres in their timeless orbits around the sun.

All of these processes take form from a spiral shape. Therefore, the spiral shape could be thought of as an energy-generating dynamo that produces a force field for making things happen. Without the order-generating force of the dynamo we would not have the compounds or elements that comprise life-sustaining masses which are necessary to promote processes of biogenic creation. On a universal scale, the stars are cooking up the elements necessary for life. Without these cosmic cookers we wouldn't be here because they produce the iron in our blood and the calcium in our bones. We need these and many other compounds to produce a firm framework for the body in addition to the planetary masses upon which we stand.

All of the examples in this book could be said to illustrate the universes dynamic production of directed or channeled energy to release incredibly powerful forces which promote life-giving order and its vicissitudes. In short, the word dynamo in this volume is meant to describe any tangible or metaphorical processes that produce action; whether it is physical, mental, emotional or spiritual. Thus the dynamo is a symbol to describe the channeling of what must be called the 'infinite' creative potential of the cosmos. Think of potential energy as information without structure, something like an encyclopedia of data that needs some form of intermediary channel to transform it into materiality. In this regard, the spiral force can be viewed as a creative catalyst for releasing information from a template, like dormant DNA. DNA is inactive information without the catalytic processes of the RNA to put it to work. For it to become active or living, the spiral dynamo must replicate the information and transform it into order. Here the transformative reformation process of the spiral is needed. In a fundamentally mechanical sense, that is exactly what is going on in the electro-dynamics of the atom when an electron is sent flying across the universe in the form of a photon, or quanta of light.

Invisible Forces Guide Us

There are many processes whereby invisible forces are instrumental in propitiating meaningful patterns of order. The unifying field that brings about the emergence of order is not perceptible by an outside observer. The process involved in the creation of the gravitational field is a good example. We can't see the process behind the production of gravity, that is, the way the instructional data guides mass to bend the space-time matrix. What we perceive in our subjective experience is a pull on our bodies that makes us fall toward the center of the earth. In this experience, gravity tends to 'guide' us, as it does every other bit of mass moving toward the same central point. We call this gravitational attraction, and we feel safe to assume that the emergence of this order comes about from the effects of its unseen field.

Thought, on the other hand, is another kind of instructional field as are the emotions. As 'instructional' fields of information they possess the power to catalyze patterns of social and biological order. Though they occupy a position in the hierarchy of fields that is nearly opaque to the physical senses, nonetheless thoughts and feelings galvanize the spiral wheel upon which the social system runs. Operating behind the scenes as informational artifacts, thoughts and emotions transform, in time, into encoded molecules that link individual to group traits via progenitor gene pools. What is collected and transferred is not the residual of mass or energy per se, but the data comprising the information field. Mass and energy are the galvanizing byproducts of the data field which produce genetic patterns. This means that mass and energy follow the dictates of the data field. As data fields, order arises from an instructional pattern deep within matter, reminding us of 'memes', i.e. information bytes.

Interestingly, informational bytes and fields of instruction seem to have much in common. Information bytes originate as subjective data trails from the collective thoughts and emotional energy discharged by the human race as a whole. In time this energy/information forms an interactive field between the surrounding environment and the resultant emergent mass that gives birth to order. Thus, beginning with the individual these subjective emotions and thoughts accumulate as information bytes shared by the collective Whole. In this a 'field of data' transports specific qualities are always being transferred back and forth between probable selves existing in an ostensive future and a current self-occupying a fluctuating boundary in the so-called present.

In this transmigration of subjective thoughts and emotions, which are the sum of probabilities between Whole and Part, one can readily assume that the sharing of these data fields equates to a sort of telepathic communiqué. I say this because, in essence, the organism is responding to information that is only tentative present from far outside its current physical boundaries. This data guides and directs the organism's evolution via data at-a-distance, far beyond conscious awareness.

But this assumption is not surprising, because, in fact, the process of following the order dictated by an information field can be seen early in infants as they respond to the emotions of their parents. In adults these feelings emerge as deep thought. In terms of informational bytes, feelings are invisible data palpable enough to be felt and transferred to others. Early on, the infant quickly learns to recognize its mother's intent by telepathically following the invisible, spiral information field. The information field, like the gravitational field upon which the Earth levitates, follows the parameters of the underlying guidance system of the template that came into manifestation eons before the baby's inception.

In a likewise manner, the galaxies gravitational field originated in the shadowy voids of interstellar space, emerging in much the same way as idea's branch out from the inner landscape of non-tangible information to form tangible biological forms. It is these non-visible patterns comprising the field which erected the neurological tracks guiding the mental and somatic activities that eventually would be shared by the species as a whole. This may explain why, though we might not know what another person is thinking, we often *feel* compelled to act because we are unconsciously following hidden tracks bearing non-verbal clues.

The track we follow is provided by a cosmic spiral guidance pattern shared by all order from a long-forgotten space and time. From this intra-dimensional spiral field there is a constant exchange of energy as biological masses respond to each other from afar. Its power to direct us is comparable to a train rolling upon rails   long ago with the express purpose of bearing passengers of today toward a preordained future destination. Bound to its track the passing train is fated to reach its destination unerringly, just as a baby is unquestionably tied to predictable parental mannerisms keyed into nurturing, predestining him/her to grow into a healthy, adjusted adult.

Put simply: as a collective whole we react empathically to each other because we all share a common system that subscribes to the same intrinsic principle. Thus, life and all order appear to mirror an invisible, pre-established inclination to cluster together; from the simplest single-celled life forms to those that evolve into the most complex. The fascinating thing about the spiral template of order is that it had its birth in the spinning orbit of the atom. Even there the atom is following an elder guidance system which in turn provides the hub around which our lives revolve. As matter evolved, following the Big Bang into biological form, this intrinsic pattern of wholeness was transferred from wave into particle over billions of years according to a common set of rules. These rules became patterns of order science has labeled constants and laws. They are the regulatory patterns by which energy/information is converted into molecular order to maintain life-sustaining systems.

In an inspiring and thoughtful book entitled *The Web of Life*, Fritjof Capra explored the holistic network of order. He made fascinating note of the success researchers such as Francisco Verela, Pier Luigi Luisi, 1989, had in chemically simulating self-regulating (autopoetic) networks in the laboratory. These two researchers believe that their experiments and findings which produced the autopoetic model meet the criteria for supporting the essential components leading to living organisms.

What was most appealing about this research, in my estimation, is that they found a formula that suggests a principle which can be repeated over and over to produce the same results leading to biogenic order. This is very important, because it tells us that there is an information template guiding that process; which also implies that order went into the formula – that is, organizational intent, like the program generated by a project designer. Here, I am referring to a self-replicating pattern from a conscious source exists within the program.

As I have mentioned in the first part of this book's introduction, it is clear from viewing the creation of order in the dusty reaches of the universe, that a spiral-shaped dynamo accompanies the generation of universes and of order. As such, this presence appears as both a catalyzing and a sustaining force to ongoing unity. The properties of this spiral process are not simply *self-organized*, if you will, but follow an inherent order dictated by an information-propagating template that gives birth to the following processes which are thereafter sustained by it:

1. The autocatalytic or self-generated; an autocatalytic system is *non-linear* meaning the output is not-directly proportional to the input, or not in superposition. It defies the second law of thermodynamics by its ability to channel and redirect energy so

that the amount of energy in the end is greater than the one originally available.

2. The autopoetic or self-regulating; an excellent example can be found in the cell processing of DNA into RNA to produce proteins that in turn manufacture enzymes that perpetuate the circle of cell replication.

3. The replication process: self-reproducing. Perpetuates and extends itself and is self-predicting, meaning it determines itself or foresees its own future.

4. The ability to self-animate or to organically transform is a trait of life-perpetuating systems. It is a process which originates in the atom. As an electron is released from its orbit it in turn manufactures a photon of light which energizes and/or feeds the process of all biogenic systems. Energetically, the nervous system conveys bio-electric (light) energy throughout the organism, thus animating it into movement, the essential feature of living biogenic systems.

5. The principle of creation oscillates in a cyclic manner very much like a cosmic dynamo or vacuum pump. From a contractive, centripetal implosion called the Big Bang, energy expands outwardly at the speed of light in spiral clusters. Once the potential energy reaches maximum expansion and is dissipated through kinetic energy, it collapses back into its central hub to renew the process.

6. Consciousness-interactive: meaning that as we expand in self-awareness of our interrelationship with the processes of nature, we transform ourselves and the world through recycling of information to improve upon our existence. Re-cycling information through conceptualization involves our ability to *holistically* self-generate more energy-efficient living systems through cognitive feedback. In short, as we become more cognizant of our complicity in the Whole, our ability to interact conscientiously improves our adaptability. These are examples of the Spiral Dynamo in nature.

7. An innate pattern, it connects the disparate intervals of space and time like scattered pieces of a puzzle into a coherent picture in the final manifestation of order. As such this space-time pattern can in turn be understood and fruitfully put to work to convert the infinite energy potential available in the Holoverse into individually useable gestalts.

Therefore, in their individual, energy-generating ways, each of these dynamic energy principles convert the innate potential that has its origins in another dimension into kinetic energy. In them we witness a universal (or Holoversal) principle at work constantly maintaining the perpetuation of ordered worlds. We also stand in awe to realize that from this fundamental core all biogenic, self-generating sets/systems produce life as we know it. Truly, we have much to learn about this incredible principle of self-perpetuation seen in the spiral dynamo. If we are fortunate enough to understand it, surely its applications in a broad panorama of processes will help us to efficiently reduce the effects of entropy upon our physical realities and thereby increase the flow of raw energy and sustain it so that we co-create a mutually hospitable world.

MEDITATION

1. Make it a habit to read more scientific articles on astrophysics, chaos, probability and relativity theory.
2. When you read these books, watch videos or listen on academic lectures strive to look for the deeper connections between your personal reality and the principles you encounter.
3. Ask yourself what is the 'bigger picture' in all things.
4. Look for the link between your thoughts and how your reality unfolds.
5. Always be honest and objective with yourself about how you really feel and think.
6. Be open to challenge your ideas and the authority of others in charge.
7. Examine your physical world with eye and ear to the underlying pulse that drives everything.
8. Strive to sense your ONENESS with ALL THINGS.

3

DISCOVERY OF A CONNECTIVE PRINCIPLE

"But I hope that it will also be demonstrated soon that in my experiments in the West I was not merely beholding a vision, but had caught sight of a great and profound truth" Nikola Tesla

The Web Work

Nature is comprised of interdependent, interwoven patterns that can be described as recurring, potentially connective wholes because they bring together (make operational or catalyze) diverse forces to become unified into integrated processes. Every part, regardless of how small it might appear, is connected to some larger whole, even though we might not be privy to the full extent of its extensions and operations. For example, if we throw a basketball up in the air gravity brings it back down to us, and we don't have to do anything about it, but so far as its connection to this process, the whole bigger picture is invisible.

Thus, any unified process comes about naturally simply because it is the collective work of a preexisting and opaque bigger picture. We don't have to worry about the process which makes this

35

happen because everything is done for us, all we have to do is pick up the ball and give it a toss. We can rest assured that it will come back down to the ground and in all probability bounce, because we can *reliably predict* that gravity will take control of its future behavior. We are also confident that gravity will keep our television stationary so we can watch it this evening without it floating about in our living rooms. It goes without saying that gravity will also provide the stability we need to amble along on that path we take this evening for our walks and even provide potential energy for the locomotion of each foot falling, one after the other, as we move along. As a matter of fact, connective principles operate together on many other subtle levels without our interferences. One that we can personalize instantaneously is the supportive way our DNA took care of the work eons ago in providing sensory processes that enable us to see, hear, smell and feel the world. Trusting the force of gravity to cause the ball to bounce, we are able to enjoy the game of basketball, precisely because we don't have to be involved in the process or concerned about how it works, everything has been already engineered in advance for our well-being. In fact, we don't even have to trust our DNA for our senses, we just awaken and there they are, all ready to use and reliable in the extreme.

As such, inter-connective processes could be thought of as transition points or windows uniting one dynamic dimension of energy and information together with another. A good example of this union is the sub-atomic world of waves and particles. Another is the world of subjective perception and sensation. Though the transition between these levels in terms of energy-into-mass is subtle, we are amazed by the impressively efficient ways these processes operate to provide a smooth transition and continuity between states of order and disorder and/or dimensions. Clearly, the origin and purpose of these links between dimensions and/or levels of energy involve far-reaching principles. The subtleness of these transition points are often overlooked at first glance, simply because we take them for granted, or because the structure of space-time obscures their nature and structure.

Immersed in the apparent solidity of the cause-effect world, scientists struggle to understand the nature of these inception points to grasp the bigger picture hidden there. If, in time, they are fortuitous in their search, which is often much further down the road, they are amazed to discover what appears to be a minute transition doorway by which these processes transform to unite variable worlds of energy. Current research in astronomy appears to confirm that the creation of the universe began, in terms of the exponential explosion from the micro into the macro-universe, at what scientists describe as one of these inception points. Our universe was said to have become at 10^{-30}, or what is known in physics parlance as the Planck length. This is the smallest, measurable point known to man, yet it marks the inception aperture through which the physical universe emanated. Named after its founder, Max Planck, astoundingly, this point is so minute that millions of them could reside in the period at the end of this sentence. Cosmologists studying the inception, evolution and transformation of the universe, hypothesize that the universe will continue to expand until it reaches a cessation or saturation status, billions of years in the future. Then, like the down stroke of a piston driven by its primary upstroke of compression, expended gases will reassemble under pressure to a central point and in a recurrent explosion will again expand outwardly as it goes through another cycle of this process. Considering the cyclic nature of the universe's compression and expansion, we marvel that it all began at such a miniscule inception point to become billions of light years across. In that explosion we get a feeling for the magnitude of the energy invested, and realize that its potential was nearly unlimited.

Awed by the thought we are led to wonder about the intrinsic energy and outcome of cumulative, connective processes of this nature and their intrinsic relationship to other forms of order in life. Clearly, the mechanics of these powerful transformative cycles have much in common with a domino effect. If you recall, the domino effect occurs as one domino knocks down first one at an inception point, which in turns knocks down another and so on, infinitum. As such, this is a principle which begins at a central inception point and moves forward progressively propagated by its own momentum. In this manner it completes a full cycle as it exposes a hidden, underlying geometric pattern.

Looking into the creation of the universe we discover that all order and life began from just such a spiraling process. Like domino's all aligned in a row to be knocked down block after block by an ongoing wave of energy started at an inception point, we sense a well thought out plan. Using mathematics to discern the origins of the underlying plan, scientists measure the energy and progress of this plan to discover how at every stage it is intrinsically interconnected. From an inception point it circumnavigates through the pattern as a wave moves on an unseen grid, emerging as connective points at precise increments. The pattern of the underlying organization which emerges reveals what appears to be a preconceived spiral route with a precisely aligned order and destination.

Of course, brilliantly inquiring minds have already discerned the presence of this well thought out, orchestrated innate design. Albert Einstein, for one, sensed the presence of this basic plan and was said to expostulate: "*What is incomprehensible about the universe is that it is comprehensible!*" Apparently awed, he was, no doubt, alluding to the realization that the universe must have had a brilliant designer to execute such a well-orchestrated plan. Surprised, Einstein sensed in that plan a predictable outcome. It was just too proportionately ordered, repeatable and holistically maintained to be the result of random order. What brings us to this fascinating realization is that, without doubt, we live in a 'finely tuned' universe with the delicate precision clockwork reflective of the keenness of a perceptive, ingenious mind.

With this idea to guide you, this book will ask you to consider two principles: one of them is known as the *strong anthropic principle* which implies that an intelligent, purposeful creator produced the design of the universe which led to why we are here now. The second theory is the so-called *weak anthropic principle* which states that the principles occurred by random chance, so to speak, that we are simply back-engineering a happenstance process a posteriori. This concept, by its description, implies that the universe came into manifestation without any pre-conscious intent. Such a principle implies that there is no plan or purpose to the universe; therefore, nothing can be predicted because there is no order to the way it works. Nonetheless, mathematics, the science of certainty disproves this, otherwise there would be constants, no laws by which it operates; and we can see that there is. Therefore, there is no way to determine the course because there is no ordered path; hence, no future. Nonetheless, the choice to believe or disbelieve is your own to decide. Whichever principle you may choose to believe is extremely important, because on one hand, if you believe in a chance, randomly assembled universe, then, in essence, you believe that life has no over-arching plan, that the connective principle described is at best hypothetical and its order without purpose.

However, if, on the other hand, you believe in the strong anthropic principle, it means that you believe not only is order preconceived, that is, follows a plan, but that its outcome is inherently predictable. Additionally, this view also presupposes that the universe is holographic, (a Holoverse) wherein the whole exists equally in every part, future and past conjoined at some point. It is the holographic aspect that actually guarantees the reliability of a Holoverse of one mind, meaning all minds are united at some level beyond the illusion of the materiality. In terms of the strong anthropic principle, this answer also presupposes, automatically includes the idea that the creator and yourself is ONE.

Additionally, the idea of the whole existing in every part implies that a connective principle unites space and time (or GUP as Einstein proposes) unites past-present and future in a continuum, which, again, in principle make the idea of prediction feasible but actual. The holographic nature of this unification is based on the interference of waves to form a connective principle where mind and matter juxtapose. These are just a few of the proposed reasons for a predictive spiral principle, for you to consider at this point in the book. Happily, we can that thank one outstanding thinker, Mr. Alex Filippenko, Ph.D., professor of astronomy at Berkeley for contributing the following six points in favor of the Strong Anthropic Principle garnered from his astronomy course on the astrophysical nature of the universe:

1) The early expansion rate of the universe.
2) The strength of the weak nuclear force.
3) The strength of the strong nuclear force.
4) The strength of gravity versus the EM field to maintain the structural stability of the universe,
5) The nuclear resonances (carbon-oxygen values.)
6) The various particle masses i.e. neutron vs. proton, proton vs. electron.[ψ]

Note: *Filippenko indicates in the course that he, for one, cannot buy the theory of a weak anthropic principle because the creation of the universe could not occur by chance because of the complex reasons needed to insure its manifestation and the issuance of life.*[ψ]

The unanswered question is what started the initial ball of creation rolling that led to life and its continuous propagation? Dare we think of this principle as mind, the shadowy silhouette of the designer in the design overlooking its creations? Isn't that what the term prediction implies, that is, to unite with the destination? Thus to foresee implies that the destination is indigenous in the inception. What we can see from here indicates that the inception or trigger point where the universe transformed from the microcosm into the macrocosm is connected via laws of holism. Think of this law of the whole as an initiating point where a large, round boulder sets perched precariously on the edge of a precipice ready to roll. Almost imperceptibly, the boulder is set into motion by the mere presence of a butterfly resting on its surface. Think of the butterfly as synonymous of the force of mind-over-matter, something like willpower directing a body at rest to get on its feet and begin to move forward.

One doesn't need to know all about the processes involved to initiate such a mind-over-matter motion, simply because all the prerequisites for predicting that it 'will be done' on earth as it is in heaven, so to speak, is already in motion. Willing it is enough, the rest is automatic, just as the imperceptible weight of a straw on a camel's back overloads it. Such 'straws or other initiating processes, act as trigger points where larger processes move forward into manifestation. The redistribution of energy when we are confronted with stress is another. It is a redirection of energy. Other common personal components acting as creative catalysts of action are fear and various emotions. The differentiation of the components that can be attributed to the general attributes of this snowball process and their activation appear to be inherently written into the Spiral Code of the Holoverse. Forthcoming examples will, of their own accord, arise that will demonstrate the outcome of such interactive, holistic connections, along with meditations by which you too can set these principles into motion to make the mechanism accessible in your life.

As has been noted, miniscule, (from our present perspective) unseen processes appear to be behind major productions, a conclusion which boggles the minds of many great thinkers. One such writer and thinker, Malcolm Gladwell, who wrote a brilliantly insightful book called *The Tipping Point*, explored some of the dynamics of how seemingly inconsequential things trigger pandemic events.[ψ] Sounding like a spin off from a principle in chaos theory known as the 'butterfly effect,' his speculations seem to imply that these domino-like productions began at precise, yet nearly imperceptible 'tipping points.' In my analogical take on these so-called 'tipping points,' these productions appear almost as invisible arrows shot by an unknown archer toward a target far *outside* the range of perception. Following what appears, at first glance to be an obscure course they grow, snowballing in time to emerge dead center in the bull's eye goal.

The most astounding of all natural processes that began by nearly imperceptible events to snowball into macro-sized productions is the Big Bang. Here in this cosmos-sized snowball of all snowball events, we discover a process that takes the same micro course into macro-proportions. According to theory all matter and energy gathered together into a tiny dot and following an explosion began snowballing to become the universe as we know it. Hypothetically, this same event is speculated to have expanded until all energy and mass is dissipated, then, at a somewhat similar imperceptible point in the future, falling into a central black hole of infinitely minute proportions from which the process, hypothetically, begins anew. Hence, the beginning and endings of the process seem to mimic each other: the inherent mass of the complete process a byproduct of its unraveling and rebuilding; its explosive release culminating in a holistic cycle – like a piston or valve from the cumulative pressure at a central point. To coin a phrase: the snowball appears to *perpetuate itself*, self-organizing as it unrolls from a central locus into the galactic spiral, uncoiling and rewinding, building power as it goes. Spontaneous, it emerges *as if* in response to a hidden channel that it follows, each convolution guided *as if* by an unseen principle rooted deeply in the process. Never varying from its course, it predictably builds as it flows, unerringly consolidating in accordance to the current of this invisible channel. In this way the snowball spirals from an inception point, self-perpetuating order and mass, all the while expanding and branching at every critical pressure point.

In a word, it is *adhering* to a primary model while acquiring mass and in that way transcends itself through its own momentum. It appears thusly to be guided unerringly to its target by a nearly imperceptible process formed from an equally imperceptible template that bridges space and time. Through the whole of this process, we get the sense that at some deep intrinsic level, consciousness of order and purpose was built in. For where else would this intelligent, self-repeating process get the knowledge that it follows, such as a template, encode or creative channel by which it moves and shapes and/or emerges from energy into matter into order and thence into life?

Trigger Points of Infinite Potential

In the fascinating science of chaos physics, researchers seek to understand these sometimes spontaneous, yet apparently 'self-generating' series of events that suddenly transpire at disequilibrium points, naming them the 'butterfly' effect. The butterfly effect can be compared to a crucial *tipping point* where small beginnings precipitate large scale events. According to a popular notion of this effect the fluttering of a butterfly's wings at some nondescript point on the globe can ignite monumental consequences globally, like a series of tornados down south in the USA or a Monsoon in the Indian Ocean. Needless to say we are often shocked and amazed when we discover that coiled up in inauspicious micro points, macro processes are about to emerge. An example of just such a powerful event precipitated from minute beginnings can be witnessed with the release of the tremendously devastative forces from within the *imperceptible* nucleus of the atom. An atom's catastrophic potential can be seen in the hydrogen bomb blast in December of 1962 at Aniwetak Atoll in the Pacific Ocean. The results were beyond imagination! Who would have thought that from such a small-scale inception this large-scale destruction would follow? With results awesome to behold, powerful, micro forces precipitate the tornado and hurricane. Swirling around a central nucleus, similar in nature to the black hole at the center of a spiral galaxy, powerful winds gyrate to create a engulfing suction that can make kindling wood out of forest of trees in minutes. Knowing the process that predicts and/or gives birth to this devastation, one is automatically given to consider that once clearly discerned, the nature of its mechanism would prove invaluable as an aid in countering such random destruction.

On an everyday level we can get an idea of the power in gyrating dynamos of this sort, how that its operation is activated by a tiny spark in your car's engine. It is this very process that furnishes the catalysts that drives the engine which in turn propels a vehicle weighing nearly a ton-up steep hill carrying many passengers for endless miles. In nature we see another example. Here completely invisible yet Herculean force scientists call gravity, labeled the great *accelerator*, effortlessly pushes the vast masses of the galaxies and planets around in their orbits. A contributory generator of all the electrical potential of the world, this same invisible force hurls objects down slopes at the dizzying speed of thirty-two feet per second.

Awed with the magnanimity at the 'triggering' of macro events by micro processes, we are led to conclude that deep within the nature of the cosmos an acausal, non-visible, miniscule force is responsible for propelling the dynamo of creation that produces the macrocosm and all its processes. Apparently, Nikola Tesla, perhaps the most prolific and perceptive inventor and scientist the world has ever known, recognized this mystical force when he was quite young. The following true story of his discovery of the generative principle, intrinsic in the heart of his alternating current dynamo's, shook me deeply when I read it; let me share it with you.

Nikola Tesla and the Snowball Effect

Young Tesla was a boy who seemed to be able to connect what appeared to be simple, often random appearing forces to reveal a far-reaching, dynamic process. From the time he was very young he was busy creating projects that coupled these invisible forces together to make things happen. For example, while playing in a nearby stream close to where he lived as a child, he created small, barrel-shaped paddle wheels and watched the current of the stream push them along. Something in his mind was awakened by the way the stream was carried forward by an invisible current. Tesla's fascination was in the same way shared by another child prodigy, Albert Einstein, who was fascinated with how mysterious currents originating in the cosmos acted on a compass to point out directions. Not surprisingly, from Tesla's early childhood experiments came the basic models for huge, powerful turbines in his future generated by titanic forces that began at 'tripping points' to achieve impossible tasks.

Though young and curious, Tesla's fertile imagination instantaneously linked the simple turning of the wheel, the force of the current and the generation of power in his fertile mind. The idea of connective interlocking processes, like gears within wheels, became an ongoing obsession throughout his life. Tesla couldn't stop the creative process because he was, in essence, doing what came naturally. You see, Tesla was the interlocutor that linked humanity to the forces of nature, so to speak, i.e., in Gladwell's terms he was a *connector*. He was a person who sensed the interaction of processes between the very small and very large. In other words, Tesla's genius was the perceptual keenness that recognizes how micro and macrocosmic forces come together. In the following story from the book: *The Prodigal Genius* by John O'Neill, you will encounter this connective principle and perceive in it a common theme that propelled Tesla's brilliant mind into celebrity and inventive prominence.

Once while still a young boy, Nikola Tesla, the brilliant and eccentric genius who bestowed upon the world the wonders of alternating current, was out hiking in the mountains on a winter day with some friends. It was not long after a fresh storm had left the ground covered with moist, sticky snow. The boys had made small snowballs and with a push, watched them roll down the mountainside. Most of them rolled a little way and stopped, but one gained momentum and suddenly began to transform from a baseball-sized glob into a massive, rounded carpet with snow and debris clinging to both ends. From a minor, unimpressive object it had gathered size and tremendous momentum until it rolled crashing with a great roar into the valley below, totally stripping the mountainside of trees, bushes and rocks, carrying everything with it.$^{\psi}$

What seems to have occurred in the final exchange when Tesla connected with the snowball and sent it down the hill with dynamic intent, came after a series of apparently disconnected actions. It was only after he'd rolled a number of snowballs down the mountain that suddenly he fully connected with the tiny snow ball in his hand, intuitively becoming a part of the mechanics by which, a powerful event would transpire. Here we need to take note that at this point in his final effort with the snowball the element of *connectedness* between Tesla and the ultimate outcome of the snowball seemed to totally jell. One might say a sticking factor was born at this point. Instead of just another snowball to roll down the mountain into the valley below, it became a process connected to a purpose. The snowball, in fact, took on the central roll of the spiral template, that is, to bind molecules of snow together into a field that would grow exponentially around the central, negative feedback hub of the original ball. Thus, the original ball became united with the virtual future target in a meaningful way – it became linked with an intent and purpose that was mutually beneficial. The snowball became, as it were, an extension of Tesla and Tesla became linked to its power. In this way the duality of the snowball and Tesla's intent became united, i.e. One Whole.

Curiosity and fascination seem to play vital roles in the acceleration of interest that binds people to repetitive activities, also the probable outcome in terms of power imparts to the process. For example, a cat is a natural predator; let them go outside and your loving, little furball with willful intent transforms from a pretty pussycat to a ferocious hunter. What drives them? It is not simply the need to kill for food. Watch them at this activity and most of the time they play with a bird, fascinated with its helplessness as if transfixed by their power to control the outcome of its life. Often, they never eat the bird, since most of our pets are well fed and cared for, they don't really have a great need for eating, they just have a drive to carry out the Whole of the process, to see it through. In this behavior we witness a goal-driven process that is built-in, that is, centralized around a specific activity. Every sense is engaged, the whole of the cat moves as One extended process toward its eventual outcome. Even a kitty evinces this behavior when it plays for hours with a ball of yarn. It isn't driven by the need to kill, per se; it's driven by its fascination with the process and its probable end, that is, his control and power over the probable outcome.

In this regard, the cats will is centralized around the hub of the activity, the Whole of the intent, i.e. to take charge over the chaotic disorder of the yarn and control it and by will direct its activities. Thus, Will times Power can be seen as a combination of unconscious processes aimed toward a specific outcome. In the same way, as people we are fascinated by the outcome, in other words we're fixated. Thus, we stick to it, like the moon sticks to the earth or the earth to the orbit of the sun and the sun to the galaxy. There is a natural process going on here, one that binds us to the greater Whole in which we exist. What is most curious about its binding nature is that the origin of its process is invisible. Isn't that fascinating! We are bound by the unknown mysterious essence of the process, the latent potential in it, shall we say, that could be captured and directed toward some virtual goal in the future. The tiny kitty is learning to hunt for its prey even though its playful fascination is carried out in a manner we associate with the Will-to-Power or to direct its destiny. But we see when looking closer, that the activity is actually connected to larger processes and that the activity is merely an extracurricular extension, shall we say. In short, little things mean a lot because behind them, big processes are at work, like the iceberg that hides a continent.

Tesla became one with the ultimate destination of his principle. In other words, he aimed with intent toward the snowballs ultimate climax as a major future event culminating in the valley below. He did this by centering his mind on the outcome, so that the rolling of the initial tiny ball and its final destination as a powerful avalanche became wholly connected. What we witness is the ultimate culmination of the role of a connector. Connectors have that rare ability of being One with the beginning and ending of a process. Hence, they are able to achieve maximum, energetic results from the smallest of beginnings. You also can learn to be a connective genius! But you must first find the single *most combining factor*, the hub which binds the project into One Single Whole. Once discovered, the power that is latent in organizational Wholeness can be transferred from the solitary singleness of the initial intent to become a magnet around which everything else can gravitate.

Enlist your senses. From a sensory level, Tesla became united through sight and sound, he became involved in the visual and audio aspect of the snowball as it grew from the tactile crunch of its tiny icy cluster in his hand, the mental picture of its powerful force shaking the valley below. The power of this whole process in the young Tesla shook him to his core, leaving a lasting impression. His entire system became imprinted, shall we say, forever more. From that moment forward he saw the event in its Wholeness. From a few ounces of unimpressive icy snow rolling down the mountain, he could trigger the tremendous latent *potential forces of Nature*. He was actually extending himself, (the extension process) connecting with the Whole of the picture at a super-nature level, so to speak. In this way he was becoming One with it. Like the kitty with the ball of yarn the latent possibility of triggering or becoming involved in the release of stupendous forces haunted Tesla from that day onward.

On another level, the kitty became a part of the forces, his awareness became immersed in it, linked to the sense of being a greater whole *outside* his limited physical self. Then, ever after, Tesla was always on the lookout for ways to make connections at these *trigger points (tipping points) to release the incredibly raw potential of nature's largeness.* Bear in mind that Tesla *and his* companions rolled numerous balls down the mountainside, but that it was only *the one which* Tesla connected to that rolled in the end with the desired results, i.e. the massive display of force and power. Tesla's snowball connected because of its spiral properties, that is, the initial ball took on meaningful mass as it gathered or connected random parts into the Whole. Driven by intent and visualized expectation it gathered momentum exponentially from the whole outside it, just as the force of gravity grows by the gross product of the bend in its field as it accumulates and subsequent acceleration.

Tesla had tuned into an incredibly valuable principle connecting space and time with order. He discovered a pattern much like the tipping point where even the minutest event is connected, or lead to large scale events. Moreover, if one followed their intuition, they could sense which one would lead to incredible results. On that day on the mountain rolling the snowball down the hill and carefully noting its results was a reality changer. Tesla not only discovered an incredible snowball-spiral principle, he also learned to follow his internal guidance system, that *extra-sensory arrow* that would take the ball unerringly to its final target in the future.

As we move forward with this text on the spiral force, you will begin to understand how the rotation of the spiral and the effects of curvature and gravity upon the snowball can channel potential energy, no matter how small from its inception to its final destination. It will become very clear as you read this book that the spiral is a self-perpetuating, process that fires its arrow of potentiality from the micro to a predictable outcome. Moreover, the strength of this encapsulating field grows exponentially, that is, proportional to its growing size. This means the spirals ability to transform within a certain length of time from a small mass into a large one at its maximum outcome, follows a specific *trajectory* that propels it unerringly to its ultimate destination. The spiral, like gravity is self-perpetuating, meaning it transforms itself by the process with which it builds. In this way it converts energy from an infinite potential source into the ultimate kinetic release to achieve its ideal outcome.

The Psychology of Energy into Mass

In psycho-physics words, the gathering of information into a concentrated focus is equal to mass and energy squared. For example: the greater the curvature or concentrated bend of the field, the stronger the power of attraction. In short, the more attention you put into a process, the greater its potentiality to bend the space-time field in your favor and materialize what you seek. As a psycho-physically concentrated process, gravitation coupled with concentration mutually act as a power-generating source in much the same way as an electrical dynamo or generator. The dynamo works off a simple principle that concentrates an attractive force around a central hub. It is this rotating central hub that has the ability to transform humble beginnings into clusters by building on momentum and frequency.

Like a vortex of water around a snagged bit of rock or twig in a creek current, all the potential force and mass of the waters flow centralizes around the whirlpool's presence. In this vortical current mass accumulates and/or bends in a spiral to form a field. In this way it uses the force of gravity which in turn acts to accumulates more mass which spirals into mega-clusters which subsequently transforms by association into even more complex events. Put simply: mass attracts mass leading to a vortex of mega-accumulations in very short periods of time. Proof of gravities ability to spiral into order from the disorder about it can be seen in the almost endless cycle of self-catalyzing replications such as the production of galaxies with their powerful black hole and in the ongoing clustering which binds mass in our solar system.

On a mundane level, an example of the spiral codes ability to create order from humble beginnings is the catapulting of a single prank video on You Tube featuring a homeless man into a viral epidemic overnight. Without the spiral's clustering process where mass x acceleration x time, or subject x attraction x timing, the video would have never gotten off the ground. Of course, there are many other subjective human factors at work in this clustering effect. Nonetheless, in a likewise fashion, the order of the galaxy requires rotation momentum acting as a current to generate attraction forces. Without these essential features, the solar system never could have evolved, the planets form or for that matter, a simple video draw maximum attention in record time. Without doubt, the process of the spiral principle to evoke mega results from humble beginnings in spectacular fashion is nothing short of amazing, albeit predictable. This book will teach you why this process is possible and how it comes about.

To begin, the spirals clustering effect and gravity at work have much in common. As an example of gravity and the spiral's snowball effect, consider the behavior of a rolling coaster. When a roller coaster car reaches the top of the curving platform on which it slides, like the top of the spiral circle, it has risen to its maximum potential energy; meaning it is at the point where its maximum potential energy is available. In short, this point marks it potential capacity is highest to make things happen. In a similar way, if you tap into energy at its central point or hub, the maximum point on its curve, the intended results have their greatest potential to manifest. Timing and frequency like gravity is a connective principle that makes particles assume organization. Gravity catalyzes events to come about by the creation of mass. The mass bends the field, thus engendering the process of order to converge and hence emerge.

On a socio-economic level success attracts success just as mass attracts mass and the factors that are involved are timing and resonance. We got a hint of the timing and resonance factors in the McDonald McNuggets in the first chapter. Therefore, gravity's ability to do work can be physically measured in terms of the frequency of its attractive qualities. Therefore, what we learn here is that the greater the resonance to its frequency, the greater the mass; hence the more clustering its field. Simplified: gravity and the spiral force are synonymous in this sense, the vortical forces that comprise them emanate outward as waves around a powerful, central hub. It is the momentum of the spin around the central hub which provides the gravitational stickiness.

In terms of the eco-physics of these forces, potential energy transformed into actual work, or as kinetic energy, derives from its ability to bind things together or to make things happen. This factor is physically measurable by the geometry of its curvature. Greater curvature provides greater stickiness, the binding ability to provide the momentum in its downward path as it rolls, until it reaches its zenith or zero state where it spends its potential in its virtual target goal. Therefore, curvature around a central hub and fixity/fascination of interest are synonymous with stickiness. Both determine potential which, like an arrow aimed 'Zen-like' at its target, can be incredibly huge in a curved space Holoverse. Consider the power of the spiral in the gravitational clusters that hold the galaxies in place, their masses composed of the sun and planets have been careening along in their orbits since time immemorial. Gravity, it should be remembered, according to Einstein, is the indentation in the spacetime field that creates the generating dynamo of the spiral by which potential energy is transformed into work.

Visualize the extreme curvature at the center of the spiral as the ring singularity of a black hole. Careening about it in a spiraling orbit controlled at its central hub the galaxy is guided by the curvature of the black holes immense gravitational mass. Acting as a cosmic dynamo driven by the black holes central field, the spiral arms reveal the flow of the field toward its locus at the center. It is this hub at the center which gathers all the light and gases and produces the dynamic turbine that drives its creative power. Immensely powerful, driven by its accumulated mass which in turns deeply carves out the shape of space and time, the galaxy unerringly follows this unseen channel (dark matter) that propels it onward.

A Self-Perpetuating System

A complete self-perpetuating system, it is the whole of the galaxy, its central hub and spiral arms that drives the mechanism in the molecular dynamo that generates life. The black hole plays two roles in the organizational drama: it is the power source for the archer that *directs the arrow of order toward its target*. In the Zen of archery, the master will tell the student, it is two things that fire's the arrow unswervingly to its target: a) gravity and b) the inner self. Subsequently, propelled by its own self-generative power and assisted by a grand, looping curvature at its hub, future and past are united. Thus, what were dual aspects of space and time unite to become One Whole. Einstein described the union of space and time as the: Spacetime Continuum. In the continuum dualities diffuse and reunite as: Energy and Mass, Space and Time, Mind and Matter to become ONE ENTITY. The divisions reunite and are no longer separated by the temporal divisions designated as independent forces. This process is a self-perpetuating system that follows its predecessor the Big Bang. Where the Whole divides into two separate states, they now reunite again into one whole to continue. The Holoverse is oscillatory, a huge dynamo of creation. Principle: Controlled by its own looping control system of wholeness, the spiral production of gravitation can be seen as a negative feedback mechanism, that is, a self-regulating loop which converts *infinite potential into kinetic energy to create a field that is infinitely self-sustaining and self-perpetuating.*

Gravity is a momentum perpetuating force, the steeper the slope and the greater the angle of its descent, the faster the acceleration of the ball. Clearly, space and time under the effects of acceleration become altered in structure so that what was once separated (space and time) now become a continuum or one continuous, holistic field. A unique process has occurred as a result of achieving maximum curvature of the field. Tesla's original snowball changed exponentially as it increased its mass and therefore, its acceleration at its critical limit. At a supersensory level, Tesla connected with the original snowball at its maximum curvature, sending it unerringly to its destined expansion in the valley below. When the snowball reached its critical limit point, Tesla's mind and the rolling ball caught the wave of the continuum, thus boosting the snowballs energy output far beyond its initial content.

It has, in fact, gathered its momentum from four things: a) Tesla's intent, and b) its surroundings, and c) the curvature of the field, and d) its connectedness to the continuum. Thus its total potential increases at the point where the curvature in the slope aids the ultimate development of mass, which in turns alters the cumulative frequency and shape of the field. The more precipitous the curvature of the slope, i.e. or critical the angle, the faster the snowball will roll, the greater its maximum force released at its ultimate destination.

Channeling, Curvature and Catalysis

In essence, Tesla's experiments in electrical potential demonstrated his sensitivity at channeling/catalyzing/amplifying and/or magnifying processes by boosting momentum at vital 'crisis' points to access the release of greater energy potential. In a polyphase motor this was achieved by adding input electrical energy at critical points along the angle of each cycle to increase output potential. In addition, using this amped up input power cuts through space and time to access greater Potential Energy from the continuum. This process automatically reduces entropy or energy loss encountered by linear mechanical processes. It's like finding a shortcut between two points by accessing the curve. Bear in mind, once Tesla was fully invested in the activity that is, linked intrinsically with the whole process, not separated from it, the more impressive was the outcome. This occurred because Tesla made a habit of greater submersion in his ideas. By first carefully visualizing the process of his inventions within his mind's eye, imagining every minute detail from the smallest part, he magnified his final outcome. In this way he thoroughly united with its maximum potential, became a part of its whole; in sum, exponentially increasing the dynamics of its efficiency. Thus, from its inception and through each stage of the project he was intrinsically harmonious with the complete process.

Coincidentally, Tesla was born during a powerful storm. Thus, from birth onward he was connected to electro-magnetism. It is not surprising that all of his inventions grew out of his innate interconnectedness to the dynamics of electro-magnetism. Perhaps that is why a jagged luminescent image of lightening and its powers were often foremost in his mind. In fact, he enjoyed sitting for hours watching lightning displays, reveling in his soul's connection to cosmic powers. Put simply: the EM field was his home turf. Thus, his major demonstrations and inventions were designed to optimally harness and convert raw potential into power.

When Little Things Mean a Lot

In appreciation of Malcolm Gladwell's 'tipping point' hypothesis, one could view Tesla as an mystic/inventor/scientist 'connector' because of his ability to bring together complex principles, become one with them and channel them into action with alacrity. In a word, his approach undeniably accelerates or catalyzes complex processes to magnify. Tesla's connectivity appears to arise due to his innate propensity to visualize and apply dynamic electro-magnetic principles and put them into action to help humanity. This would make Tesla a scientifically-oriented connectivity a tipping point 'trigger' in my way of thinking, simply because he is able to take advantage of the properties of the spiral dynamo and put them into action. One must remember that where Malcolm Gladwell sees a connector as a 'single person at the *top of the pyramid* or with a *special gift to make things happen,* he is usually referring to their maximum apex of social connectedness to the Whole. Thus a connector acts as the catalyst who releases the trigger that accelerates processes; something akin to the maximum gravitational points high atop of the peaks in a rolling coaster ride. At these maximum inception points, gravity, like Gladwell's 'connector' is at the pinnacle of the energy-potential pyramid. So in that sense people like Tesla and connectors are natural accelerators, i.e. they get things done in a dynamic way.

When we think on it we realize that scientists view gravity as an accelerator because it provides cosmic glue which brings the stuff of the universe together. Therefore, an accelerator analogically can also be a catalyst, a force or a process in the thought patterns of an individual that makes things happen, that is accelerate in a given way to automatically come together. In terms of nature's processes, it is the crisis point where objects possess maximum potential. In a comparative way, Tesla was ideally connected with that particular snowball which launched the avalanche. It was the dynamics of Tesla's connectedness to the network of forces spiraling into that whole which made the event happen in the most dynamic way possible. Looked at electro-dynamically, Tesla's curiosity spark triggered, that is, *released* the snowballs maximum potential which was converted into kinetic energy. Of course, this process can occur in nature in many different ways – but one thing is certain – it takes place when the connector is *divinely* connected or *inspired*. By divinely, I mean holistically united at a *critical* point.

On Being One with Your Target

On an everyday level, I've experienced this same kind of connectedness between my body, a ball and the hoop while playing basketball. For instance, I noticed that if I was not mentally centered or thoroughly connected with the ball, I missed a lot of shots. So, my goal was to increase the degree of my accuracy by becoming more synchronized and spontaneous in my flow. To achieve this I became more holistically united with the ball and basket. Not surprisingly, my best played games came when achieving a spontaneous, non-thinking place. Once my *ego-I* was out of the game and I became spontaneous and free, my game improved. During such times it was as though the hoop and I became one. In fact, learning from these experiences, I began practicing what I began to think of as the *Zen of Basketball*. My aim was to become an expert shooter. To perfect this state I had to become a connector, establishing greater intimacy with the whole game of basketball. To accomplish this I did lots of dribbling, ball-handling drills, difficult maneuvers and sudden shooting from all angles, *without* making an effort to think about it. I let myself *'feel'* the right time and place and followed through spontaneously.

For example, I began my practices by starting out with my back to the basket, about twenty feet away, then I'd spin in a spontaneous, explosive way and take a quick jump shot. After a while at practicing shooting in this manner, I reached a point where my spin, jump and shot became automatically synchronized in one single arched movement with the hoop. Hence, in my mind, the basketball and the hoop became One. In this manner I soon connected in a graceful, arching groove which began with an almost *mindless disconnection* as the basketball exited my hand to follow a flawless spiraling path and drop with amazing repetition through the hoop with a delightful swishing sound. I became especially proficient with a hook shot from certain points over and over on the court.

In general, this process is very similar to solving a problem numerically. If a formula is unknown, it may require numerous attempts to discover the right angle needed to *geometrically* connect order amidst the dots of chaos. Once uniting the points into a whole - the angle and flow, the same template can be used over and over to solve difficult problems easily. Often the solution comes about suddenly in an epiphany, usually after repeated efforts fail and we have given up striving. Today, computers do the work of solving difficult equations with a multitude of probabilities fast and efficiently, where a lone mathematician might have failed miserably in the past. However, bear in mind, that autistic savants can achieve incredible results with lightning calculations and abilities – *without being invested consciously at all in the outcome.* In fact, if you'd ask the savant how he does it or even to add up two plus two, he'd probably have no idea how to do it. Enigmatically, they do it *mindlessly.* Here one is reminded of the Zen practice of No-Mind where one is encouraged to pay *no mind.*

Scientists have successfully employed a method like this to solve difficult non-linear equations or to plot the trajectory of order amidst the chaos of an infinite number of probabilities. Our brain solves problems in a similar way. For instance, it is both a linear calculator that plots the course of a process in a linear fashion, but it also multi-tasked using its holistic, right-brain parallel processing capabilities. Dualistic, it senses the topography of a problem in terms of both longitude and latitude to arrive at the right solution quickly. Frankly, the holistic process takes place best when we learn to get out of the way and let it work. Once we get out of the way and trust the process, the dual processes of left and right brain merge to do their work more effectively.

Mathematicians are sometimes stymied striving to plot order amidst a chaos of apparent disorder. Their dilemma is similar to locating a black and white spotted dog in a chaos of black and white spots without knowing exactly where to look. So they go about it in a logical, cause-effect way. They know that the dog is there, just as an underlying order exists in the chaos of waves that greet the linear fixated left brain. The question is how to find it quickly? The solution remains far outside our linear methodology taken to laboriously locate it, yet very near – *if* we allow ourselves to feel or be guided by the deeper holistic pattern within. Hence, the more you think about it, i.e., add up the pros and cons, the longer it takes to get the answers. On the other hand, letting go and going with the flow or sensing its presence and following through without thinking, comes up with the right answer. In other words, feeling obfuscates the interferences of the tendency of the left brain to over-analyze. The right brain does the work all the time of coming up with answers from a 'feeling' or 'intuitive' level because it follows a curved path; which is something that is nearly impossible for a fixed, linear, straight-lined analysis by the laboring left brain.

This might sound complex, but fortunately, there is a dynamic connective principle that serves as a template for establishing all patterns of order found in the universe. When you follow that pattern without 'thinking' about it, that is, connecting via feeling, you alter the way information flows into your awareness. For example, write on the left side of piece of paper hello, and on the far side, goodbye. Now bend the paper and place both ends together. See what occurs: the two words come together so that hello and goodbye occur at once. Sure the two processes occur separately, at least in relationship to linear space-time, but looked at holistically (the bent paper) they can occur at once. The magic in this realization is recognizing that in a holistic sense, the two occurred at once – *it was the process of linear thinking that separated them.* You see, thinking divides the Whole into Parts, and adds the factor of time. Einstein once said that the purpose of time was so everything didn't happen at once, now you get an idea what he saw. He was looking at things from a holistic standpoint, that is, without divisions. Looking at reality this way the ending and the beginning actually occur simultaneously. What has happened is that curvature has overruled the straight-line reasoning so that space has been figuratively bent into a loop, or simply – you have flipped the connective 'trigger point' from 3rd to 4th dimensional awareness. So you might say that the autistic person's brain acts more from a holistic or right brain perspective (that's parallel processing), thus it is able to see the whole picture without breaking it apart into pieces.

Bringing things together into wholes is the work of the spirals intrinsic pattern-making process. As I have intimated, the spiral galaxies come together by following a holistic template that is invisible. However, it is palpable because it causes space to bend and it is this curvature that gravitational affects follow into order. The curve of the pattern lends itself to unifying holism, yet from a deeper level this underlying order is comparatively opaque to our senses. Thus, in its own way, order, like a spotted dog amongst the panoply of black and white spots, the hidden order emerges not only because of the presence of the neurological patterns by which the brain operates, but because of the underlying force of the spiral principle in the galaxy. Like the mind of the pattern maker reflected within his/her art, the source or principle that unites the pieces of the puzzle of life with the 'grander picture' is always intrinsic somewhere within its creation, yet tends to remain somewhere just outside the physical senses, invisible to only the most discerning eyes. This is because the template that brings about the patterns of order operates just outside the causal framework. Our mechanistic search through linear methods is limited by principles which naturally obscure its whereabouts though its presence hovers ever present just outside sensory periphery.

However, once individual perspective is altered or expanded, like a panorama seen from a greater vantage point or spotted black and white dog in a miasma similar pattern, it is easy to spot, its presence now readily apparent amidst the chaos. In the same way, with diligent observational applications, one can discern the intrinsic connectivity that unites many processes and tips the forces which trigger maximum organization productivity. However, as I have intimated in the *Zen of Basketball*, one must learn to reduce some of the clatter of the analytical thinking process to allow the over-arching forces operating behind the scenes to take charge. I call this spontaneous process *tapping into the groove*, something like 'grooving' to music. Once you feel the beat you simply follow the rhythm, it's easy - just let your feet follow your feelings to do the dancing. So we discover that we are following, at some deeper level, an underlying groove to which all patterns of order are rhythmically synchronized. Our search leads us to the discovery of a 'triggering process' that connects the heretofore invisible to the visible to reunite holistic order amidst the apparent straight-line disorder of the physical world.

The question foremost in our mind demands that we ask: a) what is this pattern from which order arises, and b) how can we get hooked up to this wonderful groove that guides all order into manifestation? As to the first part I would answer, all order derives from an innate principle in nature, the outermost part of which takes the form of a spiral shape. It is this principle which hooks us up as it does with any other whole in nature. To encourage it to work for us requires that diligent study of its principle throughout the processes of natural order.

In essence, that is the aim of this manual to guide and direct you toward channeling the flow of this energy into all your activities and endeavors. Once you learn to recognize the principle that induces every Part-to-become-Wholes you too can begin to:

1) Recognize the spiral principle in nature and the cosmos.
2) Learn to attune yourself to these cosmically underlying principles.
3) Reduce energy expenditures lost in unnecessary effort.
4) Increase the brain/mind's optimum output.
5) Achieve goals more efficiently and without error.

MEDITATIONS

1. If you have a goal in life, find out what its central features are. Meditate on its extensions, that is, what makes it up, especially why you are interested in it and what your plan entails.

2. Discover everything you can about the goal which fascinates you. Research it on the internet, read books, ask friends. Seek a full and complete description of it, both in terms of pros and cons. Don't leave anything out.

3. Become sensory invested in it. In other words, enlist as many of your senses as possible to feel it, see it, smell it, taste it; hear it.

4. Be playful with it. Imagine its outcome. Have fun visualizing its potential outcome in any number of different ways.

5. Now analyze its potential. This means being honest about how much of your time and energy you are actually putting into its manifestation. Is that enough?

6. In light of number five, ask yourself: compared to your investment in its potential, what do you feel is its probable outcome? How short are you in investment activity? Endeavor to make up the differences in effort to bring about a favorable balance, if you see the deficit clearly.

7. Strive to understand your connection to it. Look inwards into yourself and seek to comprehend your motivations in this process. What does it fulfill in yourself? What does the activity tell you about who you are in a deeper sense?

8. Once you have begun to explore through playfulness, imagination and contemplation your complete involvement in your activity of choice, the thing that enjoy most of all, strive to sense its ultimate outcome.

9. When you have begun to envision the outcome, strive to 'feel' its probable fulfillment in the distant future. Imagine you're a moving target aiming at moving target that you're trying to stay one with. Once you feel the connection, look for its connection to other activities that make it a central part of your life.

10. If you don't have a clear idea of what centralizes your goals, study chapter one and two closely. Contemplate the meaning of the spiral template, why it acts as a central hub around which

many things unite to form a whole. Visualize the galaxy connected to the world you're in and to yourself.

11. Next, actively apply what you've learned again to any goal-directed interest and strive to feel its outcome and its connections once again. Compare.

4

CONVERTING NOTHING INTO SOMETHING

"The physical world has at bottom – a very deep bottom, in most instances – an immaterial source and explanation. It comes from bit."
John Wheeler

Flipping the Information Switch

The tipping point is like any mechanism that triggers another cooperative process such as the release of a pistol hammer which in turn strikes the cap of a bullet and fires its metal projectile toward a distant, future target. One might describe the moment of triggering as a *transcendental* action because it involves many processes much bigger than itself. Such mechanisms involve multiple levels of energy incorporated in processes connecting us to greater and often invisible Wholes. In fact, where these connected patterns originate may be so far outside the process which we see, that they might be totally invisible to the current. Like the sum of the Whole, according to Aristotle, can be described as more than its Parts and yet each part is oh, so integral to the connected points at each separate level which unite everything to an even greater ongoing Whole. For example, the mere flipping of a light switch is more than just connecting an electrical circuit that flows between its source and the light bulb; it's also about cosmic forces that extend into the very crux of the Holoverse. In fact, many of these forces and their fields are far beyond our current body of knowledge to say the least. You might be an individual but you are connected to the Whole of the country and the world, not to mention the universe by dint of your Oneness with all-that-is, though you may feel isolated in your corner of reality. It goes without saying that everything is mutually interdependent upon the Whole though it may seem to stand alone. Thus, that any one of multiple processes cannot operate alone is self-evident when seen in the light of the greater Whole. That we are a part of a feeling, sensing organic hologram can than be taken as a given. That is why the idea of a meaningless universe, which many scientists believe, evolving out of random coincidences amounting to 'nothing' seems peculiar in the extreme.

One cannot resist asking how can this nothingness give birth to something as incredibly complex and ordered as DNA; life itself or the vast magnificence of our universe? Think on it: a "no" or "non" thing implies meaningless nihility, an empty, inexplicable void. The question is can there be such a state as a non-thing? Looking around at the vastness of the universe we might at first be compelled to remark that outer space, most certainly, appears to be a vast, empty void. But I implore you to look deeper and when you do the answer seems self-evident – that this outward appearance is deceiving. All things build on something which precedes it, though we at first glance may not be privy to its nature or physical presence.

Right away, the old tune of a great seventy's song by the cool soul singer Billy Preston might come to mind, *"Nothing from nothing leaves nothing, you got to have something if you want to be with me, yeah. I'm not trying to be your hero, but that zero is too low for me."* Yes, indeed, the zero upon which the universe is built and all things connected, is just the outer illusion. With certainly we would want to echo the sentiments – all is connected and we with it. This realization drives us to compose our own rendition of the tune: *"Nothing from nothing, leaves nothing - you got to be something, **if you want to be**, yeah,"* once again affirming that you need mass and solidity to exist here in the physical world. One thing is connected to another – the flesh to matter and matter to molecules and molecules to atoms and atoms to their components. We are affirming that reality is not so empty and meaningless but connected from one level or point to another to form an endless matrix. In fact, the idea of nothing flies in the face of existence.

Now here's the kicker… if you examine the idea closely you will discover that 'nothing' is really the something that you appear to be …depending upon another sensory viewpoint. In a very *real* sense, existence and sensory awareness work hand-in-glove to bring nothing out of emptiness and into meaningfulness. The more you expand your range of sensitivity the more you sense the connectedness we share with the bigger picture spoken of in the previous chapters. Here's an example: take for instance the wolf and his olfactory sense; researchers report that what his sense of smell tells him makes up the bulk of what he knows about his reality.

For example, it is said that the wolf can detect one hundred and seventy-five different things about another animal just by sniffing his urine. How much can you detect through your sense of smell? Not much, if anything – yet what makes you think that what you smell is more real (meaningful) than what a dog smells? Vision can be explained the same way. A hawk's eyesight is so keen he can spot his pray up to five miles away. How far can you spot yours? Probably less than 500 feet if you're lucky. You see, our senses can work for or against us, depending on how good we are using them. Truth is most of us aren't really that good at applying our senses. In fact, what some people might be able to see compared to others might seem a little uncanny, even 'extra-sensory,' when in fact, it's really nothing more than a sharpened or enhanced sense; but than, that's the nature of the extra-sensory.

What other *specialized* senses pick up may even make them appear to be getting information from far beyond this dimension. That's why it's so important to be careful about saying that you don't believe that something can come from nothing, when that 'nothing', so far as your friend's sensory range is concerned, might be something he's tuning into; it's just that you can't perceive it. This remark takes us back to our introductory comment on something coming from nothing. Actually, the subject of this chapter, *nothing,* is really a little semantics trick to get your attention so I could share with you some unique insights into the nature of the 'nothingness' upon which the physical universe is theorized (by astronomers and mystics) to be constructed.

First of all, the idea that nothing gives birth to something began with a misnomer suggesting that the origin of the physical reality defies any ability to perceive its true nature. This reasoning seems logically skewed and generates visions of an emptiness filled with a desolate, uninhabitable void. In a sense, *it is empty* so to speak, meaning it can't be perceived in a manner commensurate with our agreed-upon sensory range. This is definitely not the 'something' which could produce a reality as solid as the earth we stand on or as fragile as biogenic order, for that matter. Fact is something can't just rest on nothingness, though the orbits of the levitating planetary bodies hanging there in featureless space seem to defy this logic. For example, if you study the origin of the massive galactic systems in the universe you will discover that they appeared to spring from massive voids – apparent emptiness. Myriads of worlds erupting from nothing, could this be possible? Yet this is what the astronomers tell us. There was undoubtedly an underpinning to that void, regardless of whether they comprehended it or not and it must have been eons in the making.

For instance, a lot of astronomers and scientists believe that dark energy, an invisible force that emits an incredibly powerful gravitational field seems to exist in an enigmatic, palpable but non-tangible reality just outside the visible range of the strongest telescopes or the most sensitive radio frequency receivers. Its presence may be measured but it is relatively intangible except that it emanates an incredibly powerful gravitation field. Astrophysicists tell us this invisible but ever-present nothing constitutes over 95.1 % of the known gravitational mass of the observable universe that can't be accounted for in comparison to the net "luminous" physical mass around it.

Thus, we are driven to ask: if it is not mass, could it be the source that creates mass, the flue or channel by which the creative force crosses over from the microcosm as it transforms into spiral galaxies? After all – our universe must start from an inception point, a place so removed in terms of mass that it is, in itself, closer to nothing; a nothingness that must be directed by the purest of channels.

Something's Antecedents

The idea of our universe springing from nothing has its roots in our philosophical and religious institutions. Mystical tracts globally have made references to this nothingness since time immemorial. One of the most significant teachers averring to this void from which all things began was the great Chinese philosopher, Lao Tzu. His need to weigh in on the view of something originating from nothing is evident in the book: The Tao Te Ching:

"There was something chaotic
Yet complete, which existed before the
Creation of heaven and earth.
Without sound and formless, it stands
Alone and does not change. It pervades
All and is free from danger. It can be regarded
As the mother of the world.
I do not know its proper name,
But will call it Tao."
Chapter 25 **Tao Te Ching**

Some folks, upon hearing this enigmatic verse, might be baffled by its abstract logic and think it poppycock! Instinctively, we all know what we call nothing must simply be a hidden 'quantity' that we are yet to discover. Still, many creation myths continue to assert that prior to existence, order and life originated from a 'no-thing' which somehow gave birth to the materiality of the world. Curiously, Lao Tzu, like many contemporary scientists believe order sprang spontaneously from the mist. Think about it - that's what systems theorists insist self-organization to be, i.e. an ascent into materiality from a formless void thought of as chaos. Steven Johnson, author of the book *Emergence*, along with many scientists patently refuse to believe order has an origin, yet our mystic Lao Tzu said it was '*changeless and stood alone*,' which is interesting because it suggested that something's origins was somehow complete in itself. Certainly, this philosophical holism is well illustrated by the Yin and Yang as completing the Whole of the Tao. This remark implies that unlike our world of change, it comes from a state of being that does not undergo transformation. Lao Tzu also tells us that this state pervaded everything, indicating that it must be, in essence, hyper-dimensional.

In terms of a source, I for one am inclined to theorize that this *changeless place that stands alone* must be a reference to the 4th dimension; a place statistically containing all probabilities before abstracting (bifurcating) into any one, single line probability. This singular probability, a reduction of all probabilities to a linear path, is synonymous with the extra-dimensional origins of the fabled arrow of time. Hypothetically, this *4th dimensional space* precedes our physical dimension, hence it may not be visible, e.g. exist as an ever-present, impalpable Whole accessible only through a channel by which that singular probability can be brought into manifestation as form. In this way what was structure-less (free of order) found its first stage of becoming, as Pythagoras and Euclid implied, where a point transforms into a line, the line a triangle, and so on as the world of forms come about. It is through these abstractions that form from formlessness emerges from a hyper-dimensional space outside yet encompassing our world; like cogs-within-a-wheel that turn as the Whole system moves. One thing connects to another. You connect to your parents and their ancestors going back thousands of eons and at some everyone connects to a singular point that gave birth to all of humans and every other form of life. That single cell came from a common source is a miniscule point I call the 4th dimension. It unites all things together into ONE WHOLE. Bear in mind, that this 4th dimensional point could be said to be totally imperceptible to sensory perception, at least in terms of objects occupying the causal world. It is this 'non-visual' or wholly intangible space that comprises the dimension that unites everything. As such, it is not detectable by the range of any physical, sensory limits.

However, it is detectable through a) an alteration in consciousness, or b) by understanding the subtle properties of the spiral wave. In fact, this 4th or extra--dimensional perspective fits quite well the spiritual idea of *being in-the-world, but not-of-the-world*. In short, the 4th dimension connects us holistically to the physical plane by its encapsulating nature. In terms of physics, the description of this ever-present but intangible whole outside our sensory range has all the earmarks of an anti-universe or even the dark matter which supports it. As far as physics or spiritual ideas are concerned, than this all-encompassing 4th dimension would appear to be immeasurable, not 'of this world,' and/or containing infinite probabilities that remain 'outside' our domain of awareness, at least in the terms that we understand form and substance. Seen in contradistinction the two states - the 4th dimension, or *formlessness*, and the 3rd dimension, or *form* - are comparable to energy and mass. The 4th dimension is energy and the physical world form.

Hence, all energy emanates from the infinite source that is the 4th dimension. It is at this point where the energy conversion process takes place, i.e., it splits from its source in the 4th dimension to assume physical extensions. All energy originates in this unlimited whole; however, to use it at optimum levels, it must be properly channeled. The principle that best suits the channeling takes the shape of a spiral process. Perhaps that is why the spiral is seen so prolifically throughout the universe. Therein is the secret to a swifter manifestation of all things material. Wise is the individual who learns to properly connect to this cosmic principle because it will *exponentially* increase the amount of energy necessary to accelerate the manifestation process in record time.

During this transformative what is occurring process is that energy is being redirected, funneled through a vortical, snowball-like process where it branches into order or the complexity of biogenic form. Endlessly creative, it erupts as snowflakes, crystals, stems, DNA, leaves, florets, seashells, galaxies, cities or even ant, bee and termite hives. It can even transmogrify and emerge as a byproduct of life and awareness into mechanical and electrical technology. Or into cites and or local-into-global complexity. Its source of generative propulsion for this activity lies in its primal charge.

Make careful assessment of its monumental energy reserves, because from it our physical universe ensued. Emerging from so-called nothingness, energy appears to have been channeled, as if intentionally from a preordained pattern that crossed the time-space barrier from disorder into what we 3-d creatures call order. Unfortunately, science somehow missed the connection. That is why it tends to frown on these speculations as mere probability states, seeing them as rife with uncertainty; i.e. chaotic. Quantum physics has been thoroughly stigmatized with this messy label, and ever since has been thought of as sciences little problem. So it came up with chaos theory to bridge the gap between disorder and order in a mechanistic way attributing order to some sort of freaky, spontaneous, acausal switch, when in fact, it has all the earmarks of a causal one. Albeit, a causal principle that hasn't been provided - until now. This book seeks to offer evidence of that bridge, i.e., that the spirals we see in the galaxies come about via a template or transforming, innate pattern. Incidentally, the transformative switch equates with the holistic process by which Tesla transformed or redirected the chaotic forces of the river with his rotating dynamo, thereby channeling its riotous forces.

Coincidentally, Lao Tzu, our Chinese philosopher, seems to have anticipated modern science since he, in fact, uses the term "chaos" as if to refer to the virtual condition now known by science as a 'state," i.e., *the status of a system at any one instant*." In this spiral book the word 'chaos' will be used to allude to a virtual state possessing infinite probabilities. Interestingly, in the introduction we talked about the tendency of the template to bring order to the cosmos through the energy-corralling motion of the spiral arms. In this example random gases, which are the most chaotic of molecules, were channeled by the spiral arms to form mass and eventually, biogenic order. This is an excellent example by which to visualize the nature of chaos, since, in fact, the word 'gas' derives from its Greek cousin 'chaos' meaning *without order*. From this interpretation we get a glimpse of chaos or gas as the hypothetical 'nothingness' that possesses infinite potential from which 'somethingness,' through the form-inducing process of the template and its spiral effect. The question is *why*, not just *how*, did the template come about? Furthermore, *how* did it *'jump'* the gap between the anti-world and our own? For that answer we must delve deeper.

Ostensibly, in-between the two states, formlessness and form, one is driven to suspect that something, (in the form of a statistical reduction of probabilities into one single line framework of order) prompted the transformation. The reduction of probabilities into one timeline, if you recall, was mentioned at an earlier point. In that regard, the template appears to serve as a way of statistically narrowing the probabilities down to a few repeating series, thereby arriving at the preponderant wave(s) assuming the illuminable mass. Similar in context to separating the chafe from the wheat, this preponderant gestalt of collective energy became object-bound 3-D reality. Essentially, an unknown and quite formless quantity (even if we can't see the invisible but yet sense the palpable elements comprising it), leads to the materialization of form. To reiterate, *a statistical reductionist process led to the creation of matter or what we term as the material plane*. Like sand settling on the bottom of a moving current, shall we say, many probable lines of information were narrowed down to a specific stream of data that became the underlying prototypal model or template by which our physical world came about.

Thus, the Big Bang beginning can be seen as a narrow channel through which information burst forth as order. Its presence followed a massive compression into a single point that blew up into the bubble of our current universe. Like a balloon being inflated, spacetime continued to expand in accordance to the influx of pressure from within until it burst forth into disorder. In this way – disorder directs order to return to disorder, and the cycle repeats itself. A butterfly effect, the cycle recurs at chaos points. Seen this way, order makes its appearance with a copious serving of accompanying disorder, as if the template *needs* random probabilities to choose from in its movement onward toward replication and rebirth. If you examine the data on chaos theory, you will find that these speculations fit the facts connected with chaos. Therefore, when chaos reaches maximum disorder, it suddenly bifurcates into new order through the butterfly effect', i.e., sudden new beginnings.

So, what Lao Tzu implies may be quite true; that is, that a no-thing was in fact the very 'some' thing that gave birth to the world, but not in the same sense as we think of an object having shape and form in the physical world. That no-thing appeared in its nascent and primal form as probabilities; that is, a probability before it assumed singularity. Once it assumed a single line probability as in a template-shaping transformation, then it took form as a 'thing.' Keeping the transition process in mind; that of infinite energy reduced down to a narrow, concentrated stream, the idea that the world came from nothing may have its limitations. In fact, *nothing* may turn out to be something more closely resembling 'everything,' meaning possessing all probabilities *albeit* concentrated into a narrow framework.

Here, I am thinking in terms of the quantum wave state *hovering on the edge of becoming*, i.e., virtual, or always possessing (because it is open *and* closed) the possibility of becoming anything or everything at any moment; whichever comes first. *Open but closed -- disorder residing in order* so that it remains in a virtual state of becoming. Thus, the chicken and the egg reduce to mutually comparative states in terms of perceptual probabilities; i.e. what you see depends on from what angle or point in the cycle you are viewing it happen.

An extreme but ancient view with a distorted perspective on the origins of something from nothing can be examined in the pseudo-science of epi-genetics, a popular mythology from the Middle-Ages embracing a misguided idea of the origins of many life forms. Maggots, for example, were believed to suddenly spring up from decaying objects simply because that's where people saw them. In other words, they failed to look deeper into origin of maggots and their relationship to decaying flesh to get a clearer look at the underlying, connective process. It was only after the growth of scientific investigation involving trial and error experimentation and observation that it became clear that maggots didn't just spring up from dead flesh. Careful observation revealed that they were the larvae of flies who laid their eggs in the carrion to insure a ready food source. However, it was a hard idea to shake because of its collective appeal to the stream of consciousness in which these ideas were formed.

Today we are faced with many similar misconceptions created by the way in which we view what is termed 'reality.' Case in point: contrary to our current critique of the popular mind of this time period, many of our collective beliefs have roots in deeper processes that could be thought of as mystical in nature. For instance, life obviously originated from a no-thing state, and in fact, remains 'virtually' in that state by virtue, shall we say, of the definition. Yet one must delve deeper into the philosophy and science of information theory to understand its total meaning. In comparison, what we term life obviously came from this original nothingness but never totally foregoes it. Just as body shape and form originates in a non-tangible information state known as the DNA, an ever-changing panorama of fresh probabilities that prod it to change. I'm referring to a virtual state, hovering on the edge of becoming, open to a catalyst of probability forces that gives it a boost into continuous order. Without this edgy, probability state, order would not come about.

Thus, the problem of dealing with an intangible in a tangible way is, in fact, bridged by the presence of the spiral template. Please note: the template directs the activity of nothingness in the form of information as it is translated into form. Please recall that this is a form-engendering process. In this way what we term formlessness or information that cannot be weighed or measured per se provides a wave or curvature whereby existence is guided, i.e., birthed into form. Think about it: we come from something that is relatively nothing; we call that nothingness DNA or simply *information*. Look at this process as a form providing gestalt that began as a series of information probabilities reduced to a singular probability line. This occurred through a bridge provided by the supervisory processes of the spiral template. Thus, in that sense, what we are is, in essence is derived from a formlessness prodded by a transformative spiral process to take on form. Subsequently, in an ongoing way, this spiral process of supervisory guidance, shall we say, continues to serve as a catalyst at each point where adjustment to change is necessary to insure survival. In this way the spiral maintains order and continuity that defies points where apparent chaos begins to set in. Defined in this way, survival, through dint of the spiral principle, reduces to the ability to adapt when faced with critical limit points leading to chaos.

Once people began to put these facts together, they began to realize that a chain of events not readily observable at first observation are behind the ongoing continuity before and after crisis points. However, some people in risk management and systems theories speculate that is only what we want to see. Moreover, if the tendency to see patterns are only byproducts of our manner of looking at the world, 'nothing' or 'random disorder' would be the only all that we would perceive; which is borne out by these same nihilists who come up with these cockeyed notions. Yes, the mind gives order sometimes where there is none, but that does not mean that everything is randomness and disorder. There is a bigger principle operating behind the scenes that brings about order, and it governs the mechanics of why organic order continues to replicate itself.

Put clearly: life defies any theory that presents a meaningless, random interpretation. We can ascertain this just by asking the simple question: then why the sustained continuity? Somewhere within the continuity in all this chaos of change a principle must exist by which order is maintained despite the overwhelming presence of disorder. This fact in itself, relegates the notion of nothing leading to something as an inherent impossibility, otherwise this thing called 'organic life' could not nor would not be sustained.

One might think that science was far beyond such preposterous negative assumptions, but just the other day I listened to an astronomer say that the universe apparently sprang up from nothing. I wondered how he could be such a brilliant, insightful scientist who lectured so eloquently, but in the next moment could be guilty of such gross assumptions. But maybe that is the nature of science, i.e., assumptions based on known facts and nothing more. If one wishes to use such terminology, it should be qualified, for instance, as I do in this book by identifying how or what nothing might consist of, if you get my drift. If you don't, I hoping you will when you read Chapter Four: "Converting Nothing into Something."

Nonetheless, misconceptions happen. In fact, people often refer to the space around them as empty or absent of object-reality, when indeed, it is filled with millions of relatively non tangible things such as rays of energy or atoms that comprise a ghostly world in comparison to chairs and cars. Compared to our world of form with buildings, mountains and cars that we can touch and see, it would appear virtually empty.

Far below the surface of appearances infinitely powerful forces move toward a raw state of becoming. These forces comprise the virtuosity I've been referring to, that is, the nebulosity of the Whole beyond the Parts before manifestation. Meanwhile, upon the surface of appearances, the world of solidity is sustained by the vortex of the spiral supported by the converging streams of water below the surface pulled together by counter-currents against an unyielding, central hub. As the converging waters merge under the compounding forces of gravitation in the drive of the current, they are being forced to assume a sustained shape by the pressures behind them. The only option available is to bend and form a concentric swirl around the concave center, comparable in essence to a targets bull's eye. Thus, the vortical shape, like convection currents rising from sub-surface waves converging into molecular streams of gases in the creation of the steam (and the beginning of the universe); it begins to self-organize as guided by the template of the spiral force.

Thus, out of what appears to be nothing, unseen, lower converging streams unite at the surface as the curvature of a debris-filled whirlpool in the same manner as spiral galaxies. Another example is the enduring whirlpool of gases on Jupiter recorded by astronomers over hundreds of years.[v] In other words, if it wasn't for the dynamics of sub-surface currents the water would simply meander down the river with the rest of the molecules accumulated there in the channel. In short, the helical patterns created by sub-surface forces are caught in the merging of conflicting streams contracted around a central nucleus.

In a like manner, we know that the only thing keeping the planets stable in their orbits around the sun are their acquiescence to the curvature of space as they converge or fall into an elliptical arch and begin to rotate instead of simply continuing a natural, inertial inclination to move forward in a straight line. Looked at in another way, one might simply imagine the curving field of energy as streams of information guided into form by in invisible template.

Significantly, there are many other processes in life which follow these helical dynamics into form. One that comes immediately to mind, which at first note might appear to spring from nothing into something, is the phenomenon of viral videos. A quick glance might drive one to assume that these internets, video sensations were 'viral contagions' of a minor miracle variety. However, deeper scrutiny tells us that these videos didn't simply explode into order and self-organize as if by some acausal source. For example, the apparent random oddity of a video of a cat alternating between farting and meowing suddenly escalated from relative obscurity into fame within days.

In fact, these so-called 'viral' videos, like the vortexes in a stream, behave like chaos patterns that erupt from hidden variables that only appear to quantum-jump, as it were, from relative obscurity to fame within a few days. Certainly, on the bubbling surface of information that is the internet, they appear to explode with 'magical' ease to effortlessly pull in millions of viewers, earning their astonished owners thousands of dollars in feedback advertising offers. Amazed observers are taken in by face value when viewing the surface of the stream, thinking that these people were extremely *lucky*. It was as though their meteoritic rise from a rather nondescript, mundane lifestyle into international fame was the work of magic, or written by fate in the stars.

Surprisingly, the possibility that the video's success was written in the stars might actually be closer to the truth then one might suspect, if you consider that their success occurred because it contained a hidden encode or cosmic formula that propelled it there. One might ask what that underlying process could be. Theories abound, one is that viral videos have creative, staying power because they rely on so-called visceral or emotional 'hooks' which draw the audience to click on them, which could be true, in part. Multiple data streams obeying laws of resonance possess their own gravitational orbits; bends in the spacetime field may provide centrifugal forces for others, like the converging fluid processes in the analogy of a whirlpool forming from a river's sub-surface currents. In this case the farting and meowing cat merely served as the central hub around which the debris of interest build-up, just like a whirlpool that draws all sorts of things into its maul.

As I see it, information follows the same laws of fluid dynamics bound by hidden gravitational forces that act as a channel with its current converging into spiral patterns. Hence, the propagation of the video, a social meme, as it were, is an information virus that could be said to 'infect' the public mind because it tends to be the gravitational hub around which interest converges. Thus the meme serves as a connector or '*key word association signifier,*' data that forms hubs of socially attractive snags in the social information flow around which energy or attention converges. This convergence of information around a central hub takes on a spiral-like swirl in which a picture or gestalt emerges that surface observers aren't at first fully privy to. The perceptual distinctions that form an eventual picture take time to emerge, although the whole picture from which they emerge has been just outside their perception range all the while.

The formation of the genetic information spiral of DNA and RNA is another example in that it has been there all the stored within the helix, even though how it manifests takes time to emerge into a living organic form. In a similar fashion, what appears to be a wacky video production arising as if by magic is actually precipitated by powerful sub-social streams of energy that connect people via a hidden information field lingering just outside its serial emergence. Culture works in the same way. It provides converging social information streams garnered from religious notions, art, science and music that emerge to form central vortexes or hubs of creative energy. It's not so much the product of the information, what we see on the surface, lets be clear about that – but the non-conscious, as it were, convergence of numerous information streams that can make a 'twig' of debris dynamically spiral into the gestalt of a forest.

Predictive Spiral Factors Behind Viral Video's

Take for example a 1996 video production *Dancing Baby* which went wild and was absolutely over-the-top with near ludicrous, cartoon-like antics. One would wonder at first glance that this ridiculous theme could ever grab such social attention. However, under closer scrutiny one catches glimpses of something covert defying the assumed rational, cortex-engineered logic of the public's conscious mind. This covert *something* seems to obey a powerful, illogical current, shall we say, that feeds the childlike consumption of the collective psyche. In quality it might it be compared to a taboo side-dish of fast food, like sugared down dessert, something we are drawn to consume regardless of the warnings by the rational 'health nut' advocates. Yes, it dances to a different drummer, a signal coming from an almost childlike social appetite for the inane teetering on the verge of logical anarchy. Indeed, like the candy we hide to eat or the cigarettes we consume despite the surgeon general's health warnings about the dangerous results of smoking, many are drawn to it against the rants of the conscious mind. Below the irrational surface of consciousness, we feel the tug of a field much stronger in context to the prescribed pinnacle of approved social behavior. Indeed, people are hopelessly pulled in by an engaging current, a compelling field beyond the obvious subliminal advertising cleverly meant to generate social popularity.

I'm not suggesting that all videos which have suddenly leaped into the headlines to start a pandemic were precipitated there by this formula - there are other factors in some of them that launched their meteoric flight. Some of the video's admittedly simply struck that common, emotional cord which generates response, like a catch phrase or joke timed just right to get a laugh. It is the relevancy of the material and the timing in response to the subliminal cues (which are intrinsic factors in all 'viral' videos). Like a ball teetering on the brink of falling into a basketball hoop, it might momentarily spin there, reacting to the play of forces in which it finds itself immersed, and when the force or 'straw that broke the camel's back' taps its cumulative surface, it falls.

For instance, *Invisible Children Inc.,* the most viral video in contemporary history received 34, 000, 000 views the first day it arrived on You Tube, the 5th of March, 2012. To date this video got a whopping 100,000,000 clicks. It was about African cruelty to young boys by a certain Congo leader who forced them into fighting. Cruelty to African children by rebel forces and ruthless dictators has been a common theme, generating tons of sympathy and concern. The fact that it generated so many clicks in such a short period was truly an unusual record in itself, because most of the videos that go viral seem to take about 3-7 days. So you see it wasn't precipitated spontaneously into a pandemic, conditions were ripe for the strong emotional surge that tipped its descent (which was its ascent) into fame. One could say it engaged a synchrony of self-same feelings. In this regard, it had the earmarks of a contagious quantum event. That is, it has the ability to go from a local 3-d particle standing wave to a holo-global wave in an instant!

The Congo video doesn't have the qualities of the viral video I was referring to with the cartoon-like quality that taps right brain spontaneity. It instead appears to thrive off the collective emotional sentiment for the well-being of exploited children, something we all can relate to. Please recall, that the stronger the sentiment, the greater the bend in the field, hence duration of momentum increases and clustering accumulates proportionally. On the surface the two video phenomena's look very different, but below the water line, so to speak, their appeal is essentially driven by the same underlying bend in the field that diverts a stream of supports from millions of viewers. Entertainment is a multi-billion-dollar empire and actors are paid exorbitant sums to play roles that demand they pretend to be popular social characters they're not and to even perform reprehensible things we want them to act out even when everything about what they are doing say's not too. But we don't care, and in many ways, neither do the actors in the final gambit, simply because even negative attention can spiral into success as well as positive. The process is essentially the same, especially if the emotion or thought surrounding the accumulation of the snowball has strong enough content.

We love our entertainers and accept it when they live an anarchist lifestyle, full of libertine promiscuity, glitz, drugs and glamour. In fact we want them to, and part of it is so we can believe in their invincibility and icon-evoking otherworldly status. Something latent in us is freed, acted out, strengthening the empathic mirror and adding to the rapid clustering of the collective snowball. It makes them more believably-unbelievable which exacerbates the transcendence and social status of the viewer to perpetuate the aura. Thus we can talk about them in our awed way and promote the mythological realm in which they perform. In this way everyone co-creates a secondary escapist fantasy world free from the mundane, nine-to-five.

Shared this way, internet videos help create a secondary twilight world, somewhere between the 'mystical' and 'real world,' a kind of alternate reality where creativity is nourished in fertile ideas. For their efforts we grant the actors and their entourage all of the heady, enthusiastic props any child of consciousness can give for this Disney World of imagination. It is through this secondary route we free up potential energy and re-create the stress-free childhood realm where play gives birth to instantaneous new worlds. Clearly, through the entertainer, whether in art, acting, plays, music and song we are able to live vicariously in a childlike world where infinite probabilities emerge into reality through the convergence of agreed upon fantasies. Through this almost innocent transport into other worlds, we inadvertently activate a transformation that is crucial yet unavoidable. For example, Tesla flipped the switch that set off the 'tripping point' to give birth to his snowball effect, if you recall. He did it when his aim was invested in *playing* the child's game of imaginative possibilities, borrowing information and energy from an infinite creative source. This started the ball-rolling, tipped it in his favor along a predestined route. It was a mind-set where excitement and challenge formed the most important aspects.

Advertisers, movie moguls as well as lone individuals with dollar signs looming in their eyes seek ways of exploiting this phenomenon, scratching their perplexed heads as they search fruitlessly for methods for tagging along on the coattails of such mega-success, hoping to hit it rich the easy way. It can be done. It isn't an isolated phenomenon, but follows an intrinsic spiral path. Nonetheless, many theories abound and one of the most popular at this stage of the game is the internet meme: an idea, behavior or style said to spread from person to person like a virus. Internet information memes are theorized to spread by socially infectious blogs, email hyperlinks, videos, pictures, hash tags or websites and social networks because of the easy to use connections made possible over the web.

Richard Dawkins, the author of the *Selfish Gene* and the biologist who coined the term *meme*, informs us that the contagion of the internet virus 'hijacks the original ideal,' using its momentum, so to speak, to move and grow. Memes, in this way, are said to leave an internet 'footprint' so to speak, in the fertile electronic soil of the media which renders them rapidly 'analyzable and traceable,' and hence, easy to pick up, i.e. infectious. In terms of the theory of memes as an intellectual virus transferable through the printed word or by mouth via electronic media, the explanation is quite palatable, since it seems to fit the modus operandi, especially its initial propagation; and even more so since its growth is accelerated, fed as it is by emotion-based news commentaries, popular television with national appeal, radio shows, and the excitement generated by rich and famous people, particularly celebrities and their drama's in the news. Commercially, this method, that of feeding off the sensationalism of media flashes, is quite popular in so-called *deliberate viral marketing* schemes since it is a gestalt phenomenon propagated by a catalytic chain of associations. So in a sense, what we witness is an actual wave spreading out through the population, enhanced and under constant regeneration as it is magnified by local myths. Here, the secondary input of alternate 'time streams' shall we say, exacerbate its energy in the centrifuge of incoming collective channels to *trigger*, precession-like the meme's momentum, thus accelerating its cumulative or pandemic effect.

Broken down to bear essentials we see another example of what at first appears to be a singular event borne like flotsam upon the vortex of underlying cumulative data surrounding a nucleus of popular interest. This most certainly does not, in effect, constitute an incident of 'luck' bringing sudden success; undoubtedly there is a not-so-obvious underlying process behind the phenomenon. It is as though the picture is already there hidden in the myriad of waves, and only after scrutiny do we begin to perceive it detail by detail. Indeed, even the universe did not arise from nothingness to explode suddenly into the magnificent production we see today, it gradually emerges from a micro-level through a series of step-by-step plateaus converging from an overflow of diverse channels to emerge into a common stream. Thus, from our observation deck in the present most of these levels of accretion are obscured by a point at the end of the pinnacle of linear time. These accretion levels comprise the hidden factors that launched the Holoverse from relative obscurity into a major macro-event. From the perspective of 3-d surface dwellers, we are looking back over an imperceptible void around a bend or branch in the flow called 3-d time. It is one among many in a helical oscillation of cosmic time.

Predicting with certainty is essentially a fundamental characteristic of the so-called pure science of math. Fibonacci numbers always lead toward the archetypal Golden Ratio – numbers squared always come out times two and those which are cubed times three. If you build a house you use special tools such as a T-square for cutting and dovetailing converging parts at precise angles. If you lay a foundation, you need a balance tool for predicting that the house sits with a predetermined evenness, otherwise under the effect of gravity everything will become cockeyed and shifty. Moreover, the whole of a complex structure requires special computational data, electrical plans or schemata, and computers need flowcharts. All of these are arithmetically planned constructs containing a vast array of figures and details that in the far-reaching derivative are vital for the integrity of the construction of the 'bigger picture.' In short, plans or designs are a way of reducing the probability of uncertainty to a bare minimum or none at all. Without the guarantee of certainty random ideas could not be depended upon from which to construct a project, chemicals would not accurately blend and the results wholly unpredictable.

Predictability, than, is built into the method by which one constructs a future world from the nebulosity of theory and speculation and not the other way around. For instance, chaos or Willy Nilly randomness does not arise out of design but from the lack thereof. Thus, the rise of a great wave of order out of seemingly commonplace elements must follow a spiral pattern of organization to emerge, just as complexity from singularity or order from apparent disorder follows the *tripping* of what superficially appears to be an insignificant switch. For many this switch into order from apparent randomness is wholly discernable, requiring a return to fundamental intuition.

Thus, for many there is a nearly imperceptible process by which the switch is tripped which releases the ball to roll with great alacrity at exactly the right time and space from randomness or seemingly scattered disorder toward its probable future destination. At a fundamental level this is the process of the wave as it moves from the Whole to the Part, or from random probability to meaningful order. It does this because of its nature, that is, the pulsation of the wave, its tendency to move outward, gather information, which pulls back to the center and builds accretion levels of order. When and where it deposits this information, each time is specifically the byproduct of its wave pulsation nature; let us say it has a 'tripping point" configured into the process where it releases the information.

Let me explain this process more clearly: at precisely the angle where the incoming and outgoing wave superpose a switch is flipped; I call this the *tripping or tipping point*. It is the point where information is exchanged as the wave creates new order. When that occurs, the interlacing event precipitates a spiral bifurcation at precisely the right degree of the angle or critical energy fork to form the next accreted order. Like a snowball nearing a precipice, it appears to suddenly roll from an edge, which, in reality is a point in which the curve in the spiral field is the greatest. In this way we see a new leaf or branch phyllotaxis, or a new invention, philosophy, law, change in an entire way of life; or as in the Big Bang, a new universe.

This is the convergence arena where many streams of incoming energy explode, a veritable Niagara with its hub remarkably resembling the Horseshoe Falls. What power! What force! From that point onward its cumulative rise to meteoric proportions expands exponentially, in much the same way as the escalation into galactic clusters. Sensing this many people have unconsciously exploited the falls natural fluid dynamics, coasting down Niagara River and over the brink into the majesty of roar of fame and furious power that catapults them into national prominence. These cosmic snowballs gather into globular extravaganzas that warp the structure of space and time so much that light coming our way (carrying information from extra-dimensional sources such as the continuum) provides a look back 100 billion years into the birth of the Holoverse. Holo-leap from the macro with its space-time bending, to the clustering of data around an information meme, and you get some idea why this phenomenon has such bizarre ability to cumulatively attract.

In fact, what we are seeing in the cumulative snowballing of the internet meme virus is very akin to the fabled 'butterfly effect.' This effect is familiar in chaos circles as a new pattern which suddenly erupts at a critical frequency point (sharp bends in space-time) to create a new frequency pattern (alternate universe). The contagion that takes place at this bifurcation fork has all the earmarks of an overflow of mass and energy from diverse information streams to create viral clustering. Like the damming of a river, which has much in common with gravitational bending of the matrix, the input of myriad streams of information act to catalyze and hence perpetuate at critical limit points sudden, powerful transformations into new order. Interestingly, in fluid mechanics chaos is often described as a torrent of conflicting currents which suddenly emerge into an ordered systemic flow. What we have discovered in this analysis is a separate current that carries information over chaotic white water upon which we can flow to collect into a vortical pool beyond. A good example from the forces of the cosmos is when two galaxies, one larger that the other are draw together so that they suffuse, in time, to form one mega-galaxy.

Followed step-by-step from its inception, the evolution of information into 'data-verses' that gather into opaque vortical pools of dark energy, can be predicted if one learns to follow the spiral eruptions from its apparent inception beyond the void. Unseen but sensed, beyond these points the spiral progressively emerges at bends in the field where the template is strongest and the clustering of mass to form order unfolds.

MEDITATION

1. Look for the Wholeness in everything that includes you as a vital Part.
2. Strive to see everyday events throughout the world and universe as inter-connected to you by an invisible channel that begins with your deeper Self.
3. Sense that the cosmos is because you are.
4. Look for 'trigger points' where large processes are connected to smaller ones.
5. Learn to exploit them by surfing their currents.
6. Find out where and how your presence gets the ball rolling. If it doesn't move on, the event isn't for you.
7. Learn to recognize your connectedness to processes 'outside' our space-time continuum.
8. Think of déjà vu, as you coming home to yourself.
9. Look for ways of transforming infinite potential into practical usages.
10. Realize that you united with gravity and the spiral.
11. Envision ways of making things work more efficiently in your life.
12. Think of how to reduce entropy or energy waste.
13. Contemplate the nature of the Strong Anthropic Principle. See how it works intricately throughout your life to make things snowball into awareness and manifest.

5

PREDICTION AND INTENT IN CREATION

"God has put a secret art into the forces of nature so as to enable it to fashion itself out of chaos into a perfect world system." Immanuel Kant

How to Get Your Snowball Rolling

For the untrained eye a tree in a forest remains hidden somewhere within the abstract of apparent disorder until the search of the intentional focus of the individual viewer uncovers it, albeit as if by accident, rather than design. For example, trees are a standard feature of the forest but without them forests do not exist. Truth is we don't really notice an individual tree unless some distinct feature draws our attention such as genus, height, thickness, the color of the leaves, a gnarled branch or a twisted trunk that makes them stand out from the rest. Then we see a connectedness to others like it and a distinct whole begins to branch out from this singular individual, and it is not an illusionary whole, I might add for those who surmise that mind makes these associations up. For example should we add another big factor such as the emotional impact that this particular type of tree has on the observer, such as its significance in regards to a specific childhood memory, then its meaningfulness becomes even more important.

When that happens, the tree stands out as unique in our minds; in other words, it not only grabs our full attention but we become a part of its fuller meaningfulness. This same reasoning can be applied to people, or individuals. They don't grab out attention when they meld into the passing movement and anonymity of the mundane world. But put a flashy suit, jaunty hat, cocky gait or a pearl handled cane in someone's hand and everything begins to change. Presto! You have an individual and moreover, a chance for the observer to participate in the experience! A good salesman has a sense of the pulling power of uniqueness. For example, he knows that nothing sells better than the look of success to those who wish to be successful. The smart salesman dresses sharp and even when he is broke acts as if he has a hundred dollars in his pocket. In a sense something of his 'apparent' success begins to rub off on you.

In short, there must be a 'pulling point,' a center hub of energy that draws your attention regardless of what you are doing toward it. A case in point: every day enormous crowds of people pass through Times Square but few miss the singing cowboy in his fruit of the loom underwear, dressed in nothing more than a cowboy hat and strumming his guitar. He's a walking billboard model for the company and it has netted him a handsome contract.

In a similar way but perhaps with far less attention-grabbing sensationalism, businesses hire someone to hold big signs and spin them in an erratic manner. Others use colorful, wind-jostled flexible manikins, or pay bosomy girls in short-shorts to stand around the entrance of their businesses. Life begins, in this way, to take on a grander glow, appealing to the theatrical in all of us. Therefore, lights, music and action have a magnetic draw, especially if they are mounted on a flickering neon sign with a bright, blinking, pointing arrow. Loud music together with bright lights can transform a plain attraction into an exciting marquee that harnesses our attention to its message despite efforts to simply ignore it and walk on by. On a hyper-dimensional level, the energy of the display is transferred to us and in turn we are entranced and excited to participate in its message. In other words, we are drawn by the sensation-clustering nature of its mystique; and yes, something that goes back to the birth of the universe and beyond. It's that powerful!

Going back, we can understand more clearly our singing cowboy's uniqueness as the brazen, near-nudity in the middle of a busy, downtown square in New York. It is this shocking quality of starkness which both isolates yet enhances him and to be effective, it crosses all lines of conventionality. Attention getting by perspective it isolates him, acting like a vortex to draw us, even unwillingly, in his direction. Without doubt, this attention-generating semi-clad spectacle of a near nude cowboy receives a fat kickback from the local businesses, plus he capitalizes on his act by raking in piles of coins and bills that fill his basket generated by hypnotized, gawking passersby. In fact, the area where he stands, nearly naked, has become a vortical energy center drawing flocks of people who become swept into its unseen but felt eddies of current. Without being fully cognizant, they discover themselves slowing down to get a look at this bizarre individual. Business grabbing, retailers and advertisers vie for the backdrop space.

From this observation an important detail arises: any outstanding point that engages our senses acts as a spiral energy vortex for centering attention. Like a hidden-in-plain sight path through the woods to an animal's den, it is obvious to those who recognize the signs. As such it has a personal or resonant frequency, which means it has a numerical wave ratio with a square root exponential that unites a person to a much greater picture or whole. Like a family draw together by a common bond or a nation, it acts as a collective magnet. Intuitively, it is quite obvious to the members as a mother's baby is to her though she may have not even seen it yet. The wave draws her to it and like a smaller piece in a bigger picture its relationship is integral because it is connected to a gestalt or collective frequency pattern. In this way an individual is connectively linked by vibration to his numerical resonance in which he synchronizes like a card key in a modern hotel lock.

This is the vibrational neighborhood in which we operate; the same is true of job, spouse or friends both in terms of space they arise and in terms of the path through time that draws us to our destinations. When I say "in terms of space" I am referring to the geographical area and in terms of time – to the progressive notes or stages by which the composition of one's life course evolves. One can think of this as the amount of entropy in a system based upon the factors that lead to it.

Iteration or flow charts[1] do this to a certain degree when they demonstrate the amount of work and cost involved in the development and sale of product over a period of time. In other

---

[1] Burndown **Charts**. The burndown is a **chart** that shows how quickly you and your team are burning through your customer's user stories. It shows the total effort against the amount of work we deliver each **iteration**.

words, a linear graph that seeks to determine or predict how much time is necessary to complete a job and how feasible it is to agree upon based on the data collected. The spiral forecasting way would make this determination based on a flow chart that incorporates both the interfering global as well as local factors in terms of entropy or durability in time and space. It would also incorporate bifurcation or potential and 'real' crisis points where adaptation to other factors may change the dynamics of the flow of outcome of the development and longevity of the system in question.

Seen dynamically, this predictability is based on the intrinsic numerical ratio or vibrational rate of the convergence of these interlocking factors. Thus, one could think of one's personal gestalt or whole as a rhythmic, interlocking pattern of order which links them to a hyper-dimensional matrix. United this way, the individual is a part of an ongoing whole that in the physical world appears as a linear series of interconnected vibrations. It is this sort of vibratory, pattern-linking gestalt or process that unites everyone to holistic patterns, biogenic and otherwise that extend over predictably long-term periods of time. Through this linking-up spiral process, a person is reunited, tonally with interrelated increments of space-time. I mention 'tone' because of the importance the frequency quality of the state or stage that a person is in, attracts corresponding qualities in others. This also includes circumstances that surround the person and the event. Here, we are back to the tendency of people, places and events to synchronize or meld into resonance with similar vibrations. This could be compared to getting into rhythm or timing with things of similar frequency. Therein one can discover a 'pulling attraction' that draws you into the vortex of energies which comprise that event.

Interestingly, and not just as a side note, researchers have discovered that although Alzheimer's patients have significant short-term memory deficits, they don't seem to have problems in remembering things that happened long ago when it is accompanied by enchanting music. This is possible because music links them or magnetizes them, pulling them by the tonal resonance of their limbic systems emotionally to the larger gestalts of similar vibration. When these gestalts are stimulated, they reactivate or temporarily restore identities contained in invisible increments of space-time, psychologist's term memory. What connects them to these long-term events is that the memories are emotionally tied up to clustering wave patterns which form the nucleus of time-space increments with similar tonal quality. These patterns of memory operate on the same basis by which the spiral came into prominence in the inception of the universe.

By the same intra-dimensional token, patterns in waves link us to so-called linear events far ahead in time. Seen from a hyper-dimensional level, the predictability of these patterns in terms of wave resonance are why it is possible to predict or forecast the future. We are attracted to our own tonal qualities or frequencies. When you begin to understand and integrate the awareness that tonal quality attracts you to an energy gestalt, you will not only comprehend why you are unconsciously attracted, but learn how to recognize, control and link up to any patterns, macro or microcosmically, or local-globally, through conscious alteration and manipulation of your tonal or emotional frequency patterns. In fact, social systems emerge and subsist on the emotional links binding together centuries of feeling through the strength of their emotional bound group needs. Think of the history here as the global wave and the world of the current individual the local. Together the two come together to forge the space and the time ratio by which events evolve.

Linking up Emotionally to Bigger Waves

The layout of the city is said to self-organize as it emerges out economic necessity. Yet, this only accounts for the horizontal aspect of its growth in terms of the individual or the group; there are many other levels. Seen multi-dimensionally in terms of necessity, it is clear that not all enterprises simply emerge because of their location which is based on the availability of rental properties in the area. This popular notion of how cities grow when in fact, they expand and arise around a central locus from a converging vortex of interfering waves or forces. A department store's attractive power, for instance, pivots on its ability to generate revenue which reflects a vibrational spiral wave of core emotional resonances. However, what sends out a tone that is appealing, must strike a similar cord in the receiver, as an ear is to language and language to the voice of the nation. All resonance in its turn is reflective of the tonal quality of the areas general mood and there is something greater in it which appeals or does not to the individual consumer who is drawn there. This means that tonal quality reflects something more than the general social climate; indeed, it strikes a resonant note that fulfills some quality that is needed in those that are drawn to it from a much wider gestalt of information. What this suggests, is that growth follows local as well as global cues, some acknowledged consciously, others intuitively.

The local one's are those that are most obvious and immediately important, while the global tones are not so obvious, at least to the left brain preoccupied with serial or singular data processing.

Musically labyrinthine (or maze-like) in nature, like the ancient power of its mystique, a business's power to attract, lies in its hidden gulf or resonant archetype of wholeness. That appeal is like a promise that shall be fulfilled and the receiver must sense this deep within or its attractive quality would bear no monetary consequence. The archetype of wholeness, as intimated in the foregoing section, is the vibratory frequency of its wave pattern. Tonally, it has an evocative force that might appear, in part, to have magical properties, so much so that certain tones or pitches can actually make someone stop to take note of what is going on there. In other words, it forces a person to acutely invest the nucleus of their sensory range in what that store has to offer. It is true to say that we all have tonal qualities and are a part of a tonal whole that extends beyond our consciousness and draws us like the gong of a dinner bell draws the hungry.

For instance, have you ever noticed how certain high frequencies sounds can make your dog stop and shake his head or peer curiously, perhaps with irritation in the direction from which the tonal resonance is emanating even though he may not see the source from whence it emanates? The quality of the sound both annoys and attracts him. On one level he is attracted but on another forced away. The vibration carries dual meanings or perhaps is layered with myriad messages. Cats also respond in a similar manner and so do people, though they may have little awareness as to why or what stopped them in their tracks at that moment, or more importantly, what dissuaded them. In fact, that is why certain kinds of music are used during movies, plays or radio broadcasts. The purpose has a wave like pulse, first pulling us one way than pushing us another. These dual pulses draw our attention too and fro to certain kinds of scenarios, especially where it can enhance in some way the quality of the presentation.

Just think of how drab or uninteresting a film might be without the intensity of Dolby sound to highlight or mystify the emotional backdrop of a dramatic scene. Every little event takes on monumental proportions. Your heart speeds up and breathing accelerates, hands become sweaty and you fidget in your seats, than laugh at yourself suddenly realizing that it's only a movie. The quality and timing of the music has covertly drawn you in, transported your mind beyond the chair or theatre.

Music has motivational evocation power. It evokes a wide array of emotions, especially sentimental feelings when scenes are cast in moody drab colors. It can also inspire patriotic feelings or direct a charge. At times the tempo of the sounds pull us into the past, while other's make us fearful. Overall, color, lights, sounds, especially if portrayed in unison, envelop and/or captivate our attention. In so doing they do another thing which even more important – they *prepare* us for what we must do with what is forthcoming. Unconscious clues make us wary in a darkened forest at twilight. Deep instincts are awakened and our anticipation expands exponentially; and not all of it rationally,

We know, for instance, without being fully conscious of why we are fearful for the well-being of our heroine, (and ourselves at another level) that in the next scene a villain will enter who will threaten her (our) life. Sometimes we are even driven to jump up and check the windows and doors. We lust with her desire and wish to flee with her fears. Somber music can suddenly change the atmosphere of the theatre. A lonely blues can be agonizingly painful or a dreadful rise in sound will send our hearts pounding and some of us will let out involuntary screams, or hide or eyes with anxiety or disgust. The music leads us forward, like soldiers marching off toward war. Unconsciously, we anticipate the future and deep down our knowing comes from a hyper-dimensional level where waves prevail in an interconnected soup. From this admixture of energies our intuitive senses warn us when danger is near, or give us the sense that love will triumph; even if we're not fully committed to the lines of the movie. We transcend the moment as we are driven by the tonal quality of the music.

One might say that tonal quality has the power of a strange attractor to either disrupt the chaos and suddenly bring about order or send us scurrying in another direction. Where and how we react all depends on the receiver who provides the observer that collapses the wave and governs the reality that ensues. The wave generating source acts as a catalyst to bring the vibrating dimensions into meaningful wholes. From this we can rest assured that the ability of the wave to be replicated and passed on is all the interactive work of the receiver. For example, someone doing something strange or slightly off color, teetering on the edge of bizarre, unique or unusual goes socially viral, does so not of its own accord – but because of its appeal to its attentive audience. Of course, the effect can also be catalyzed by inanimate objects and things. Legends and myths associated with a hotel, for example, can almost by itself bring flocks of people just out of curiosity alone. Still, the information must be generated and received in the end game. The trick in this end game is the in the quality of its uniqueness. Memory works like that - the more the emotional tonal quality of it stands out from all the other moments in our life, the more it tends to jump out at you.

Hence, the more power these kinds of events have to draw people to gather into clusters. Just a tiny tip from the right kind of energy can set this ball rolling, and once it begins there is no stopping it until it fulfills its mission, so to speak, and reaches it predetermined point in time. Like the accumulation of high- and low-pressure convection currents, they rise and dissipate according to the momentum predetermined before their descent down the slope into materialization. Look to dreams to teach you because they transcend the rational boundaries of your awareness and penetrate into the depths of the mysteries that cannot fully be comprehended by the conscious psyche – except through symbolism. Look to Carl Jung's brilliant insights into the myths and symbols that abound in the collective unconscious for global-to-local events that are about to transpire. Archetypes are transcendental, for example, meaning they possess global elements and personal symbols come with subjective impact or personal connotations. In the mosaic created by these dual forces, you will discover the meaning and purpose of why events take place within your personal reality and what to expect in the near future.

Dream example: A dream of a woman who is a close friend began with her standing outside while dark clouds suddenly began to accumulate under a sunny sky. Suddenly, out of this accumulation of boiling tumescence came a great fish which leap forth and swallowed her. Afterwards, the skies cleared and the day appeared sunny and bright. Interpretation: dualistic forces dual for supremacy in a conflicting morass of emotional energies, both negative and positive, i.e., angry versus peaceful search for a resolution of the stress. The fish, a spiritual symbol frequent in the Western world represents her final resolution of these conflicting energies via being 'swallowed up' as it were, or taken – over, by the higher mind of God. Thereby, bringing about a swift end to the conflict and directing her behavior in terms of the future to a peaceful and insightful finish.

In another way, clever acts serve as energy funnels to channel the flow of attention toward a desired ending: a local magician with a gift for illusion, a man juggling five balls while bicycling along on a unicycle, a midget acrobatic group, even a troupe of Capoeira practitioners doing difficult martial arts flips. If the magnetism or uniqueness of the event, person, place or thing is eye-catching enough, then its ability to catalyze the flow of energy into a powerful '*snowball of activity*' is greatest. Thus, any eye-catching event: an accident involving sound, lights, explosions (if they aren't dangerously violent (and even then, sometimes when they are not continued too long) can draw enormous crowds of rubber-neckers together quickly. People are pulled into the growing, glowing gestalt of energy by its intense spiral vortex. But like I said – they aren't consciously aware of the field they are following. Only the unconscious knows where this field exists and reacts automatically (intuitively) to its presence. In fact, you will only be subtly aware of its pronounced ability to draw your rapt attention into its central hub. It's like sensing when and where to move to avoid an object thrown at you, though you might not be aware or consciously involved in the process.

One might refer to the intensity of its drawing quality as *its* **attraction frequency**. Seen as a formula, the AF (or attraction frequency) is a wave's number of oscillations per second in terms of its ability to draw your attention. Hence, if its oscillation frequency (frequency = energy = attention) is very high, it emanates an intense AF. Seen as a vortex, this oscillating wave rotates around a 360° circumference within a given time period; that's its RPM, so to speak. This rotation within the given period is an oscillation around a circumference, or circle and can therefore, be referred to as its angular velocity. Angular velocity is its speed in terms of degrees around the circle as it oscillations along the curved path. Thus, the higher the frequency, or oscillations per second, the greater the angular velocity and the greater is the curvature of the field. Greater frequencies amplify the curvature of the field which draws more people into its central locus or tipping point, sending the energy ball rolling at greater acceleration toward its destination.

In short, varying oscillations between high and low frequencies have correlative ability to either attract or detract attention through the AFQ or attention frequency quotient. Therefore, events with the greatest AFQ are higher in energy, giving them stronger ability to accelerate the momentum that brings about the materialization. Lower energy balls, such as though which work off of depression, doubt, anxiety, unhappiness have less ability to generate the speeds which tighten the loop between past and future, in terms of time-space; but they can, nonetheless galvanize the manifestation of dark events. Consciously, we may simply feel attracted to an event. Superficially, its colorful or musical appeal or *unique* appearance demarcates the particle state of an opaque symbolic association that covertly draws you with energetic intensity. That's why we stop to check things out –

they have an attraction frequency that activates our energy field in some way. Or so we think – below the surface we are following a wave.

Natural phenomena such as Snoqualmie Falls in the state of Washington evoke our resonant emotional frequency response of awe, because they have tremendous, spiral drawing frequency power. The frequency oscillations are amplified because of the falls sheer, precipitous drop, hundreds of feet straight down into a central chasm. That's like being dropped into the very heart of the energy field and depending upon what the wave suggests to us, we are drawn accordingly. Correspondingly, it accelerates our resonance field as our excitement level shifts into high gear while the sight literally carries us 'inspirationally' along via the sense of awe. In fact, look at the whole scene as a helical vortex of sheer, precipitous forces descending to a central hub, with powerful impact, into the valley below. The breathtaking drop of the falls is awesome to behold amidst the flat, stark backdrop of a placid, bucolic countryside. Here we have a powerful, abstract catalyst that draws energy from one space-time level and redirects it to another. Like an Escher tessellation, its central maul or hub bifurcates or cuts vertically through the horizontal linearity of our conscious landscape, dropping us into a vortex or breathtaking pit where we are shaken from the mundane placidity of our lives to suddenly reawaken with an alternate view of reality. Visually, it's comparable to changing gears in a sports car on an especially curved section of the tract and accelerating forward along a vast, linear path.

As I have intimated, people sometimes have this same stark drawing quality too to suddenly shock, disorient and reawaken us to something deeper convening in our psyches. This occurs when their abilities, uniqueness or appeal seemed timed to a tee juxtapose with impact with trending interests and seem to suddenly capture our attention. Such people can seem to reach right out and grab your attention and when they do, they pull you at a great rate into a new world view. Let us say, they act as a window between worlds.

When this happens a person in the news can suddenly become a hot item in mere moments. They seem to be suddenly blown out of a cannon, so to speak, in a meteoritic rocket to fame, when in fact, the spiral wave that generated the event was on a descending curve long ago in space-time. Their life reorients and in doing so has, in effect, cut through the linearity of temporality to dilate space and shrink time.

Then there is the effect of other energy catalysts, at least at an intuitive level like that of *shock jocks* like Howard Stern to centralize interest-bearing circumstances through attention-getting acts. Sensing that situational events have the power to attract and centralize energy-generating balls, publicists and agents often encourage celebrities to do something risqué or patently unusual to get the public's attention. Thus, in the case of many celebrities, the express purpose of their socially hub-centralizing disputes, especially the violent confrontations and fighting such as that between Tommie Lee and Baywatch beauty Pamela Anderson carries a charge; that is, an *attention generating frequency* that drove their careers nearly overnight into seven figure paychecks. The snowball was exacerbated by the tons of publicity it generated as a hot item because it followed the powerful explosive current of notoriety and sensational the public was longing to see at that time and place. A dynamo of converging waves, it instantly turned their career around and carried them effortlessly to financial riches.

Suddenly, the public's attention is drawn into the spirals' powerful vortex of forces. To achieve this space-time alteration in record time, it had to change its perspective from a wide angle (chaos, forest) view to a narrow (single tree) perspective. In other words, it closed on the forest and funneled in on the couple and when it did it began scrutinizing minutely everything about them. What is most interesting about this phenomenon is that under the focused spotlight of collective attention from millions of watchers, the snowball of success that became this couple's private wave, surfaced from a celebrity ocean.

A powerful energetic force, the snowball began to descend with enormous gravitational pull into the valley of their dreams. Once what they were doing grabbed the public's attention it automatically released a powerful avalanche of current which carried everyone swiftly along with them, toppling social issues and taking out competitors helplessly caught in the flotsam of its great velocity. Of course, bear in mind that individual spin-offs had its rewards and anyone touched by its dynamics were swept along too at an awesome rate. Drawn into the spotlight by this swift rush to fame, however, this couple (as is true of anyone caught up in the maelstrom) was instantly expected to account for every little variation in behavior, each conflict magnified under the public's curiosity lens, adding particle to ball until its magnitude was internationally stupendous.

What we see here, in effect, is that the focus of all the attention upon their private lives activated the snowball to tip at a crucial fork.

When it did it gained incredible stickiness and force as it picked up momentum, like a car racing down a steep grade, which made it begin to roll and as it rolled, generating into an even bigger and more powerful ball. Curiosity in the spotlight is a powerful force. As it grows the issues that comprise, those scrutinized at every level grows through the cluster of rubber-neckers invested in its potentially disastrous outcome.

Though the force and momentum of this powerful snowball as it gained incredible size and attention seems phenomenal, its course moved steadily toward a target source in a virtual future that was totally predictable from its inception. One thing for sure, it wasn't going to die down and dissolve until it reached its crescendo point and when it did, the results could be guaranteed to be spectacular not only for them but for everyone, including the viewers. Every step from the primal moment that it began to tip toward the edge of a magnificent precipice of potential, to its final resting point far down the slope of the probable reality that manifested in its powerful climax, followed a *geometrically precise spiral pattern*. The pattern occurred just as predictably as the first galaxy that ever emerged to produce mass, order and life from information in a bleak, empty void.

At first glance this process might not seem like it has a lot to do with the chaos theory mentioned in an earlier chapter, but it does. The primary state of chaos is disorder, like the tree lost in the forest. When a single tree begins to stand out, such as one that suddenly is hit by lightning, or the fabled 'widow maker' that without warning comes crashing down, that's chaos followed by a strange attractor. It's the type of event which leads to a shocking, noticeable, sudden emergence of new order. As to Pam and Tommie, though this couple was not altogether nondescript at first, they were comparably lost in the obscurity of thousands of other actors and actresses all vying for some sensational event to highlight their existence and pull them out of the random number game. Being unique is akin to acquiring the prime number of one, or anything near that is nothing short of a stupendous feat in itself. The ability to suddenly rise up out of the obscurity of the masses and be noticed and in demand can make you a rich man or woman overnight. It happened for them suddenly, in this case by conflicts and confrontations in public view. This energy, coupled with their reputation, tipped the ball and sent it rolling with devastating force.

However, their case is not unique, it can happen for anyone. At these moments a nondescript couple can emerge from chaotic nothingness, so to speak, into social prominence. Presto - everyone comes running to see what the ruckus is about. There are a lot common things that can get just as much attention quickly. For instance, have you ever noticed how much energy fire engine's get? When the sirens blare everyone comes running to have a look. The same thing can be said for car wrecks. They draw attention because of the danger, which triggers the greatest of all draws beside love. For stars whose careers were fading, enlisting people to invest emotion in them is difficult. Getting noticed is a godsend – you can count on in an instant to put cash in hand.

Of course, there are other bonding factors leading to their explosion into eminence, After all, Tommie Lee had earned a reputation as the bad boy of rock. His uncontrollable, unpredictable temper (emotion) and self-indulgent, libertine character also acted as an element for activated the attractive force. Of course, Pamela's sexy body and sensual looks had made the Baywatch episodes a hit, this much you'd have to give her. But she wasn't all that big. But together, now here we have powerful elements: sex and conflict, two powerful forces. On a scale of frequencies both aspects occupy a more negative range of emotions, according to various psychological sources, but not always. However, in this case, libido and violence fuel a materialistic society's fixated greed for money which feeds off primal, lower-level limbic system drives generated by the rise and fall of the social status wave. But not seen, hidden in this exchange of energy, is competitive emotions such as hate, envy, anger, fear, rage and anxiety; all elements comprising the underbelly of stress. On the surface we are only privy to the negative offspring of monetary competition such as graft, corruption.

On a positive side there is the joy of success and the material things it can buy, including power and social recognition. Below the surface, a seething cauldron boils and without its generative force there could be little if no change. In fact, one major reason war is so 'in' in our contemporary world culture, is that it helps release the 'maximum potential energy' necessary to propagate changes that are stifled by surface social adherence to convention and the pretense of peace. From a deep libido level conflictive energies jostle about in the creative, yet volatile soup of social unrest. Connect your financial vehicle to that energetic wagon and your chances of success are maximized, for good or bad. The reason for this is that much like the internal processes that go on under a placid earthly crust, molten magma is being disturbed by gravitational vacillations and in time released during powerful seismic cataclysms. The cataclysms are the inner organic life of earth mass and consequently, social transformations during chaotic interchange in forces.

Fired by powerful adrenaline catalysts high frequency information snowballs propelled at a speed tantamount to a speeding bullet into collective prominence. Swiftly drawing a wide matrix of people together into gestalts, all feeding off lower limbic system boosts these transformational changes are literally catapulted into sudden success. Transformation elements feed the vitality of greed, aggression exacerbated by the competitive Darwinian dangling carrot in money, fame and power. All are fight, flight, fright impulses generated by the reptilian brain of our earliest ancestors.

Of course, these are not the only emotions that have the ability to catapult social frequency exchanges from the primal centers of the collective brain, but they are the ones currently activated in this socio-economic morass. Materialistic snowballs catapulted into prominence, in terms of predictable monetary value, reflect the popular mode of social exchange. Bear in mind, that all modes are experiments in growth and adaptation, not so much in Darwinian terms, but in a deeper examination of the roots of creativity. The degree of interest generated is reflective of the sum of the audience participation just as movies, books or science and art reveal collective levels in creativity. All reveal a much deeper and more intrinsic factor which might at first be overlooked, and here I am referring to the degree of the spiral angle propagated by the experimentation with information flowing into the 3rd dimension from the 4th. In short, the potential of the emotional wave to attract interest lies in the associational resonance. It tips the snowball to roll and the energy to flow.

The quality and content of the associational resonances can be thought of as the spirals curvature signature. The signature has associational attraction, or repulsion, depending on its symbolic, data content; hence, the more the context juxtapositions with the collective mind, the greater is its chances of snowballing. From its contents, social clusters evolve to give form to space and time. According to the receptiveness of what is popular in the social mind, the wave is repulsed or attracted, enlarged or dissipated. A socio-economic wave rises and falls – that is, conjugates with the 'bigger picture' or wave pattern, or it doesn't. That is why it is so important to 'feel' for the coming trends, by sending out dry runs with different items. For instance, if you want to find out where the big wave, first of all keep up with the media, movies, celebrity spotlight, import and export business and the general mood of the public emotions. Think in terms of a flowing stream of water, a poorly built craft in a powerful stream might get dashed quickly for many reasons. The reasons might not just be the availability of products, but the materials needed for its construction in a competitive market where the current is trending toward conservation and your product smacks of excess and exploitation. Social mind says everything, but not everything vocally. Sometimes the repressed elements may speak louder, in a rebellious way, and you may miss the boat trying to appeal to the popular market.

Bear in mind that these energy prominences represent forks into totally new universes of information. As such they have many elements in common with the originating model as they reform into a new order. Think of this alteration in information as wave-bonding and rebuilding. It is a natural transformative process and represents a change in angle of orientation; with it comes a comparatively different pattern. The wave patterns that generate these transformative forks are a materialized energy-matter version of the forecasting graphs used by chaos theorists to portray a strange attractor at points of transition. If you recall, a strange attractor is a sudden alteration in a feedback pattern displayed on a forecasting graph that predicts deviations in environmental and weather trends at chaos points and are undergoing change.

When these changes occur an alteration is sub-surface patterns is underway, and a catalyst is releasing energy that transforms into epic proportions overnight. Anticipating these processes, wise businessmen and clever media advertisers struck by the probability of riding the wave and making extraordinary momentary gains resulting from such exponentials are taking advantage of the game. Energetic dynamics available in these currents have affected many areas, especially the writing and publishing game which is presently changing right under our collective noses.

The Black Hole of the Publishing Dilemma – Solved!

One of the most powerful and important strange attractors that functions as a bridge between consumer and business is collective information dissemination. Information transmission is vitally important in generating the attractor because it serves as a powerful current to rapidly propel a socio-economic ball to a grand climax. The attractor will ascend into social prominence through a Trojan horse process, transmitted via the subtle yet eruptive dynamics available in the television, movie and publication industries. That's why celebrities wear complimentary gowns and suits made by enterprising fashion designers to television interviews, award ceremonies and galas. Knowing how to ride this wave's powerful potential is a feedback pump shared between publishing houses, publicist, agents, writer and media industry. The real reason of a social network such as Facebook is gossip, exposure and the recognition by word-of-mouth to those people who in the end game will be buying the product.

That's one method but the following is another: it used to be that every writer desperately sought an agent with high hopes to place their paranormal romance thriller with the right publisher. In this highly elusive milieu, lucky breaks came mainly by referrals; dinner with an agent; or by bombarding a publisher until he finally gave up on rejecting or simply ignoring your manuscripts. One such book was Conversations with God. This particular writer, as the story goes, sent many, many query letters until he got through. Though it proved to be a top seller once it was placed, the writer had to jump through more hoops to get the publishers to read it than Carter has little liver pills. Once it got to a large publisher, it sold for seven figures and more.

In some ways you can understand the agents, they no doubt are overworked, harassed, pursued and most of all - over paid; and let's not forget spoiled with stacks of great material and people who would give their eye tooth for a shot at the brass ring. Knowing how desperate people are, agents can't help but keep one hand in the writer's pocket and the other in the publisher's coffer, working it from both angles. Publishers aren't exempt because most of them come off as money hungry tyrants, cut from the same fabric for power as agent, all fueled by the worst emotions in the lower limbic system – such as greed. In their lofty world of dominant control, they dole out pennies to the writer's (8 cents on a dollar if you're lucky). That tiny stipend goes to the people who've put endless hours into the gestating the books they make millions of dollars from; that is, if they sell. From a publisher's standpoint their caution is warranted, since their monetary risks are greater. They inform us that the big problem isn't writing, its promotion and marketing. Thus, if a clever writer is perceptive, they will need to know much more about their audience than how to appeal to the genre. They must already know how to get inside their head and stay there.

This means the snowball has to start in the emotional gratification of the product. In other words, it must have visceral impact in some way – to stand out emotionally and by that token, connect them to something bigger. Then it will have sensational, momentum-engendering properties such as an exciting subject-matter issues that are couched exactly to feed the right emotional frequencies. Frequency of emotions is everything, because not only are they contagious and energetically engaging, but they are the properties that can predictably determine the future of the writer and hence, the books rise to fame. With this coterie of emotional appeal one might also add that should the material reduce stress in the long run, carry the reader, if you will, it can definitely add to its probability of being a winner in the publishing game. Emotional frequencies are the trigger, the catalyst that generates the added energy that boosts the book from an interesting to a sensational level in record time. Scenes that reach out, as it were, from the two dimensionality of the written page and pull the reader into the aura of the scenario can be quite gripping and sometimes even overwhelmingly transporting.

Much of the initial 'tipping' force needed to generate popular appeal isn't as necessary if writers are celebrities, prominent people in the news, people with impressive credentials or sheepskins, political leaders and other sundry pack leaders in the game of life. Those people have a lot of visceral momentum. Then the bridle that controls the cash flow is not so wieldy. Thus, finding a famous name among the writers is like manna on the waters since much of the work of emotional marketing is already done. Therefore, these people get prime billing and the best percentages, money out front and the ideal interviews and monetary backing. Publishing and being an agent is big business, it's all about marketing and knowing how to stimulate your audience's emotional frequencies is paramount. In yesteryears when the market wasn't so saturated with tons of out-of-work dreamers desperate to be discovered, writers were a bunch of major ego trips and petty quibbling over contracts a foregone conclusion. Thus the trine of agent-publisher and writer sometimes turned into a major ball of wax that had much in common with the nauseating temperamental actor's syndrome.

Big change now is that old game is very much passé' because modes of information transmission are different in more ways than one. To get your book noticed now there's a new snowball in town and it sort of evolved out of the desperation of the little guy to get noticed in a sea of competitive chaos. What's great about it is instead of working through agencies and publishers to trigger the snowball effect, to get the ball moving requires a reversal of the old 'trigger' or tipping process. Today the snowball must be made to come rolling to the writer; something like psychokinetic writer's energy. Here the ball must truly be your buddy, especially when you start getting money calls from big leagues players who checked your site out and discovered everyone loves your stuff. When that happens all you have to do is lay back and wait for the right deal – and believe me it will come in time; if you're book is engaging, it has emotional pull which means its energy generating.

Emotions=Gravitation=Energy Generating=Cluster building.

Are you doubtful? You might ask how this is possible. Well, that's all taken care of through blog sites, for one thing; You Tube for another. Then there's special writer's posts like Watt Pad where hopeful writers can go to hang their prosaic dirty laundry out for others like them to enjoy, or critique, whatever floats their boat. What's great about the snowball building here is that there's thousands of writers each reading each other's books, plus perhaps millions of reader's visiting there. Mutual interest stimulates the flow of raw and most importantly – competitive creative energy. Thus, not only do others get off getting into your inner creative world, but it forces everyone to dig deep and come up with uniqueness. In short, it gets them into their works not just from an intellectual level but from that emotional level I've spoken about. Emotions feed the meme of ideas. Emotion adds dimension. Thus, the potential of your book, once it gets attention, is relatively exacerbated. True, a certain percentage of these manuscripts may never see an agent let alone a publisher, but who cares – they get something else which is priceless, especially in the long run when you log those wonderful things called 'clicks.' Clicks mean recognition and if you get enough, the snowball will come to you, you don't have to start it rolling - everyone else will do it for you. When that happens than who care's whether publishers are snobs and agents are hustlers, just everyday people, writers like yourself who've never been published before will see your writing and if they like you, and click on your stuff, tons of other people will get into the feeding frenzy just to see why the others are biting. Another element which really increases the momentum of the acceleration is something benign as comments. Comments are great for spotlighting your dangling hook and starting the feeding frenzy.

Here's how it works: remember the fast-food parable? Okay, that was about reducing stress, but they're reverse engineering on Watt Pad by stirring up the feeding frenzy first to draw in the attention, which will pull the agents and publishers who are snooping, but intentionally staying incognito. Well, the reverse fast food of publishing is creating a big fuss by getting your name up in those nauseating emotional bright lights first so the right people can see you. Yes, that means getting your book plenty of ample cheap illumination. You know like a fireplug in a B rate movie that a drunken driver runs into and draws the sirens from emergency fire trucks and police cars. Right away all the people come charging over to see what all the hullabaloo is about and bam, you got clicks, you got rhythm and you got clout! Who could ask for anything more, as the old song goes!

Like a glowing bulb to a moth, it brings the buyers into your arena. Now remember there are a wide spectrum of emotion's all running the gamut from the most sublime feelings to the lowest depressions. Think about your book – examine its emotional contents; obviously there are many. Like a marquee of colored lights, you need to pinpoint or highlight, shall we say, those brightest or darkest points and make a noise. Again: controversy attracts. If there's hostile controversy in the central protagonist or theory, make a big flashing light out of it. Challenge people with it! Shine in it on every issue big or small that even remotely has anything to do with it. Stir the wasps up! Get the messages buzzing! That's what they do on these sights. Stir up muck! Muck-raking has predictable results. The stink is like the smell of riches, its offal to behold, but boy does it add to the fertileness of the soil!! Mike Tyson was one of the meanest S.O.B's to ever walk into boxing. He had a reputation for having a raw, street tough tongue and muscle and heart to back it up. Everyone wanted to see him knocked off his cocky throne. The emotions around him were overwhelming. Usually, his pre-fight interviews would end in a down and out brawl with plenty of threats. Both fighters were so caught up in the violence that it acted as a super-powerful magnetic field that drew millions and millions of viewers from all points across the globe to see this vicious animal of a man rip another victim to shreds. The betting and money involved was over the top, perhaps higher than any other paid performer in boxing history and that includes Mohammed Ali and Rocky Marciano.

In fact, on Watt Pad, using this same technique, there is one female writer (who I won't mention) that has made a habit of enticing people to comment, even if it's negative, because she seem to sense that any comment adds to her sites attention-getting interest. And if you think about it, this makes sense because making snowballs requires packing ice together in a tight cluster and adding more on top of that. Did I throw you for a minute? Well, the point is little by little once you got enough interest generated and you've given your snowball a little roll, without much effort you've got a couple thousand clicks. A lot of people can be fishers of men, but people who know how to draw them through interaction become embedded in the process. This automatically enlarges the scope of the energy body and it enhances its ability to grow exponentially. Regardless of whether it's negative or positive, because – like I said with the publicity stunts to draw attention – let's get down with the facts - controversy sells. Like hungry piranha, just seeing the action all around your book will start a feeding frenzy and your snowball may include over 100,000,000 clicks which will definitely bring the likes of the big boys like Random House and Paramount Studios, who are the hardest to sell unless you have all the 'right' connections. Then – something happens – a miracle of all miracle's – those hard-to-reach publishers who never looked at your query letter and those agents who tossed your writing in file thirteen because you haven't been referred, will start flocking around you begging – talking those six and seven figure numbers. Suddenly you're in the driver's seat and guess whose riding shotgun? Yes, you got it – a flotilla of agents and publishers.

From an on-looker's position, you are changing your position constantly, even redesigning your character as you go along, so much so that it's hard to keep up with the alterations. In fact, you and your site, including your site looks like a battle zone of re-writes amid pugnacious controversy and still you emerge Phoenix like out of the chaos unscathed and highly buyable commercially. You're digging down into some really deep, dark dredges of creativity here and it has all the earmarks of a living hell, but you know what? It's child's play to the right ears…

Generating Unlimited Creativity is Child's Play

Paradoxically, we've talked about doing nothing and finding everything. Here's another perspective twister: how to get inside chaos to find order. How does this work, you might ask? Well, there are naturally occurring cycles behind chaos and order in every organic process, like growth for example. We are constantly transforming and we're not even aware of it. Every seven years each cell in our bodies are totally regenerated, so in fact, we've technically died and been reborn right under our noses. Life learned a long time ago how to conquer adversity by giving up being fixated on each point. In this way it is always predicting its future. It does this by looking ahead, beyond the chaos to the order beyond. It developed powers of precognition which evolved from, of all things, learning to make use of everything so that nothing goes to waste in the creative energy game. So, if you feel all mixed up, blocked, there's ways to pull out of this creative dive into darkness and to make all the tragedy work for you. But first, you have to get inside the head of creativity and see it from a personal perspective, then you're not guessing at its works – you're on the inside looking out at the process as it starts rolling.

A good place to start is learning to get acquainted with the order in disorder. Discovering that you can make what you've been calling 'reality' do a back flip as you conjure up your own strange attractor; as it is called. One of the most impressive and unusual places to see some conjuring at work is in the difference between the adult world and the children. Children, for instance, creatively play within the relative obscurity of their chaotic little worlds, living in their own space, almost unnoticed by adult's busy making a being orderly. Most adults don't recognize the order in such disorder at these levels. They tend to overlook the depth of the childhood mind, often seeing only raucous behavior and an annoyingly messy room. However, should we stop for a moment and examine what is going on more closely the stark differences between an adult's and a child's perspective of the world begins to emerge. For example, contrary to the irritating display of disorder adults encounter when entering a child's room full of a chaos of sticks, rocks, splintered toys, torn pages, scattered marbles and other sundry items, children see a fun world that in their imaginative hands can become anything at any moment and does in the next. Children, in fact, appear to live in a 'twilight' world of pure imagination teetering precariously on the edge of chaos. It is a place where all possibilities abide *in potential*, a place dreaded by adults immersed in the frenzied economics of order.

A child's world lies in a kind of raw, creative possibility space filled with infinite probabilities. Once focused upon, the probabilities are reduced down to a few distinct images, thus a rock might become the baby Jesus while a lump of clay transforms into the Holy Mother, and, alas, reality is no less profane for it. Like a waking fantasy, everything has an amorphous plasticity to it. Hence, its structure can change instantly into something new in the whimsical sea of emotions and images swiftly passing through the creative lens of the child's mind. Unlike the steady-state need for order of adults where reality must be rigidly maintained in an unchanging pattern and persistently relied upon to be there from moment to moment, childhood consciousness is more closely allied to random chance and the true meaning of the word 'state' or *in process*. The difference between these two world views is like an Alice in Wonderland looking glass.

Here an adult step through the mirror and enters the chaotic wonderland of the child and the child steps outward into the mundane, ordered world of adults. In effect, we get a split vision of two dimensions - the 4th and 3rd.

Perhaps the plasticity of appearances and the free range of the imagination explains why children love cartoon's so much and clown's, i.e. because their playful patterns, defiant of order, more closely approximate their own inner visual world. It is a chaotic place of infinite potential. As such it allows spontaneity to flourish, the stuff of imagination and endless possibilities; a wonderful place subject to change at a moment's notice. Even a clown's costume fits in because it assumes a broken kind of order by its illogical, playful nature. Thus, it is readily assimilated into the cartoon-like malleability of a child's mind. Like villainous figures in a cartoon, the figures can assume any form and are impervious to repeated assaults, even explosions and come out of it unscathed, something in their essence unchanged and applicable to the next imaginative lark. In short, the child's world is surreal, similar in context to the changeable visage of a dream. Ironically, their inner world is taken for granted to be, by adults, a sort of 'delusional' ignorance of how the world really is. Adults feel they have to tolerate children and pacify their fanciful make-believe with objects that fit into their silly little world, when in fact the world of a child is closer to the true nature of reality than the adults. Secure in their rigid metaphors of reality, adults talk about their child's strange little habits of chatting with imagined ghostlike playmates they can't see and assume they made up this nonsense in their heads to be entertained to tolerate an adult world; yet how wrong they are.

Here's the creative sum of it - children actually live in a world like the original nature of the inner cosmos before we evolved into the macrocosm of rational beings, i.e., the dreamscape. It is a place where an object can assume any dimensions, becoming many different things in an instant, and often does. I arrived at this realization through many years of studying the nature of my own dreams during altered states of perception. One of the things that allowed me to get into the gist of my dreams and see them as they really are was achieving a non-striving consciousness. With this method I could get an '*in potentia*' glimpse of the dreamscape without imposing too much conscious order to their meaning. This means I could subjectively stay aware while in the actual dream and review *it as it occurred* without imposing my preferred need for order onto what I saw.

For instance, if I saw a peacock turn into a chicken that turned into a car, I wouldn't interpret the dream as - I saw a peacock that I almost ran over with my car. In this sequence of events, I would have imposed a cause-effect order upon it force it to get in line with the kind of reality that adults strive to make and expect to be there; i.e. one that appeared sensible and left me feeling sane. This need for structure and its alliance with sanity seems to be a big fret for adults – a fear of seeming crazy or what is sometimes considered worst - childlike.

This creative world of the child's mind appears to be the same space that inventive or brilliant humans like Albert Einstein, for instance, who valued imagination more than logic itself, seeing it as the creative hotbed from which all intellect arose. He valued it because without its plasticity the creativity of the world of form and function could not arise. There are many stories and images abounding of Einstein riding around on a bicycle, hair askew, oblivious to the world of adults, with his tongue sticking out, refusing to adhere to the rigid sense of order demanded by the collective masses.

Another individual who portrayed this clown-like visage of the creative mind was Salvatore Dali. Here was a man who was often seen with a zany, villainous upturned mustache and pointed eyebrows designed that way for the express purpose of freeing his surreal vision of reality. We must recall that as the author of the surrealist art movement, Dali painted plastic, dreamlike images that seem to defy the agreed-upon order of the conscious world. Like his cockeyed paintings, he was an individual who lived in the super-fluid and cartoon 'ish' circus of his imagination. Oftentimes his behavior was thought to be closer to the antics of a deranged mind, when in fact, his creative, childlike behavior revealed how deeply he was immersed in that magical, twilight space between the unconscious and the conscious mind. Simply put, he dwelt in exactly the same inner space as a child inhabits and because of it came off as rather bizarre and theatric in comparison to the conservative and often snooty adults.

Clearly, it is in this malleable, flexible, plasmodial clay of disorder, if you will, that the fertile great mind resides. In its morass childlike minds ceaselessly invent, taking advantage of its limitless potential. Think on this: the key here is the possibility factor – increase its space *and potential* (its power to be) and you exponentially perpetuate the probability of its persistence in space-time. That is why reality teeters on the edge of change at crisis or transformative points. These potential energy points are creative gaps between order and disorder that catalyze the 'cutting edge' of reality. Interestingly, these points are synonymous with the distribution of angular, progressive, trigonometric curves on the phyllotaxis distribution of florets of leaves, the invaginations in cones, twists or spin of helical structures, and many other forms of branching. It is at these points where catalysts in the chemical hormones of plants are released to boost ongoing change which insures the prolongation or survival of the plant. Analogous to bubbling foam upon the surface of social change, social growth and transformation at these breaking or critical points, skims its white water in a levitating rubber raft of creativity to arise out of the chaos to emerge into new wholes. Thus, these points of change at the edge between dissolution mark expansion or rejuvenation to another level of energy. One is reminded of the current chaos in the Ukraine. Regardless of the ensuing chaos, it is undergoing creative transformation, like other chaotic regions in the world where conflicting streams/visions of order battle for supremacy in the converging riot of energies merging on the cutting edge of a changing, disheveled world. (June 2014).

What I discovered in these glimpses beneath the veil of conscious order, was a creative morass that is more like clay in route to form just before a potter gives shape to his emerging bowl. In a word, we see infinite potential en route to form guided into new order by an underlying principle of expansion following critical limits. Here another stream of order not fixed in the rigidity demanded by the particulate world exists; its order feeding off the relative chaos of subjective emotions which finds expression through the language in subjective perspective. Thus, emotions can be said to act as a booster rocket to energetically propel the self into new order. Intuitively, we all recognize this language, even other life forms and respond from a level of consciousness that is wholly different than the accustomed cognitive rigidity found in the formality of social life. In this intermediary world of visceral communication where the 'so-called real world' plays a second fiddle, information flows to us from a common base that all life shares. Its attractive force feeds a playful field of impulsivity and often downright zany, cartoon-like silliness that comprises the underbelly of the social mind. It is also the signal level of unconscious knowing we share with other life forms, who respond knowingly to our intent, through body language, smell, sound and somatic presence. In short, it is the sensory world dominated by our emotions, an original place of knowing that existed long before we imposed the rigidity of meaningfulness, we call language and cognitively oriented object-reality. Once imposed the creative life follows a fixed stream so alien to the youthful malleability of the virtual state.

On a visceral level one communicates in a pop-cultural voice that has its own tempo; ad lib's without need for proof, playing off innuendos without worrying about the content. Collective history bears this out. We need but go back to the medieval world, a turning point in consciousness before the advent of modern scientific reasoning and the rigidity of logic dictated rules of communication. It was also a place when myth and prose ruled and there was a god/goddess dwelling at every fork in the wayside waiting to appease every emotion. Those days at that stage of consciousness were a Barnum and Bailey sideshow of creativity where muses poetically rang out the daily word and you were amazed how mystically insightful; they were and wondered how they did it. They did it because everyone lived in a different virtual modicum of order, where language appealed to another completely different level of our awareness. In essence, that same state of information sharing harkens to the mental pliability of the child's mind, a riotous and veritable Pandora's Box giving birth to the chaotic panoply of possibilities known as the creative process.

For adults time and order are in servitude to cyclic goals and if this orderly interrelationship changes, they must be replaced and new items like the old put there in place of them. This is the world of order imposed upon the backdrop of nature, another kind of spontaneous reality more closely approximating the constantly transforming world of objects in the timeless realm within a child's mind. In a sense, adults have become victims of the ordered world created out of logic, technology and work. They rely on technology to keep them in check and to adults anything with any 'meaning' and 'purpose' are things that can be relied upon to be there every time they return. Adults need the reassurance that the world in their mind, that the world outside remain stationary, so to speak, so they are busy maintaining continuity in terms of relative order. They forget that the world of permanence they put so much stock in, is only a fanciful, changing state subject to the whimsy of lurking chaos.

But despite their care, foresight and inventiveness, uncertainty rules and randomness is always lurking about imposing on moments of secure tranquility. Undoubtedly, something in humanity responds to the memory of a deeper call to order, and it is right there in the midst of the proud proclamations of science reminding us how we got here in the first place. Something knew billions of eons ago and the result of its careful planning drives us through the fog of doubt.

MEDITATIONS

1. Lie down on a couch or bed, even the floor. Take some deep, even breaths and tell your body to let go. Breathe this way a number of times, getting a feel for how you're breathing affects you mental and bodily states. (Of course, breathing exercises can also take place while walking, sitting down, or during deep sleep once you become proficient at it.)

2. As you breathe deeply note how images change inside your mind. Random thoughts will flutter back and forth through your head - don't worry about this. Actually, this is good, because it automatically tells you that you are in an altered state.

3. If you follow these thoughts they will branch into emotions and images, pictures that will take you on journeys into other realities. Bear this in mind as you encounter these impressions.

4. You probably won't be able to affectively follow your thoughts as they change, but if you continue to practice, soon you will recognize these states and learn to relax when you confront them.

5. Once you reach this state of recognition, the imagery will carry you to places, so to speak, outside your immediate spacetime. Again, you probably won't recognize what these first impressions are telling you, but it is important that you learn to go with them.

6. Imagine when you contact these states that you're floating on a river, like a log, down a stream toward the ocean. Just go with the current, let it take you where it will. In time you will become a master at going with the flow. Try to transfer these thoughts into your life. Go with the flow and flow with the go. Imagine yourself in the river channel just floating along like a raft or log. Breathe deeply and try to notice what is occurring around, whether you are relaxing and meditating, or going about your everyday activities.

7. Strive to imagine your daily activities, whether thoughts or actions, as *bifurcations* into other realities. Study how dimensions come together to get a feel for whether you are entering into a holistic or transcendental state of unity, or whether you are merely branching into another reality. Time and space changes occur very subtly, so it takes time to notice any transferences of energy from one state to another.

8. When you encounter people during your everyday interactions, try to pick up on where they're energetic state is focused, especially taking note of how you are interacting with them.

9. Become actively involved in striving to alter you brain waves at will during everyday interactions, and watch how the energy changes between you and the other person. Don't be surprised to find yourself picking up specific things they are thinking about or planning. On the other hand, don't be surprised to discover what they pick up from you. After all, you are exchanging energy and information on a hyper-dimensional level.

6

FORECASTING CYCLIC PATTERNS

"Good timing, tick-a-tick-a-tick good timing...
Timing bought you to me." Jimmy Jones 1960

Emotional Rhythms: Keys to Your Success or Failure

Most people range between a series of cyclic emotional highs and lows, and this is to be expected since we are emotional beings caught up in a web of visceral interactions that follow like clockwork the daily rhythms of our lives. However, these currents of energy can change radically. In those moments we find ourselves adrift in a vast interactive ocean of competing waves, many of them not observable on the external ocean of emotion, until we find ourselves out too far in deep waters struggling to get back.

The fact is emotions can and do change daily with the competing, myriad, tributary streams of the world in which we confront each other. In this milieu of constantly changing circumstances, pressures come at us from every conceivable social direction. The energy seems chaotic and unpredictable and at first we feel dealing with it is hopeless. First one minute we feel ourselves being pushed this way, than in the next, another. It's tough for many people to remain calm as social stresses invariably push our most secret buttons. When that happens, we fly off the handle despite our best efforts to hide our true feelings. Not wishing to admit our lack of preparation for these pressures, we often try to cover up the sudden explosion of feelings with explanations that more often than not seem pretty lame.

At best the truth of the matter is we more than likely were out of touch and never saw the big wave coming until it swamped us. When such an emotional deluge occurs, people are astounded with their behavior. They don't understand why they reacted the way they did and must admit that they weren't paying attention to what appears to be subtle, unforeseen forces which brought those conditions about.

Frankly, I feel most people have good intent and would choose to be kind to one another but become overwhelmed at times and simply vent. Afterwards, they are absolutely dismayed to discover themselves in the midst of an emotional monsoon. The trigger points might appear to be food prices that suddenly skyrocket. Stock whose value seem to have plummeted overnight or the tragedy of discovering that the value of their house has fallen, perhaps is even much less than when they brought it.

Everything just seems to have gotten out of hand when in fact they were out of touch with their emotions and the change of the cycles about them. Dismayed when counseling with a therapist, it is no small wonder that they are stunned to discover how out of tune they were, plus loaded down with much buried emotion. During those moments people feel like battered shells in an alien sea of emotions, social trends and patterns. But there's an upside, regardless of the apparent chaos.

Have faith my friends, it is possible to become fully attuned with the waves and anticipate the coming of these moments. However, to do so require close observation of the social climate in which you are immersed. The emotional climate is an ocean of which your own feelings are a pulsating river of waves, like interlocking cogwheels within a clock-work that drives the counter-surging personal and social trends. Being out of tune with either emotional pole can lead to devastating crescendos of loss and despair, or on the other hand, to soaring feelings of joy and placidity.

Emotions: Now Trending

To find equilibrium in all these waves we must stop for a moment to consider how emotion leads us back to the initial trigger point where it all started. Thence, we shall discover how we arrived at these emotional transition points and find what set them off. Again – as intimated, a primary fact to realize is that emotions are waves, as are all trends. In fact, the two fit together like glove and hand. Where you see a trend beginning, emotional content preceded it. Hence, knowing this, one can predict its arrival and exercise better control over the outcome. To check them and perhaps take better control we must get to the gist of the emotional content that generated them...

To begin, the question that must be answered is how well do we know this wild creature that lurks within this thin veneer of social decorum? What are these emotional energies that lurk within us? Why are they always at the edge of a precipice ready to go off like a volcano, to consume our reasoning with such passion? Can we track their path and therefore predict their cycles? Can we forecast them like the weather - possibly, in an objective sense? If so how about subjectively? That part is questionable, because often, by the time we're aware of the emotion precipice, we're rationalizing the reasons following the aftermath of our passion.

Clearly, we are in great need of confronting our emotional self to find out what governs the patterns that sets us off if we are to comprehend the trigger which sparks them objectively or subjectively, for that matter. Part of the problem is that we are schedule bound and time conscious and anything that interferes with the process is aggravatingly acting in their activation. Plus, there seems to be far too many catalysts that ignite them to make a reliable determination. That fact alone is frustrating because it suggests that the accumulation of emotions over time add up to more stress; an unstoppable everyday issue that is unavoidable. Hence, the acute need to recognize a) the sources of these emotional waves, and b) reduce the moment of their presence. Another issue to deduce is the milieu of conflicting currents in which we are immersed. Many people might find it difficult to know where those generated from others and their own begin or end.

Regardless of the confusion, rest assured there is a point where your personal emotional waves conjugate with others like the tributaries leading to a major river. These emotional tributary or forks may flow upstream or downstream yet each provides a path you can follow back to source. These means forwards in time to predict the future course of the wave or backwards to their origin. We have but to examine them in light of a reliable analogy – the watercourse.

Each emotion is a tributary path to its source; that is, a watercourse by which underlying factors coalesce and come together as they follow a common current, just as a river follows the underlying currents of the planet. At these forks even miniscule social pressures can tip the collective emotions to generate a snowball rolling in the form of a commanding trend. This is a trigger point and where it occurs is a point of potential energy, similar to a ball rolling down a hill along its course to a certain crescendo or outcome.

In fact, emotions are building up as we speak, seething just below the surface of the changing social climate, waiting to surge forth at any moment. Within the cauldron of the social emotional climate, they bubble and boil, welling up from within you. Thus, it is important that you remain aware of the fact that you are literally creating your immediate reality from this personal emotional climate. Ironically, its presence is so powerful and overwhelming that you may fail to sense its proximity and assume what you feel entirely comes from the climate about you. In a sense it does and it doesn't. In reality, your emotional life feeds off the collective climate. Moreover, it personifies the greater emotional whole in which you are immersed, and yet, in your own way, you are independently feeding it. To make it clear right now – you abide at the central coordinate point between your emotions and the collective emotional climate which best resonates with you. In few words, you dwell smack dab in the center of your emotional neighborhood.

What is most interesting about this neighborhood is that like your own emotions which rise with your successes and fall with your disappointments, this arena of interaction resembles the highs and lows of changing weather conditions that reflect the greater fields of energy about us. Therefore, it goes without saying that staying abreast of the changing climate can give you a leg up on the energy which drives the collective emotional dynamo; i.e. climate. Once attuned and aware you can out-step the competition, automatically reduce the stress that leads to your emotional reactions and get a clearer picture of what lies ahead.

Should one plot these veritable but predictable patterns on a seismograph scale they would appear as Fourier frequency waves? The collective psyche is constantly sending out and receiving frequency signals. Patterns of the collective, they represent perturbations arising in the climate and accompany or precede currently trending patterns of social change. Like forecasting stock market trends with cyclic patterns on a chart, anyone can learn to read these patterns to determine exactly where they stand in the 'bigger picture'. Consider it somewhat like turning on your television and tuning into the specific channels that carry varying events such as news, international affairs or various advertising or media broadcasts. Each channel or interfering wave transmits a specific, interactive, social frequency that channels data from the 'big picture.' Like your television screen, the big picture is governed by the exchange of energy waves coming from your subjective trans-ciever (transmitter-receiver) of the emotional-intellectual input and output exchanged by the world mind.

Physically, your personal input emanates from the lower limbic system and mixes with the world climate slipping by the observational rationale of our intellectual radar. For the most part, the 'big picture,' reflective of the grand emotional climate of the times, transmitted by the world mind, represents the myriad input of millions of emotions in the mixing bowl of civilization. Visualized, they would appear as myriad merging tributaries joining to create a huge main stream. The powerful current of the bigger stream comprises what might be termed the social or collective unconscious.

Consider its evolutionary origins. Many sociologists and anthropologists suggest we are just wild beasts dressed up in pretentious, superficial, civilized garb, while underneath we're a seething volcano of powerful, primitive emotions. Like a bomb about to explode, we are all impatiently struggling to burst free at any moment. Surging forth at any moment as the main stream feeds into our lives, we are powerful forces that can trigger major events. In fact, at the tributary points where events occur, our emotional responses act as catalysts with astounding tipping point potential for creating change!

Perhaps the conversion point between lower limbic system energies and the screening mechanism of the neo-cortex is what Mary Shelley had in mind with the Dr. Jeckle and Mr. Hyde character who at one moment behaved as a kind, intelligent doctor and the next a diabolical, vicious mad man. That might sound a little scary, but well, one thing is certain, the rational mind and the beast are competing characters in nearly every great tipping drama, whether it's man versus machine, emotions versus intellect, love against hate, or god versus the devil. Interestingly, the bible with is good-against-evil them is still the biggest selling dramatic emotional trend of them all, bar none, and it's been that way for centuries. Regardless of the drama itself, the struggle between these dueling psychic aspects and control over them are usuable factors that can give you that special advantage in the socio-economic race to the top of the monetary heap, should you wish to tip it in your favor.

How these dynamic forces operate as a powerful draw in the subtleties of the individual brings to mind a television episode on HBO featuring the psychological conflicts of Dexter, its leading character. Portrayed as a psychopath, he struggles with an obsessive-compulsive rage to kill others, of all things, like him, as if by doing so he is controlling his own inner conflict with the beast in himself. Well, not altogether, because somehow this character comes off as a malfeasant with a skewed empathic urge (or so the writer's and producers would like us to believe) with the need to protect and defend his fellow citizens, which seemed dramatically opposed to the nature of this anti-social psychological illness.

Nonetheless, classically characterized in the clinical definition of this disorder, the episodes anti-hero is emotionally closed off except during moments when his own personal tributary merges with the collective. Grossly unaware of his emotional blocks even as a young man, he is hopelessly driven by horrible, unconscious compulsions which at 'trigger points' transform him into a murderous killer. By the way, he's, quite literally, also OCD (obsessive-compulsive), albeit, a killer with a penchant for cleaning up every drop of blood spatter. So, you can magnify the horrifying impact the episode generates when you consider the rift in his personal – from pristine presence of mind to evangelical puritan justifying each bloody execution. So you see it takes a lot of conscientious pre-planning to pull it off cleanly. Oh, well, you get the picture.

Similarly, the civilized mind compared to the inner beast, the sociopathic youth growing up as the progeny of a police officer might be emotionally conflictive, to say the least. He must learn to straddle two worlds - one in which he is forced to conduct himself in a normal, conscientious manner, and an alternate in which he is driven by a beastly, unreasonable violence which must always remain hidden. Paradoxically, it is his father who rescues this individual's social graces by encouraging him to adopt the pretense of normal, so to speak, emotional feelings to hide his inability to relate empathically to other people; otherwise, his secret life risks exposure. To achieve this disguise his father gives him a special code to live by. His father's main caveat to avoid detection while interacting with other people is: "There are only two things we can know for sure about another person, *1) What you think you know about them and 2) what they want you to know.*" Obviously, the leading star, bereft of normal social emotions is being told that the surface personality of everyone we meet each day is not the true, inner self. Instead, the true self is hidden from the outer world, concealed within the confines of the brain and inner psyche. In short, the father is suggesting *we live within a web of deception woven like a tapestry of pretense about us.*

Whether this comment is entirely true or not is debatable yet what does ring true is that there is a deeper, emotional self often termed the unconscious. Proof of this deeper self's existence, surfaces through psychological tests or patterns. Over time as we confront others on various issues, it is this inner emotional self that appears to form the nexus of an unchanging center. In short, behavior studied over time reveals spikes and troughs of strong reactions that differentiate peaks and valleys of high and low feelings that will gives you a fairly good read out of the hidden self, even if people try their best to hide them. In this center or nexus one detects a range of vibrational content that comprises the varying frequencies making up the self. Now transfer this reasoning to the collective social climate and you get a big picture of the true inner self that comprises the central river that feeds off all the little tributaries.

In this analogy, several things emerge which can be relied upon as true: each one of us have our unique frequency 'fingerprint' shall we say, that is our own and no one else's – plus, the climate of the social mind also has its own unique pattern. The uniqueness of this pattern furnishes a lens through which we can get a glimpse beyond the wall of the outer self. It is important to not only get to know your own emotional frequency (s) and others, because it is this frequency self that connects and triggers the snowball which connects you to everyone and everything else in the Holoverse. Inside this wide range of emotions, the true, inner person resides in a compact, primal ball. When it begins to roll its movement and momentum is pulled toward or away from the billions of other emotional centers. Each, when they connect, form larger and larger clusters that eventually become avalanches of information that can have devastating effects.

Bear in mind as you read this that the direction in which we are progressively moving from individual frequency centers to conjugate with others emotionally, represent similar fields of vibration. In time these fields form ever increasing aggregates or matrices where millions of interconnected points pool to create far-ranging, complex Wholes. Put in holographic terms: our individual intersecting wave unites in a wave-merging holographic 'big picture' that reveals the undercurrent of emotions – (like streams of water) leading to central social movements.

Now, one thing which can be ascertained from these observations with certainty is that to every individual there is a special rhythm, a beat which is their own. Strangely, so busy are most people at erecting and maintaining high castle walls to protect themselves from others, that they are unaware of these inner rhythms though they relate from that space at every moment. Ostensibly, the attempt to remain hidden or isolated could be a vestige of an instinctual survival memory; for instance, the desire to evade a predator in a primitive, dangerous environment. In those moments it might have been in crack or crevice, up a tree or in a cave, some place where concealed them from predators, intruding eyes, thievery, or in some cases, from themselves. The latter is especially true if the inner self one flees brings anxiety or stress such as taboo thoughts, compulsive and annoying impulses and inclinations, or reactions that are embarrassing and over-powering. In any event much of the process goes on in an unconscious manner; so one goes about hiding in effort to achieve a modicum of anonymity from the world at large. Nonetheless, in the interim, the attempt at evasiveness becomes a habituated, unconscious mechanism running on automatic and as I have mentioned, so much so that most people probably are only vaguely aware of it.

To get an handle on where this reasoning is going test yourself by asking these questions – am I aware of my moods, feelings, thoughts as I act on them? Do I sense the cycles of my moods or the underlying emotional rhythms that comprise my habits of relating or reacting to the world? These rhythms, again, refer to cyclic patterns of behavior patterns which represent the status of one's use of space and time increments; something we will deal with in depth in the last three chapters of this book. This can include the length of the time you need to adjust to sudden changes. These rhythms also reflect how you interrelate as you adjust to the demands and presence of other people and the world in general. If might also be called your 'comfort zone." If you are aware of them, then you have a sense of your rhythms and perhaps even have some control over how you respond. FYI - you may expand or contract your personal space (comfort zone) by changing your accustomed responses or your ways of viewing them.

If you are aware of your comfort zone, you are well on your way to sensing the hidden or 'true" self and your energy rhythms abiding with you. The next step is getting a sense for the hidden rhythms of your fellow man or woman. For instance, you might know not to push your mother or spouse to hurry when you're anxious to get on the road for a trip. You can feel their frustration and perhaps sense the limitations in their ability to adjust to change, so you back off. Your close circle of friends have similar rhythms to you thought you might not be aware of just what it is, even while feeling comfortable in their presence. The same goes for larger groups, the city you live in and the geographical area you have chosen to raise your children or to work in. In fact, your job reflects tons about your personal rhythms; also if you like music and not math, or art instead of writing, competitive sports or lone walks and private moments. In short, the rhythms inside reflect the external environment you prefer to be in or the people you choose to associate with. Without doubt, based on those rhythms it could be said almost everything about your future emanates from these rhythms: your personal life, ambitions, spousal choice, behavior in general. Thus, what is thought to be ahead of you, is predictably well within your present reach. In fact, once you get on top of it, you will be, in effect, ahead of yourself and everyone else. The primary trick though is first getting to know your true self. Not surprisingly, knowing self is one of the central quests and tenets of all philosophical and spiritual endeavors because it is the key that connects you to all other patterned wholes and to our 4th dimensional Holoverse.

To begin this pursuit, one must actively strive to sense one's own rhythms. This you can do by noting how you feel and react to the other people you meet and to the world in general. Be as honest as you can and take time to objectively get to the bottom of why you're feeling what you are when you react to others and the world. The knowledge received will help you begin to recognize the flow of your moods and the rhythmic patterns that come and go. Your moods are linked to bigger patterns around you. Though yours may vary individually, they can reflect many things about the climate of the neighborhood in which you are located, the level of ambition driving you, your economic situation and so on.

In general, moods say everything about you and so much more. They reveal why you associate with the people you do, belong to your political party, work on the job you think you feel forced to take. In short, moods form the parameter of the vortical nucleus of your emotional field. The field is a powerful attractive force. You can't see the field, per se, and you can't see yourself at the central loci of its attractive epicenter until you make a habit of discerning a) your personal emotional field and b) the central neighborhood

The reason you probably won't see the field (though you might sense it) is because most people haven't taken time to make a subjective study of personal emotional patterns and daily cycles. Being aware of them will give you valuable insight into how to connect better to others and move up in the world, plus it will eliminate the need to maintain such a rigid shell around you Rigid shells have all kinds of ramifications such as making you a wall flower when you'd really like to dance, or finding self-confidence to move out of your neighborhood, go to college, or advance materialistically in the world, plus many more things.

There is another great bonus it will eventually provide and that is the ability to overcome bad habits and approach the world with as a completely new person. The biggest plus of all, is that it will also get you connected to infinite potential. That is the middle of the central current flow where small ideas, ambitions, desires and dreams can snowball into big successes quickly.

Anticipatory Rhythms and Prediction

Psychologists studying the evolution of consciousness, such as Julian Jaynes, discovered that the earliest form of divine communication came through muses in poetic verse. In fact, the poet would go into an altered state to transmit the divine word from God. This ancient poetic delivery of the word, especially revered in Grecian times as an oracle such as the one at Delphi, became what we now know as prediction, i.e., the ability to channel information from a hyper-dimensional source while being in an altered state. In that regard, one could loosely typify such communication as a form of verbal geometry. In this description I am suggesting poetry acted as a holistic wave field uniting the immortal or *limitless* mind of all-that-is with that of the relative, fragmented individuality of mortals.

Seen in terms of the ascending structure of our neurological hierarchy, the lower limbic system, our first line of communication, the lower limbic system, unites with all-that-is. Thereafter, the information is transferred to the rational or intellectual centers of the neo-cortex. In this way a geometric bridge spans the holism of divine order to connect with the disorder of human life. So we see that poetry, a step down from the ONE, serves as a resonant bridge. Thus, divine order became aligned with worldly disorder.

In a similar way, art seeks to bridge the same intrinsic need in human life, which is to capture and express something of the beauty and wholeness which is other-worldly and thereby raise it to a higher vibratory level. One might say that the higher mind inspires us to reach for something perfect, some Whole, as it were, beyond ourselves. In a similar manner, in the human world sacred geometry than, became a method of uniting life with the rhythms of heavenly cycles. By staying in alignment with the rhythms of the cosmos we extend our consciousness toward the potential of the divine.

A good example of this is the Fibonacci numbers. Discovered and written about by "Leonardo of Pisa," in the book entitled *Liber Abaci*, it contained calculation sacred numbers in both Hindu and Arabic script. The Fibonacci numbers have many spin offs cascading infinitely into diversity yet staying connected to its originating source in the 4th dimension. In short, these celestial numbers symbolize and reveal the presence or imprint of divine balance and order in all number throughout its many higher numerical sequences which manifest in the physical world. This adherence to what may be called 'divine or sacred geometry' is a fact that also illustrates why you can rely on certain numerical sums to always turn up regardless of how many times you add them up. For example, on a mundane level, probability mathematicians inform us that if you put 23 people into a room, two of them will predictably have the same birthday. This you can count on, double the number and you double your chance, but the end is always predictably the same.

Though geometry and trigonometry are generally considered to be the math of physical planes, their pristine certainty hearken to heavenly origins as they transfer divine sensitivity and utilitarian guidance down through the age via seasonal cycles of seeding, husbandry and harvest aligned to the ellipse and cycles of the moon and sun. To align with them is to stay connected to that which is divine. In this way human life manages to stay in contact with the divine. Sensing divine guidance architecture, music and art strives to demonstrate elements of that consciousness as it makes an enthralling effort to be more like the creative source in all that it composes. Each composition in its own way a mortal adaptation to the ebb and flow of preternatural forces evinced through metric cycle, all the while guided as are the seasons to heavenly forces.

This adherence to divine guidance can be seen quite clearly in Paleolithic cultures such as the early Egyptian where geometry was implemented as a way of measuring acreage to settle land disputes devastated by the deluge of seasonal floods and the rise and fall of the river Nile. Its specific purpose was to establish boundary points designating land areas hopelessly altered by the flooding of Nile waters that had washed away markers, redistributing the shape and structure of the terrain of neighboring domains. Trigonometry, which is used to measure the pulsations of the waves, such as its curvature, amplitude and phase, is than an extension of geometry in 4-D time, whereas geometry relates more so to 2nd and 3rd dimensional frameworks. Calculus gave way to relativity theory and Riemannian math and so on. In this steady progression from wholes into parts we can trace the circumambulatory movement from sacred to the mortal frameworks of reference. Subsequently, in these transitions we also spiral from poetry to math and musical resonances during one complete 360° cycle. In terms of spiral evolution, this is a gnomonic progression which follows an intrinsic Fibonacci evolution by magnitude in time.

Gnomonic progression, if you recall began with a base, in this case the rhythmic meter of the poem. All poetry is built upon different metric patterns of progression such as iambic and pentameter verse. If you recite a poem, or when a person's 'raps' they are unconsciously creating a topological space-time flow which has its own landscape tonal cadence. Taken as a picture of a transcendent whole, cadence represents numbers in sequence from an unknown holistic source, which when combined with musical notes and their corresponding instruments in a score connect us to varying geometrical emotional places within us that strike a compelling, common chord. For example, where there is music there is rhythm which draws people into clusters through the emotional undertones. This occurs within the groups that cluster into bands that evolve into an orchestra, which in turn draw enormous crowds; all pulled together by the vortical spiral's gravitational field. Bear in mind that it is a wave field which is, for the most part, invisible.

The clustering doesn't stop there, it reaches out beyond with its tonal frequencies when recorded in DVD's and CD's which in turn draws millions of people over greater periods of time into greater and greater crowds. So you see the spiral extends itself in time as well as space. Thus, its transcendent qualities have the ability to straddle both the world of particle and that of wave. For instance, 40 an ongoing Fibonacci number, is guaranteed to be a multiple of the number three. This means that in terms of the progression of the gnomonic spiral, at exactly point 'x' in time its wave curvature will juxtapose with that number. Taken as an omen with predictive portent, this is great news because it suggests that transitions between waves needn't be haphazard, they can be correlatively determinate. Coupled with strategic data, a calculated wave can predictably determine exactly how well a product; will do as it expands exponentially outward from its initiatory point of origin. More importantly, these Fibonacci figures can all be forecasted in terms of a time-space flow chart. Moreover, our intuition, which is centered in the old limbic system, is directly keyed into the rhythms that comprise the patterns hidden in our emotions. This can't be emphasized more, simply because the limbic system is our emotional epicenter where the interplay of cosmic and personal waves conjugates.

Going back to our original point, harmony will most assuredly take place if a pitch-trained group follows a musical score freely and spontaneously. In that way each can collectively learn to anticipate tempo changes intuitively, something often associated with acquiring a musical ear. In essence, this breaks down to getting into cadence with the beat through iteration or syncopation and learning to follow the tempo; a binary sequence of up and down strokes of a drum rhythm's wave, for instance, which is actually following an underlying numerical progression leading you toward a magical crescendo with a predictable outcome. In the same manner attuning to the poetry of life, such as the rhythm of the times, can activate certain intrinsic centers in the limbic system, which will also bring into play a wide array of latent archetypal symbols, collective waves that have correlative emotional counterparts.

Once activated a person can, figuratively speaking, take a journey into other alternate times and get a sense of the rhythms prevailing during that period. This is often intimated by the analogous idea that music has the capacity to transport you to other periods, vaguely remembered realm or even identifiable eras of earth history. Indeed, sometimes it is almost like actually being carried back in time, so strong is the emotional and tactile sensorial experience.

Such rhapsodic (enraptured) musical journeys, so to speak, are possible because numbers and meter join together certain rhythmic sequences to spontaneously form aggregate wholes. If that reasoning is applied to music, numbers or metric beats on human emotional centers, can build unifying wholes from memory, symbols and social archetypes. From this morass the emotions associated with them have immense drawing power to bring about group stickiness. One could say everyone in this harmonious group is dancing to the same primal symbols. In this cacophony of musical input, the quality and nature of these symbols and their associated emotions also have the ability to magnetize greater and greater clusters, creating masses that have exponential quotients the outcome of which is predictable over time. We can see elements of this in the litany of Catholic masses, Islamic recitations and prayers, Buddhist chanting and Hindu dances all are based on evoking these associative compounds.

Again: numbers progressively aggregate into gestalts to become new wholes, such as when the square root of 2 becomes four. Great speakers know to begin their speeches when people are slightly tired, so their guards are down and unconscious emotional contents has greater strength without the cognitive functions getting in the way. I like to think of this as 'jumping the barriers of the senses.' At these times when the gathered masses are in a slightly altered or alpha state, then information can be implanted in a meme-like manner, slipping unnoticed by the radar of the conscious mind. Mesmeric speakers of this sort are using a form of subliminal programming allied to sleep learning. Recitation of a litany as in Catholic Masses, dutiful prayers, bowing over and over to the sound of bells, blaring horns, chanting, playing drums or other percussion instruments has the same effect.

These methods are simply bypassing conscious thought and going directly to lower limbic centers where emotions released are connected to archetypal symbols that have deep, conjoining connotation and meaning. Thus, the power of the unconscious mind, as it is known, is released and a person spontaneously dances, sings, chants and for the most part goes into an altered trance-like state and carries out the subliminal content of the information transmitted.

The power of the trance state can be seen best in a chorus of people singing together to create melodic harmony. They are, of course, learning to give up their individuality for the ambient harmony found in the whole. That is why music universally has the power to build virulent circles of attention, like a contagious fire which warms a large group of people from the epicenter of a tiny hub. As such, the fire acts as a generative, transforming force altering the individual vibration, so that each resonates to its heat.

Arithmetically, when people learn to harmonize, they are following the sum of the syncopated notes in the score to a dramatic summation. The strength of the numerical attraction intensifies when everyone sings together or bangs instruments and, in general, creates a din of harmony out of chaos. And what is great about this raucous display is that there is it offers freedom for self-expression outside the prying eyes of convention, or the scrutiny of social criticism. Typically, in the progression from the one-two beat of the basic rhythm a meter is created with a unique tempo coupled with the sounds from instruments or a group of voices, blending yet teetering on the edge of sending the snowball of emotion toward a glorious crescendo or new whole.

Socially, individuals combine together in a similar manner to form groups that progressively reform into larger wholes, all following a basic underlying rhythm or tempo. Extrapolate to vehicles assembling as they converge on a highway, self-organizing into aggregate wholes as they suddenly change individual speeds and move ahead as one. Ants follow pheromone trails to food sources under a similar cadence, led by the strongest Pied Piper of pheromone scouts. Also, we might mention that this same form of harmonic clustering is the means by which termites build mounds upon a common soil or galaxies emerge from the underlying spiral code within the dark matter from which they erupt.

Trusting such evolution of natural events to follow this same function, so to speak, the same can be said of individuals joining together within a group to harmonize. They are spontaneously, self-organizing in form a harmonic union. To an outside observer this union appears to spontaneously emerge into a Whole, but we know that the groups are following an invisible score with notes on an increasingly progressive scale to an eventual crescendo. In addition, we know that, in time, it will end at a progressively determinate crescendo. A group of jamming drummer's do the same when they let a lead player beat out a primary rhythm which they all embellish or improvise on. In time the group gradual blends together in syncopation to produce a resonance. In reality, each separate drummer adds their own contribution to the sounds that emerge, yet unconsciously, shall we say, remain close to the original tempo. The music represents a progressive exponential which moves like a living organism toward a predictably probable climax.

In these exponentials, one gives birth to two which in turn gives birth to three and so on reforming over and over into unlimited wholes. In this way wholes evolve from a spiral gnomonic, that is, they progress from a basic root number or meter and move forward along a straight geometric line that gradually curves as its angle adheres to the changing space-time rhythms that bind it to its underlying whole. Like the Golden Mean, or the Sum of Pi, the radius remains balanced and predictable though time and spatial changes though it curvature might alter as it evolves. In this way the spiral brings together, over time and space, gradually increasing aggregates from a singular beginning, building on itself to unite into ever-increasing wholes what was apparently fragmented into parts.

Thinking in terms of the spiral's application mathematically: if we calculate the angular velocity in terms of time for order to emerge, we can use this formula: $t = d \div v$ over $360°$ (time is distance divided by angular velocity) and you get the sum of the spiral's emergent curvature over time. In this pattern one can recognize the emergent aspects of the spiral curve. Apply this formula to music and it increases the harmonic proportion in musical notes over the length of the score, song or musical composition. It will also reveal the shape of the composition's variations over time. If you were calculating a gnomonic progression, so to speak, from an original function, that is, the number you started with, it's square or cubed root divided by the curvature of the spiral in terms of distance and time you can precisely predict its probable future outcome. So you see the spiral curve acts as a gnomonic progression toward a predictable outcome that can used to forecast. This the way the brain, using Fourier analysis, navigates the sea of waves around us and plots, with astounding accuracy, our course through life; i.e. if we don't interfere with it too much and distort the quality the feedback in the data wave. When this formula is applied to musical harmonizing, it too follows a probable outcome over time and space that can be determined by the notes in the layout of the music.

If we apply this reasoning in a practical sense, when you are willing to conscientiously share your input, that unique, singular quality which is 'you' with others, it blends into a symphonic, musical harmony that brings about a united, happy people. Now, I said all of this to say, you're going to learn something extra special in this incredibly exciting section of the book about your individual contribution to the collective rhythm or harmonics of the whole. It may come as a surprise to you, but music, like love, is a universal language, which teaches us how to follow a score or pattern toward a tonal, anticipatory outcome that exponentially leads to synchronized wholes.

Try this as a group: everyone grabs something to bang on and someone begins to beat out a basic rhythm or tempo. Then slowly, one person after another adds in their input. Note that in time everyone is beating out a collective rhythm that is the sum of all the drummers in the room, each with their own individual contribution. Also you will notice the natural camaraderie that evolves. Gradually, a variability sound wave will begin to flow back and forth between the group as you beat out your individual rhythms. The overall effect takes on the oscillations of many parts to create an emerging whole. As the vortical center of the playing changes drummers, the wave plays back and forth. What we see is the submergence of each part through the convergence which produces an emergence, in time, of continually new wholes.

The outcome, though veritable, can be predicted based on the sum of the tonal contributions of each participant, even though it may vary over time. Visualize this process as a flowing stream with many eddies contributing to a collective current which carries the water as a whole downstream, snagging on rocks and submerged stumps and trees, building vortexes that emerge and submerge periodically. The sum of these individual eddies and their contribution to the collective stream is the eventual force or power it has to bring about change downstream.

Spiral Gnomonics and Prediction

In short, the sum of the flow, in terms of its collective union downstream, illustrates the contributory energetic factors of spiral Gnomonics. Seen as a collective principle, in terms of its work, spiral Gnomonics, like electro-magnetic force can be beneficial in bringing about predictable outcomes to many points simultaneously. Thus, *SG,* when applied to the feedback of contributory emotions to a social climate over increments of time, can be quite useful in determining the probable future of any given project. In that regard, Gnomonics serves as an energy barometer to gauge the ebb and flow of variable emotional climates of emotional energies over time. It also furnishes a useful, interactive, historical picture of the patterns that evolve of the collective, emotive climate over time. Though our feelings may vary at different points, or from one situation to another, visible patterns, like weather conditions, will gradually emerge. Even though the angle of the collective current may change as energy builds and flows around different interactive centers, the overall story that will emerge will have many qualities in common with the emotional content of subjective readings.

Subjectively, there is a story available to read here, and if you are willing to study carefully the contents, it can reveal much about the hidden aspects within each individual. That picture which emerges will symbolically reveal the contours of the common patterns where detours and blocks encountered the habits, we build emotions in life. In short, in time and over distance, the story that emerges will reveal the underlying wave and its patterns can be studied to foresee the outcome of interactive individual and social patterns. For instance, it can be used to determine, according to the reactions to varying emotional patterns, if an individual will finish schooling, or be a drop-out. A reliable timeline can be established that can tell you if your child will become influenced by peer pressure and join gangs or use drugs. Of course, feedback through learning and adjustment patterns must also be fed into the data to get a final read-out.

This same gnomonic reading can determine if a person's business investments succeed or fail in the long run. A spiral read out chart can faithfully reflect not only what you believe, but track any pessimistic, ongoing habit patterns of reacting to variables affecting adjustment to change. Everything reflected in data feedback can help to prove that you are on the right course, i.e., hoping for the best, but expecting the worst – to coin a phrase. These things and more are possible because once you sense those subjective rhythms than you will understand much about the moods which control your anticipatory responses.

Memory serves a similar function when coupled with emotional feedback over time. For example, it provides a sense of anticipation to future change; which is a natural warning signal from your physical security system. When it isn't working effectively, you get bad feedback, particularly if the data is skewed by negative habits such as expectations of failure created from an ingrained, early childhood fear of rejection, etc. Why you behave as you do reflect these often hidden, subjective (unconscious) rhythms which rule your overall attitude, interests and behavior. Get to know these rhythms because they rule our lives and most importantly, *predetermine* our responses to the world in general and more specifically - to others further downstream. Because they predetermine our responses to others and the world, they could be said to foresee our behavior before we act.

Think about the patterns of other people you already know and others you have just recently met. How much do you already know about them or feel you know? From an outsider's position you get the impression that you can pretty much predict certain things about their responses before you ask them; such as whether they will respond favorably if you ask to borrow something. Sensing a negative response, you may find you don't want to ask to borrow anything - intuiting that it's futile. However - and here is where a general caveat as to this rule would apply: sometimes they may actually change their behavior suddenly and you wonder what made them do this. Something about their rhythms has changed. Can you guess what it is? Next time you tell a friend that you feel you can predict their behavioral responses, note what general tonal quality it is that they seem to be acting on. In other words, try to get a feel for the rhythms which comprise the way they respond. If you achieve some insight, change your approach. What you are doing here is manipulating their wave field.

The reason this method works is because rhythms or cycles are patterns form an unconscious field or barrier about us. Thus the field is actually a security perimeter closely monitored by the person/subjective entity in charge. Like a security unit that guards the perimeter of a valuable resource, they monitor the movement of those about them very carefully to protect their anonymity. But there is one chink in this armor and I think if you considered what we just touched on in the foregoing paragraph, with changing rhythms, what actually is occurring is that they are, figuratively speaking, changing guards. In short, at that critical point (and a very tense one) there's a shift in the authority voice of the psyche; emotions are switched and a new personality takes over. When this occurs there's a vacillation in the wave field. What is actually occurring is that in the multiplicity of parallel worlds which make up a Holoverse, the focal self is changing identities. This actually goes on all the time because we are comprised of multiple selves, many identities or epicenters; each moving in and out in a wavelike manner from the central hub of self to the perimeter.

Again, to repeat – if you are not aware of your field you are definitely unconscious to switches in your own subjective rhythms, which comprise the timings or patterns that release the assignment of changing monitors. Thus, you will not understand why you feel as you do, and furthermore why people react to you the way they do, or, more specifically why your life turns out the way it does. Like a person dancing to the rhythm of a drum beat, people move back and forth through the perimeter of these unconscious rhythms that rule their lives and determine our future as a group, nation and world community. The fields we share unite us at an interactive wave point to form a quasi-rigid information grid. By quasi-rigid, I mean that while appearing to be rigid it has flexibility and/or the ability to reshape itself according to the incoming nature of the information we share.

We can penetrate each other's field and when we do we get a better picture of the true person inside. In the same way the information we share as a group contains a holistic picture of what the people who make it up really think and feel as a group. It contains their mythology, beliefs, fears and desires. As the field around the individual forms a projected barrier it is also an information-reading filter that deciphers the intent of friend or foe. Hence, its feedback to the unconscious of the individual is multi-leveled because it has many purposes, most of which is to maintain and provide a stress-free subjective environment.

Because it works through the unconscious much of this information exchange is lost to the conscious mind. But you can become aware of it and when you do use it to enhance your communication and control your reality. I like to think of these rhythmic patterns as precognitive, meaning they see our future because in a very deep sense they carve it out of our emotions make-up. Groups of individuals are brought together because their cycles synchronize. The same may be said for how they relate to things such as jobs, sports, music, art and so on.

As I mentioned, these rhythms form what could be thought of as a force field. Everyone can feel them to some extent and more so if they are in touch with their own field. However, caught up in the external artificial rhythms and fields dictated by our contemporary world makes it difficult for some people to recognize their own. Hence, to find one's own pace and understand its cycles can be a chore for people lost in their work-a-day life and out of touch with listening via their own inner ear. Thus, the adage: for he who has ears, let him hear takes on important impact because it means staying attuned to your rhythms within. When you do you will know without asking why your life turns out the way it does, simply because you will have acquired a natural intuitive sense of where others are coming from.

In this process getting your sense of timing is everything, especially if you got it, because it's that inner, rhythmic sense that automatically helps you adjust to everything and everyone else. Furthermore, timing, as the Jimmy Jones' suggests, is what synchronizes our energies and draws us to others, i.e. our mates, friends, as well as protecting us from negative situations and dangerous foes. Getting timing can save your life and put you in sync with the flow of greater current flows in the 'bigger picture' that can carry you to your destination, or on the other hand, effortlessly pull us into a whirlpool of negativity and failure.

Clearly on every level of life, we humans depend upon order and are fixated by cycles. We build our whole lives around artificial schedules based on compulsive repetitive emotional patterns that we arbitrarily dream up and then wonder why we feel so out of sync with nature and life about us. But that's not how it always was years ago. Some cycles were good, meaning synchronous with the cosmos. For centuries we lived in accordance with naturally-occurring periodic cycles – hunting and food gathering when hunger drove us, responding promptly in the manner that the situation demanded. We learned to obey the revolutions of the heavens, planting and harvesting in accordance to the moon cycles and steering weathered crafts through tempestuous waters by the signs in the heavens.

But that was long ago, before the beginning of the nineteenth century when we started getting into the monotonous, mechanical metronome of clock time. Attuned to metallic, interlocking gears, clocks became the great 'regulators' replacing the elder rhythms, imposing increments of time that were thought to bring a uniform consistency to our lives. But still the old synchronization we shared for eons with the cosmos continued deep inside us, regardless of the impositions of our newly acquired habits of order.

Still, gradually a mechanical kind of uniformity covertly took over human affairs. And as it did it began to impose rigid schedules, we all had to abide by. Gone were the flexible periods of change we knew as the time we shared at the organic interaction level of our biorhythms. Some people have remembered these elder cycles and returned. They were cosmic tracks to natural ports we knew and followed without hesitation. What we might call an hour today was a plastic, open veranda of possibilities. Some tribes simply followed the migrations of the animals they lived off. Moving when they moved and remaining while they grazed contentedly on available grasses. In this kind of super-fluidity time was more like space in that it wasn't so uniformly structured. In this setting the animal that became a human being, responded as the day and the life style demanded, regardless of the need for adaptation, life took on an easy flow. Interestingly, Native Americans still think of clockwork time by which contemporary societies live their lives, as rigid and unhealthy and pretty much ignore it unless they forced by convention to adhere. Undisturbed, they live their lives according to their own inner rhythms, and to modern travelers regulated by mechanical clock time, they seem quite out of sync with those of us bound to mundane schedules. (See: Edward T. Hall).

Under the influence of modern mechanics, the circumference of the whole became divided into twenty-four, inch wide periods called hours. Wedged into larger sections between the tick and tock, varying increments known as minutes and seconds were doled out like parceled candy treats at the last chance café called 'real' time. Altogether, these digits became the given order by which we marched out the cadence of our days. Thus, we became prisoners of robotic beats which drowned out our deeper connection to that past stream of signals from whence we came.

Way back when, before clock time, earth-based cycles were divined by geomancy, a now lost system of time known by the ancient Celts. Geomancy gave a different sense of synchrony with all-that-is. Only the disintegrating presence of stony outcrops mark these mystical networks dotting the landscape. To those in the know they point out the path where the energy flowed by which rituals, such as the equinox and solstice were aligned. There were no artificial orders by which they planted their crops and prepared for changes, nothing superimposed from the outside. Patterns attuned to these obscure rhythms by current standards of clock time might seem too magical, that is, to possess, a very mystical mapping of life's course. Though laid out long before the rise of contemporary science and mathematics, the geomantic sense of timing was highly accurate. It did this in spite of the fact that it was intellectually antithetical, constructed on intuitive synchrony for planting and harvesting which it was said to maintain without failure. As it was in those times, so it is today, the rhythms come as surely as the sun flashes brightly through Stonehenge, yet we witness only decaying relics of its wave path in rows of stony monoliths.

For the most part, we have forgotten much of the old ways. Without realizing it, clockwork time overtook our sense of the rhythms change as we became habituated to newly allotted increments of space and time which now block out those other worlds. In that sense, our rhythms became 'dissonant' with the resonances of the underlying order of the cosmos, as it did for those now indistinct oscillations of information emanating from alternate routes and ports which once riddled space-time. Hence, we have fell prey to a kind of superficial meter of order, one that grinds harshly against well-worn gears that no longer have traction.

Without realizing it, we have become once more hypnotized by a completely new way of viewing the universe in relationship to ourselves, and for what reason? True, this new order gives us continuity and a border by which we can relate to which differentiates what *is* and which *isn't* us. To do this we must adopt certain notions of time and space that provide a modicum of security within a pattern of consistency. Consequently, we cling desperately to beliefs that what we experience as cause-effect is the way reality works and refuse to believe that have been or will be other time streams or patterns outside of the ones we are used to.

Nonetheless, as collective inhabitants of the world grid we have learned to adhere to an unspoken but felt formal cadence that demands our collective attention. In short we have adapted a censored view of what is 'out there' that appears to be *real*. To get a peek into the underlying streams laden with probable order, we must diverge into signal processing, that is, the sending of patterns of order from one spot to another via energy channels called electrical wires. In a carefully insulated parameter of order, electrical waves carry data piggy back to a receiving unit such as a television or radio, (just like our senses) where the information is transformed by electronic components into a readable pattern such as a movie – a show comprised of light and sound. To achieve this transformation the process requires a 'stepping down' of mixed signals into a controlled or pixilated pattern that converts the waves sent from the other end of the line into a picture.

Now consider: in terms of energy, one could describe the admixture of innumerous waves as chaotic, riotous energy, without order or meaning – *until* it becomes transformed into a picture complete with sound and a readable story line. That story line is a feedback of wave patterns that your particular culture, with its language and archetypes, mythology and social ideas of order can comprehend. Our audio receivers are in our brain-mind even though these organs we call ears receive it when we tune into a telephone call sent to us. It's up to us to translate its meaning. You're Uncle Bob or Aunt Mary mean something to you, not everyone else, and all the data centers around things that are usually (outside of crank calls, telephone solicitors and others) pertinent to you and your family.

The interesting thing here, is that sound waves are carried by an electrical current that have traveled across miles of wiring where a receiver in the form of a telephone broadcasts a mishmash of vibrations the brain re-interprets as a message we recognize. If you interrupted a telephone wire without a proper receiver, all you'd hear is white noise, not even an ear or a brain could interpret it. The same happens with television, when our receivers are not working properly, all those black and white spots dancing on the screen, are waves that haven't been translated into recognizable data. Without someone who understands the information coming via telephone wires to our phone receivers, through the medium of language, that is, (organized waves united by a common pattern), the information would remain nothing more than gibberish. In short, translated into comprehensible information is a snowball that hovers on the edge of a precipice. Just like a physical one, data is a potential energy cluster of that handled the right way can be incredibly cumulative (like Tesla's youthful avalanches) and directed properly. Indeed, the mind, like a pen is mightier than the sword because it has the ability to isolate a singular wave in the midst of white noise. Focused it determines the difference between the noise of dissent or jubilation of assent, depending upon its translation into palatable bits that provide a common pattern everyone can easily comprehend. The point of translation between these two opposing degrees represents trigger points.

Trigger points like these, whether in the form of math, science, music, art, literature or entertainment are the subtle, yet incredibly titanic forces that precipitate world change. For instance, a revolution in consciousness was catalyzed in 1915 by the mere arrival of the gifted pianist, Glenn Gould in Moscow when he played his own uplifting, inspirational interpretation of the Viennese version of the Bach overtures Bach. Before that moment, musicology in Russia was drowning in materialistic depression bought about by repression of the collective spirit. Little did they know the light, dancing, lyrical poetry that free-spirited music could provides. That discovery rocked the Russian group mind Music, expressed in this way, serves as a stimulant to produce change, like enzymes in an organic system, which hearkens back to what must have be the nature of the first inception process.

Thinking carefully about it one can deduce that there must have been a time and space where all information began from what would appear to be a chaotic jumble of information bits, without specific purpose or meaning until they were translated by a transferable template. Following that point it would appear that the data became forthwith organized into a pattern or program which registered as a meaningful sequence conceivable by the whole as order. From thence forward that order became the straight-line series of events (like a sine wave) known as the cycles which gave birth to the physical order of the world. A good analogy would be a spectrum of multi-colored hues emerging from one solid, white light. Through this template or medium, information would appear to cross-over, as it were, from it origins in another dimension. Like dissonant sounds, from that point onwards, meaningless data would recede into the white noise or chaos. In this way order conceivably emerges out of chaos.

Of course, science has began to sense this, and now accepts that all those other waves out there really aren't chaotic, to the contrary, they're just systems of order without proper translation. Thus, we see that chaos and order are merely selective ways of dividing a whole into meaningful and meaningless arrays of signals. Know that they merely need processing in order for them to take shape and form into a pattern we can recognize and put in motion; e.g. to render useful. Knowing this, it is not difficult to see that order appearing in the universe required a cyclic-based template that served as a translatable key or pattern to unlock or channel its meaningless content into usable information. Once achieved, this pattern was repeated over and over again from one level of creation to another. Indeed, it is the pattern which appears in the holographic creation, that is, the integrated whole shared by every part in the cosmos. In fact, it is the central key to collective resonance. By far resonance is the most important property affecting the collective consciousness of life without which, there wouldn't be any harmonic's to bring about organic unity.

A harmonic bridge, resonance is by its nature cumulative. This means it builds worlds of order from harmonic vibratory convergence and in the process acquires volume and/or mass. One could say that it accumulates mass which in turn bends the field. By this process the structure of space-time continuum is altered to the collective will of the people. In fact, today scientists looking for a *theory of everything* have come to rest on a belief that harmonics may be the central basis of creative order in the universe. Quantum physicists call this system of harmonics collectively 'string theory' because linked strings resonate or pulsate in harmonic wholes.

Returning to our musical analogy, the creation of Holoverse is a resonance process, hence it would appear that before any order came about a musical ensemble of heavenly forces must have settled down to one melody, so to speak. Apparently, scientists, like musicians, comprise those special groups of people who need the numerical reassurance of repeated cycles to believe in. A drummer is captivated by the pounding beat, enmeshed in the rhythm, bound to it, but not like Prometheus. Drummers have the ability, like the mathematicians to change the patterns by combining them into polyrhythms, that is, to create more complex wholes of the ensemble of metric feedback. These new rhythms or patterns of order have a way, in turn, of captivating others, uniting them to a growing snowball of common meaning.

Bound by left-brain logic, mathematicians often find it hard (except for Rene' Poincare, Edward Lorenz and others) to visualize that behind one set of numerical order another pattern exists. Yet, numerically patterns like these can designate cascading underlying rhythms that comprise nature's laws. Following them faithfully, as did Edward Lorenz who developed chaos theory, composers and mathematicians can unerringly predict the outcome of a given future order or crescendo. The ability to transport individual consciousness far beyond the temporal confines of the present is one of the hidden mystical elements inherent in math, art, poetry and especially music. In that regards the latter reigns as the universal language because it has the ability to transcend, as it were, language and custom, reaching the inner world of feelings where everything is connected via resonance to the cosmic beat or heart of the Holoverse.

Cycles or pulsating rhythms have binding coherences, thus creating geometric mosaics, labyrinths uniting converging dimensions. This is the resonant hierarchical or gnomonic basis for the evolution of life. Though what we see on the surface of organic material mass often obscures the deeper unions between these resonant dimensions, each system of order from the atomic to organic fields progressively builds on its process. Still skeptics tend to reject the notion that we are bound to other spacetime orders or that they might co-exist nearby. Nonetheless, we are vibrantly united holograms beyond the organic picture of our singular sensory stream. In a Fourier process of analysis, the brain acts as a wave decoder which translates incoming patterns into readable bits, reshuffling, if you will, meaningless *disorder* into *meaningful* order rendering what is necessarily relevant to the individual and collective mind.

Like waves within an ocean, we are adrift in divergent and convergent data streams, the greater content of which are nebulous waves, spaces in mathematics left to probability theory. To the logic-bound scientist, these realms might be thought of as steeped in mysticism, chaos and uncertainty when they are simply discarded, irrelevant data, for the most part because they don't resonate with the known patterns. So you see, what the brain is doing here, is extracting, evaluating and predicting or dissecting meaningful patterns in terms of future trends from chaos. In short, separating certainty from uncertainty, and determining the parameters of the Part as it relates to the Whole.

Through the course of evolutionary unfoldment, primordial patterns link us altogether into comprehensive Wholes. At the level where isolated behavior branches into the language of various groups, tribes, nations, people are separated according to the cache of unique symbols or vibratory patterns relevant to their signals. As each primate group branches into separate symbolic patterns, on the surface of communication the meaning can become quite diverse. Hence, smiling to a chimpanzee, contrary to homo- sapiens, actually signals danger, the showing of teeth, grimacing associated with aggression. However, in human society these gestures has become associated with friendship, i.e., we smile to indicate all is well. Nonetheless, if we look deeper a great whole transcends the differences of outer social behavior relevant to each group, transmitting a higher order information that is common to all. For instance, have you ever prodded a praying mantis and watched stand defiantly to fend you off? This common factor is all part of the core bond that unites the hologram of life. Seeking deeper confirmation, if you continue your prodding, sensing imminent danger to his life, he scurries off. This you instantly know, without doubt is a transcendental signal that he is frightened.

You might wonder is this tiny creature defying you or is he merely reacting to your aggression? Universally, this behavior is reminiscent of human as well as every creature's behavior. It is here at this unified field of communication that the questions confronting signals, incoming information and its interpretation, are transcended by a common resonant Whole. In this case, the binding Whole which brings about the emotional clustering stems from the realization that we all instantly comprehend the message this tiny insect is signaling; so we let him be. Emotion, especially if it is coupled with recognizable behavior, offers all life common information bits that acts as a sticking factor to seal our union, thus leading to greater snowballs of comprehension. So in looking for strengthening bonds that lead to greater snowball effects, and therefore more predictable outcomes, look to behavior which transcends the relative social etiquette of each apparently independent group order.

MEDITATIONS

1. Take some time and sit back to think about how you spend your life.
2. Concentrate on what your goals are and how you want to achieve them.
3. Calculate how much time you are using to get your goals accomplished.
4. Ask yourself: how can I get them accomplished quickly and more efficiently. Take another look at your goals and your methods of getting them accomplished.
5. Once you've calculated and did a rough estimate of the amount of time and energy, you're putting into getting your goals accomplished, make another list of what you're doing that you call 'free time', plus consider any negative health habits that may interfere with your ability to accomplish your goals.
6. Ask yourself: is the amount of time and energy put into accomplishing your goals balanced by what is getting done?
7. Again: ask yourself if you feel good about the amount of 'intent' compared to the accomplishment of my goals? Is there a great disparity between what you 'want' to get done and the 'way' you seek to accomplish it?
8. Additionally, be honest with yourself and ask: where do I spend the largest amount of my time? If you find it's on the couch watching soaps, sleeping, doing recreational drugs, or

partying with friends, began to reduce that time and change the patterns.

9. When you are lying down relaxing and cruising in your mind, are you thinking about your future and how you'd like to be somebody years from now? Where do you stand in relationship to your dreams? Are you happy with the feedback you get within yourself?

10. Strive to spend time when you are relaxing and lying down, or just sitting in a comfortable chair to repeat your own mantra of intent. For example: *Forever and ever more, I am active, wealthy, happy, healthy and secure.* Something like that. In fact, feel free to do your own thing with your mantra, but most of all make it catchy, hopefully like a little rap; something that will stick in your head.

11. As you're meditating on your little mantra, visualize yourself the person you wish to be. See exactly what it is you want coming to you.

12. Learn to rearrange your space and time and when you do, you'll discover not only that your whole life will change, but that you feel better about yourself in so many different new and exciting ways. Don't be surprised to find opportunities falling in your lap that heretofore you wouldn't even have dreamed of receiving.

13. Remember: The world is the result of your imagination backed up by will power in the way your use your available space and time. Master those two aspects, and everything else will fall in place so fast it will make your head spin!

7

FORECASTING – THE SPIRAL WAY

"The spiral is still our most profound image for the movement of time and therefore it is central to our visions of evolution." Robert Lawler author of: Sacred Geometry

Predicting Outcomes based on Variables

At first glance, predicting the future seems no more than determining specific, recurring wave patterns. Superficially, all wave patterns appear to represent no more than numerically recurring frequencies within a given time period, comparable to the two plus two sequence that adds up in time to equal four. Nonetheless, even these simple, repeating numerical patterns can be affected by the variables they encounter. Sometime two plus two doesn't equal four, and that's scary for people depending upon certain numerical outcomes to recur predictably over time. Anticipating this, life built into its recurring patterns replication adjustments based on the constant reintegration of new information from changing variables. In essence, this is the purpose of evolutionary DNA trait variation data used by biogenic life to navigate change. Moreover, the data served the purpose of adjusting to constantly changing variables while maintaining the basic, original pattern. That is one reason why I trust my intuition over physical charts, even though forecasting based on recurring cycles can work, if the variables added in are accurate and reliable.

Nature therefore, teaches us, if we wish to reliably predict the outcome of a process, it is necessary to consider the elements that affect its recurrence over time while maintaining some semblance of the original plan. Apparently, the cosmos perfected this process so far, or we would not be here. It was a forecasting plan that included a means by which to ensure the inclusion of these variables affecting the new creation. The full implications of this feedback cycle, which can be described as a negative feedback system, similar in context to a thermostat, continues to stabilizes the changes at crucial point and bring them back to an ongoing plan. Hence, like nature, when planning for success the plotting must include a constant checking back with as to the subjective reason for the project, (going back to source) which is one of the most important but overlooked aspects to consider when preparing for future growth. Further investigation in the vacillations of the stock market will explain what nature teaches us. Think on the following.

In financial terms, to reach desired outcomes in the future of any economic endeavor depends upon our ability to monitor our resources while trying to adjust to variables controlling the supply and demand of stock. For example, special consideration must be given to the trends from comparative patterns over time and the effects that led to specific outcomes, if one wishes to insure favorable long range or even short-range forecasts. This means one must consider when plotting the effect of variables on the outcomes the adjustment rate to recurrence of similar wave patterns over time. Taking a cue from the preceding chapter, for instance, the objective wave may include the emotional climate of the country during highs and lows over time as well as the subjective wave of the investor's personal emotional state.

Though the general or quantitative emotional content may never change, the quality of the individual content may act as a prime element affecting the outcome, since each individual may react differently to the data which is presented to them, depending on how the subject views the data in personal emotional terms. Therefore, including subjective emotional reactions into the prediction automatically increases the probability of accurate forecasting. In terms of eccentricities in the wave, its shape bears great significance on the outcome because the acuteness of the angle reveals the degree of the amplitude and therefore, the intensity in the angular velocity of charge. Emotional charge and frequency are essentially synonymous and the shape of the wave reflects this. An acutely bent wave has the capacity to alter the time-space field, which means it can accelerate the turnaround time by inflating it. The power of the field to alter lies in the intensity of the emotional charge. Put simply: change the frequency and you change the field. Frequency changes have the ability to tip or trigger a larger wave into rolling; especially those created by the collective social climate.

As I have intimated in earlier chapters, frequency and amplitude of the wave reveals much about its contents. Not every wave is equal, and this is true especially as of the frequency of each individual wave and the way it interacts or conjugates with other waves. Everyone reacts differently to the collective wave. Therefore, our interaction with the social wave bears the imprint of our own unique personality signature. Understanding this interaction with emotional waves can be pictured as the waves which carry ships on the ocean. The quality of the wave, whether it is large or small in amplitude, placid or tempestuous is crucial. Moreover, the nature of the energy affecting the central wave determines its shape and usefulness based on its motion. Think of the waves affecting the orbits of planets around the sun. The internal status of the sun governs the gravitational waves upon which planets orbit. Thus, their individual eccentricities or perturbations are the result of the effect of changes in the sun upon the gravitational field. Shake up the wave and you rock the boat. An evaluation that might be useful in determining its affect over time is its general composition, temperature and age upon the shape, amplitude and phase relationship to the planets within influence of its presence.

The sun is the central force ruling the gravitational field upon which planets orbit, thus it dominates every aspect of their individual existence. If changes occur it will be because of its field. Yet, as anyone knows who has studied gravitational theory, all bodies exert individual gravitational fields, including you and me. Within the individual and the collective mind, subjective emotions act like the sun's gravitation field on the planets. They dominate the epicenter of the converging field and are the primary force that exerts pressure against the collective social climate. The individual wave feeds information in and receives information back from the collective.

Like a powerful force field, the central emotional wave in society transmits the general trending weather conditions and as such reflects the collective feedback of people reacting to political, military, economic waves. There are of course, many other elements to be considered, but in general these are the predominately influential forces. The emotional wave transmitted by the migrant children during June of 2018 at the Mexican-American border crossings that were separated from their parents, sent a charge that swept round the world. It drove an adamant right-wing president to soften his anti-migrant status and change his rhetoric almost overnight, so much so that his wife hurried down there to reassure people that they had a heart. They sensed the building emotional storm that was about to rock our nation and realized they were the target of Tsunami of outrage and familial sentiment that could rock his leadership and threaten the very fabric of both our society, not to mention political state. Trump knew to change his stance and to do it quick, to stop the onslaught of forces from happening.

In short, change the nature of this central emotional field governing the collective wave or one's subjective emotional response and everything changes or is affected accordingly and vice versa. Going back to our sun analogy, the sun affects, in a general sense, the wellbeing, so to speak, of the planets in their orbits and likewise the planets in turn reflect in the vacillations of their frequencies the sun. One might describe this interrelationship between the frequencies in the state of the sun with the orbit of planets and what goes on within their atmospheres and core, a harmonic, or in some case inharmonic attunement or convergence/divergence. Obviously, if the conditions within in the sun are out of balance than the planets in their orbits and within their atmosphere and core will likewise be affected.

An example of this can be found in the discovery by astronomers that as the planets pass closely to the sun's orbit, the powerful perturbations in its gravitational field change the shape of the wave from circular to elliptical. This change of shape in the wave is very important because it tells us a great deal about the strongest governing variables affecting current flow, long range rotation and movement of planets through the matrix of time-space. What I'm alluding to here is the bending of space and the alteration of time, which can be compared, in pedestrian terms, to the socio-economic climate. It is these alterations in frequencies, (changes in the conjoining fields) that produce the vary patterns in market fluctuations, supply and demand trends and the economy in general.

The structure of these waves can be seen in their amplitude and cycles per second/frequencies which in turn controls the shape of the wave. If the frequency is consistently harmonic the vibrations produce evenly spaced waves with symmetrical patterns. On the other hand, if the frequencies are extremely high the wave becomes bent into a loop pattern. Bends of this sort produce fluctuations in the trends. It may help you to imagine the bending of space and time by taking a piece of flat paper and bending it until both ends touch. On one end you can write 'beginning' of the universe and on the other the 'ending'. While these points only represent hypothetical beginnings and endings, they symbolize how the bending of the matrix can reunite the beginning of the universe or pattern and a hypothetical ending. What we have is the union of two variables through a spatial loop in time. Here, two diverse points converge into a new whole, comparable to the notion physics calls a continuum.

Now let's apply this idea in relativity physics, the bending of space and time, to the dual ends of rising and falling stock prices affected by subjective emotions and the collective socio-economic climate. This image of the bending of the space-time (beginning and ending of the universe) gives you an idea of how when these apparently fragmented opposites merge, we see how they conceptually reflect the union of individual with collective orbital frequencies. Such mergers can have long term affects. Caught within the orbits of these mutually interactive waves within waves, like the changing of interlocking gears in a clock, our lives faithfully reflect any slight change in recurring, periodic cycles which show up in the general socio-economic emotional climate.

Moreover, in terms of the ability to produce change, any alteration in the intensity of these waves, represent the potential available energy being used by the socio-economic system to catalyze the emergence of new order. Change the convergence of the space-time loop, its cycles per minute, and you change not only the availability of available energy and the flow its data base, but the time in which the convergence into new order comes about. What this example demonstrates is that space is equally alterable as is the flow of time. In a simple example: if you were traveling toward San Francisco, which was seven hundred miles away from your take off point and your velocity was seventy miles per hour, you could, hypothetically, be expected to arrive in approximately ten hours. However, changes in speeds are controlled by variables (interfering waves) such as rough terrain, a heavy flow of traffic or inclement weather conditions. When this occurs these logistics could drastically vary.

It is the variables you encounter that alter the status of your arrival time and simultaneously the relationship you might have when facing the variables. A desire to maintain the primary speed even though the variable may be inhibiting forward movement such as detours, a wreck, snow, etc. decreases the accuracy of the logistics and increases the chance of an accident. Therefore, time adjustments, both personal and incidental must be precluded in the potential variables when making plans. To compensate for the potential interfering time increments, precautions must include a flexible window of at least two hours.

Coupled with these changes in the window of time based on the variables expected to be encountered, another major, potentially unexpected variable arises: adjustment to stress-inducing factors. Unfortunately dealing with stress throws the proverbial monkey wrench into the trip by introducing a subjective emotional variable, which is a crucial shadow factor affecting the outcome of all changes in the matrix. Overcoming that variable at the get-go changes the relationship by a tremendous degree before you encounter the obstacles. Emotions, in this regard symbolizes the most powerful inner forces at work producing the vacillations in the field which bends the space-time matrix.

Understanding the effect of emotions on the time-space variables in relationship to the individual reaction response caused by the presence of blocks, teaches us that one can accelerate or reduce the velocity at which future events come about. Going back to the speed in which the president acted to avoid anger from the country over the migrant crisis at the border over the separation of children from parents is a perfect example. Let us say he acted in a 'timely' manner to alter the manner and speed at which the anticipated wave would sweep through the nation causing tumult. That is why knowledge of emotions and the willingness to control your reality by understanding their nature and production is so important. This means getting in touch with who you are emotionally to effectively predict and control in advance what you anticipate will come about in your future. Expectation is composed of ¾ feeling and ¼ thinking. This disparity explains why emotions rule your Intuition IQ.

Nonetheless, as I have intimated before in this book, knowledge of inherent human factors makes forecasting more plausible simply because human emotions arise according to set patterns, which for the most part rarely change unless the individual is willing to take charge of habitual habits of responding to stress. Of course, this is not always easy. Becoming familiar with the nature of human emotions and their effect on the production of frequency patterns that alter time-space conditions can prove a valuable tool to avoid costly mistakes in planning. Such insights can be garnered by studying personal habits and chart them over a period of time. These are wave patterns depicting the rise and fall of problems encountered and how you responded to the pressure. This means a portfolio of patterns must be amassed. The portfolio will reveal predominant patterns that have recurred more often over time.

Knowing this one can get to the heart of the preparation issue and detour the problem, thus reducing unreliable preparations due to poor predicting. Usually a physical chartist, someone who predicts according to a graph, will base his/her determinations solely on the technical appearance of jagged lines depicting variables on an arithmetic or logarithmic chart. Those determinations often fall short of fully revealing the emotional climate of both the individual buyer and seller in relationship to these transactions.

The Frequency Status of the Stock Market

Clearly, the stock market controls the socio-economic climate but it is also affected by many variables, the central aspect of which is the emotional status, i.e. climate or well-being of the world. Borrowing from some interesting examples of changes over an increment or period of time, we will begin with a real-life scenario. For example, we will examine the effect of fear and greed, which are essentially co-elements, on the buying and selling of stock in the Dow Jones Market between the periods of 1903 and 1932. During that incremental period the stock market underwent a tremendous vacillation in the amplitude and frequency of the selling and buying phases of the wave. At the beginning of the phase, in 1903 during the period known as the "Rich Man's Panic," the selling of stock underwent one long period when the frequency of the emotional and/or socio-economic climate was low. Therefore, the so-called 'bull' market ruled until the selling market was at its peak, indicating that the availability and hence the price of stock was high because the probability of the market ahead was more certain.

During the middle to the latter phase, the market seemed to become more certain in the late 1920's and transformed into a sellers' market. At that time frequencies escalated and when it did the results were the riches of the Roaring Twenties. Clearly, what we discover at the initial inception point on the graph is a period dominated by the emotion of fear with its negative anticipation of failure when seller let go of their stocks. Stock became almost valueless. Unfortunately, it was this devaluation of stocks that stymied growth in the market leading to a period of depression.

Fearful, anxious expectations in turn altered the degree of the angle of the wave, until – and this is very important, people were willing to trust in the future. Thus, in space-time terms, the future was forestalled or slowed down, meaning it was bent in a concave fashion rather than convex. If its shape was convex, the market would be expansive and healthy. Until the climate changed at the economic depression's inception point began around 1929 the country suffered accordingly. It was not until public optimism rose and its emotional frequency changed to hope with the anticipation of good times ahead that the investment climate changed. When it did change frequency, it led to the manifestation of a very positive value wave. Seen as a whole, it is clear that in 1903 the seller's market was catalyzed by depressive expectations, people who believed that the future would not get better. Fortunately, on a plus side, this made it a buyer's paradise which, in time, eventually led to a socio-economic boon. However, that panned out as the 30's approached; the worse part of it settling in during the year 1932 known as The Great Depression.

As we have learned, knowing something about the nature of the emotions which promulgates the rise and fall of these patterns can be a huge factor in favorable predictions of long-range forecasting simply because it controls the way we react to variables. Hence, if this knowledge is acutely integrated into the analysis, not only will the reader be able to reach a greater degree of accuracy in predicting the future, but understand why the frequency and hence its shape is so affected by emotion. Once understood, it gives the reader that proverbial leg up on controlling the outcome because emotions catalyze the degree in the shape of the wave. Emotions can be predicted and in a precise way, the desired outcomes controlled to a greater degree.

Elements of Spiral Metrics

In the preceding chapter you were introduced to spiral Gnomonics, which is essentially building on gradually ascending exponential factors from a primary inception point. To picture this primary inception point think in terms of the construction of the sacred temples in India which was built on a central block or point which gradually grew in squared increments. In this book's application of the same principles, we are going to apply that pattern to the spiral curvature. Rather than starting at a one foot by one-foot square block, we will start at a central point and gradually create a spiral curve. From that point imagine the spiral gradually expanding outwardly along a curvilinear path just like the patterns you see around a plant stem, the shape of nautilus sea shells or the helix in pine cones. In the patterns that evolve, the spiral shape will grow exponentially according to the input of various data. This data should also include its frequency quotient which influences the shape of the spiral produced, and in turn reduces or accelerates its growth rate. Thus, the progressive evolution of the spiral pattern that evolves will, hypothetically, seek to predict the eventual rate of growth affecting the outcome of your enterprise or investment and hence, determine its rate of dependability in the long run.

Remember: the emotional climate controls the rate of the frequency. The higher the frequency in the intent behind the emotion, the more positive its outcome and conversely, the lower the frequency, the more negative will be the outcome. Functionally, the evolvement rate of growth of each plotted spiral is influenced by the following factors: a) the type of data you input, b) the shape of the wave which evolves, c) the length of each periodic increment and, d) the spiral's growth constant or acceleration in terms of time. Arithmetically, these factors can be read as distance divided by the variables inhibiting or increasing the rate of growth. This can be written as: $D \div V =$

SPR/T. D equals distance, v the rate of acceleration and SPR the growth of the spiral over time.

In short, this chart will reflect the rate at which your investment will fan out on a spiral curve; its angular momentum over time. In essence, the rule is quite similar to discerning the speed it takes to get from point A to point B within a given time, except for the fact that you are adding in the underlying factors (variables) which alter the degree of the curve and therefore, its end sum. The structure or degree of the emotional curve is the determining factor which acts as a major influence on the rate of the final frequency in the sum of the outcome. The shape of the sum wave will often vary radically from its original pattern – from broad and rolling, to narrow and choppy. Excited or happy emotions produce waves which have high pitched, narrow, pointy peaks and deep troughs, while somber, depressed or negative emotions reveal longer, deeper, often pitted troughs and flat peaks. Joy and exaltation, positive waves tend to travel fast through space and unite points in time quickly while hatred, envy or disgust move slow and laboriously and are broad and flat. The spatial sequences for joy are comparable to the illusory passage of seconds or minutes and depression would appear to span vast lows comprised of hours and days. Thus, time and space are drastically different in the way they are altered because of the velocity or frequency (shape) of the wave. Positive waves move in a clockwise spiral and negative waves counter-clockwise. Of course, as I have mentioned, all waves are composed of many different waves, so in summing it up, one must consider the variables which give it its final shape or structure.

This brings us to the fun of applying gnomonic principles to a spiral chart which I term Spiral Metrics. Formally, SM shall be defined as the structure producing the shape of the order of events affecting the growth of space-time increments over time. The following material will explain the physical mechanics and purpose of charting metrically, but the final three chapters will focus on the process from a subjective level. For now we will do some imaginative charting.

Conflict and its Spiral Ramifications

If you plan to be buying or selling stocks and would like to make a chart, they serve essentially the same purpose that planning your grocery list does, since it reminds you what you need to do to prepare for during a given increment of time. However, a spiral chart achieves this in a more organized and systematic way since it also reveals the future of your own well-being in the next day, week or even month ahead. Everyone can make these charts. Instead of a linear chart like those used by horizontal forecasters who are mapping trends to predict stock growth, your imaginary chart should contain a curved and perhaps broken line in the general shape of a spiral. The broken line will indicate periodic variables over space and time in its shape that disrupt the otherwise straight lines of forecasters demarcating perfectly symmetrical peaks and valleys. Among variations in the growth of the spiral are political attitudes, threat of war, world or local weather trends, pandemic diseases, general mental health, scandals, government chaos, employment, a terrorist attack, embargo's, strikes, cold wars and so on. Such problems can devalue the dollar nationally as well as the status of the Euro dollar. As a whole, all of these elements are caused and/or affected by the general emotional climate of the country as it relates to the emotional climate of the world.

The purpose for a portfolio of elements, such as a tracking chart for the stock market, will be to present a more detailed analysis of the variables affecting trends or changes in trading between buyers and sellers as these factors relate to your personal and the collective emotional climate. To become acquainted with some of the terminology used in the stock market: buyers are often referred to as the bears, and seller's are the bulls. Bears try to buy stock at its cheapest rate and bulls seek to retain it unless they feel the market ahead is going down. Beneath the surface of affairs, business is conducted totally from a visceral level because trading is Darwinian in nature, simply because it grows out the competitive greed generated by competitive lower limbic system emotions such as fear, anxiety and sometimes hatred. The following description of the process will give you an idea why this is true.

For example, when buyers are more powerful then the seller's prices move up, but when the sellers are more powerful then buyer prices move down. Thus, when "A" buys stocks from person "B" the seller, "A" believes that stock is going up (meaning he's selling too cheap) and "B" believes he would rather have cash that the stock (meaning "A" is buying an over-valued or at least fully-valued stock). Though the transactions are done from a business perspective the battle between the competing forces is much like any power struggle.

As I have suggested, for the holistic minded trader, including comparative emotional frequency data into your chart gives you the added advantage of a perspective which views reality from the *bigger picture*. Remember - anything affecting the lower limbic system automatically alters the relationship between buyers and seller's because it inhibits or encourages spending. Interestingly, the emotional climate is nearly invisible to buyers and sellers of stock without a careful examination of the state of the intellectual-emotional mind-body of the world.

The Emotional Pulse of the Socio-Economic Spiral

All of the foregoing factors governing the rise and fall of the economy and consequently, stock prices follow the socio-economic curve which has ramifications in both the cosmic forces as well as human nature. But these factors, especially those arising from within the emotional and psychic field shared by all life, is oftentimes overlooked. Thus, when considering the growth of a spiral curve most thinkers tend to envision it in terms of the cyclic convolutions of the planet under the influence of the sun and moons gravitation field, but there is a far more powerful force field within. This field is created by the emotional content of the times and loosely referred to as the collective emotional climate. It too includes the thoughts and beliefs making up the world mind. Many subtle and generally overlooked elements of the spiral, its overall shape, including the structure of its spiral curve must be considered. All of these aspects in the spiral's generation are affected by the collective emotional climate.

Nature contains many examples to draw from, e.g., distortions in the smooth invaginations of a nautilus sea shell reflect cosmic imbalances that affect the smooth development of the spiral shape. Similar alterations in shape and pattern can be found in the phyllotaxis generation and distribution of growth in trees, branches of plants, the florets and leaves of a shrub. Such distortions in patterns reflect the effect of forces to produce distortions in the quality and continuity of the spiral wave. The same could be said of evolutionary growth spurts; hence, periods vary according to perturbations in the wave-phase interrelationship between the sun and the planets.

By the same token, disruptions in growth patterns in the helical evolution of socio-economic spiral patterns, like any that occur in natural processes, have their origins in the mood and behavior of people on a mass level. Everyone, unilaterally, are affected by perturbations in the emotional climate fields. Conversely, should the factor's giving rise to the evolution of the wave stay constant than the pattern, its shape and consistency will remain equilateral throughout the spiral growth.

In nature or in human fields the spiral, its general growth pattern, especially the shape of its curvature responds to the periodic release of catalyzing hormones which normally occur at precise points in its evolution. On a physical level, additional factors can influence its growth such as magnetic perturbations in the gravitational field, eruptions of magma on the sun, orbital wobbles of earth or astronomical effects like asteroids or changes in earth's greenhouse effect. In all these you will discover serious vacillations in the time-space growth patterns of the spiral. Again, the same thing can be said of the socio-economic spiral. Interfering perturbations affect the stability of its growth, and reflect the polarity of the emotional climate.

As far as normal, uninterrupted growth - should the ascending, deeper processes that activate periodic bursts by catalysts remain equilaterally constant no evidence of changes in its structure will be observable. Importantly, in terms of the emotional climate and the development of the social climate, as a whole, cosmic processes like those occurring in nature do affect and influence our emotional trends. Severe internal perturbations can give rise to a war like the one that rages in the Ukraine which erupts on a social level from an emotional mosaic of anger, paranoia, fear and hatred.

Coupled with the repression of amassed, historical fears and suspicions commonly known as the *cold war*, these vacillations in the international shape of the spiral force expresses itself in the conflicting personal agendas of Russia, European nations and the United States. The world emotional climate accumulates a snowball of resentment, anger and hostility, all given momentum by the catalyst of revenge. America and EU decide to apply sanctions to control aggressive-subversive pressures levied by Russian military under the command of Vladimir Putin. Suddenly, the emotional memories of old Soviet KGB mentalities spill over from sub-surface collective innuendos to add their emotional spillage into social cauldron of mounting hysteria and paranoia.

When the right elements fall in to place past unresolved fears and hatred billow up from parallel planes and collective emotional repressions gather potential energy to produce the momentum generated from skewed logic. Few researchers I studied considered the spiral effect as a valid process in the creation of varying kinds of order in the macrocosm. Likewise, they did not think to consider that the collective emotional climate behaved in similar manner as naturally occurring reports of weather changes.

Unexpectedly, the social climate, like a dam breaking can release a veritable hidden Pandora's Box of repressed, paranoid past increments of emotions into our time stream. Similar to a log jam, these elements can cause havoc in strong emotional currents as they explode into manifestation. Most of it comes from buried archives of collective data dredged up from that time period and before you know it, all the worst emotional elements from the cold war era erupt. Bare in mind that we are linked by emotional associational content to all periods of time in which similar collective feelings existed by frequency.

Fears accumulate and the anxiety creates a tit-for-tat retaliatory reaction, and both countries impose more and more import and export sanctions and pretty soon, the world economy freezes up on both sides. The Russian ruble is devalued and the Russian people become depressed, angry and revengeful and the U.S. and Europe suffer from the lack of trade interactions with a country the size of Russia which has heretofore done enormous trading with them.

On the surface when this happens, the growth of the economic spiral nose dives and the world economy undergoes a block, detour and dwindles not just in terms of the present condition but has far-reaching circumstances. On the surface we see war, stock trade blockades, economic problems affecting the well-being of the countries involved, but underneath the conflict and its vicissitudes we detect the evocation of long-standing emotions that reflect anger, hatred, fear, anxiety, resentment, paranoia and revenge. Put these elements together and you have the seeds of a major socio-economic gestalt and none of it good. That internal morass of emotions is like a hurricane and as it builds it gathers steam from the resultant clash of emotions it generates. When this occurs the spiral is undergoing a levogyre or left-handed reversal of the good feelings built up since relations between U.S., Europe and Russia after the Soviet era and a detour of the flow in the generation of collective potential energy. Clearly, what has happened is that within six to eight months of conflict the world has detoured its progressive flow by borrowing negative stockpiles of emotions from past situations thought overcome, but piling up like unexploded enemy shells from a former war.

These kind of negative unexploded emotions from past cold wars are like land mines and as such have the capacity to set the growth of world nation back fifty years or more. Furthermore, they hopelessly stymie the mental, physical and emotional health of everyone. Hurling hatred missiles in veiled innuendos is akin to fighting mind wars. It generates 'alienation' diseases and releases plagues of emotional memes that infest morale and act as a catalyst for manufacturing of real disease in time like the Ebola virus. This virus, like all viruses, as Richard Dawkins suggests, is first generated as a parasitic meme that clings to fear, paranoia, hatred and revenge. Its origins are deeply rooted in our collective subconscious symbolized by its eruption as a physical virus in Africa which represents the negative, superstitious elements of the unconscious or dark side of human nature. This is also the geographical origin of the zombie virus which symbolizes alienation from the planetary soul, a sort of wandering of the spirit brought about by too much immersion into fast foods and their psychology, plus the alienation of a mechanistic society. Unfortunately, the collective psyches nightmares show up first in darkest Africa. Tapping these elements in our collective psyche brings about rapid escalation of the levogyre or negative, reverse spiral, while blocking creative energy flow.

Examined more deeply, the antipathy that has arisen between East and West could have been predicted and controlled if the conditions of poverty, war and famine in Africa had been averted by more collective aide from the world gestalt. Without knowing how to read the quality of the collective emotional energy and understanding its relationship to the world mind, it is impossible to understand the exponential growth of the psychological snowball that is being produced by these volatile negative energies. The same can be said of Middle Eastern violence and mayhem. Bear in mind that a 'middle ground' symbolically is important in the analysis of these alienating spiritual forces at play throughout the world. They reflect a line drawn between dueling spiritual camps. In short, these violent eruptions are reflective of unresolved spiritual competition and conflicts in the undeveloped male spirit of the world mind over whose god is greater. Resolve these issues and the wars will dissipate. End the competition between U.S., Europe and Russia and the Ukrainian conflict will disappear. Disintegrative economic spirals are only the tip of the pyramid, and the greater problems are all below the surface in the subtle, boiling cauldron of the limbic system battles which in time erupt into major differences and wars. Getting an idea of how these emotional elements work toward creating world changes and conflicts gives you some insights of the chaotic forces propelling your personal endeavors toward future goals in a sea of conflicting or potentially supportive emotions – depending on how you prepare the way.

Profit Acceleration Points and the Snowball Effect

One of the essential things we have learned in this book is how the snowball is connected to greater forces far beyond itself. It is these cosmic forces that propel its momentum. On the physical surface of things, the area that physicists refer to as the causal plane, physics is thought to be ruled by the EM field and gravity. However, order and consistency of energy flows from the 4th dimension releasing enormous power that terminates in the stupendous avalanches of order we see in the multiplicity of order and life found here at the 3 rd dimension end of its journey into manifestation. It is this type of cosmic force that produced the physical world - all the order and biogenic life found through the myriad reaches of the Holoverse. So when I am speaking of hooking up to these super-conductive fields of energy, I am referring to connecting to forces far beyond the physics of the material world. Hence, the high-speed acceleration seen in a myriad of the processes is, in truth, exacerbated by omnipotent pressures beginning far beyond it in the 4th dimension.

Going back to our examination of the phyllotaxis process in plant life, we see that when the pressure behind the next generation of Fibonacci florets, stems or flowers encounters a stagnation point, a catalyst is released by the plant to boost it to the next stage of growth. Pressures at these *critical stress* points, between counter forces holding it back and the forces behind it, both within the plants DNA and in the cosmos, drive it forward beyond a sticking point. However, in terms of its potential energy for forward momentum, that angle of the curve represents the trigger or tipping point which can predict the moment when its future manifest. As such, this point now has accumulated incredible potential energy to produce all the transformations necessary to get it down the road, so to speak, triggered by an energy catalyst beginning in the fourth dimension. The ability to flip this incredibly powerful switch is your hands.

Not surprisingly, resistance is a vital factor and often overlooked factor in the process of growth, without which there would be no growth beyond the angle of this curve where the barrier is encountered. With it, however or because of its pressure-inducing resistance, enormous potential is generated. In essence, the presence of stress at a crucial point in the cycle of growth and expansion serves the same purpose of a dam in the propagation of electrical voltage. Depending on the amount of the potential current and the pressure of the resistance in the dam, we can determine the precise point at which the outcome will come about.

Thus, it comes as no surprise that when the stock market encounters a sticking point which brings about the accumulation of pressures, it is about to boost it forward at astonishing speeds of accelerated growth in future profits. The first stage of this process can be seen in what forecasters of the market refer to as *support*. A support stage, in terms of the sale of stocks, is the price level of growth where there is a pause in its value or movement. Unless this level is violated or broken through, there will be little if no potential for a buyer to make money fast. In short, they must break through the support lines. Though pressures develop and stress often rises during these phases, the upside of this apparent down point, is that an increase in potential energy is escalating. Hence, forward growth with sudden great profits is possible and the longer the resistance the better is the possibility of a bonanza!

Typically, at this point three things occur: 1) buyers overcome sellers, 2) volume increases as excitement builds, and 3) stocks rise in value sometimes as much as 50% or more. (See: Tim Knight Chart Your Way to Riches.) The type of resistance referred to her should not be mistaken for 'overhead resistance,' which is the point where stock value will not rise any higher. These ceilings in stock value usually can best be recognized by studying the charts provided by professionals such as Tim Knight who has made a habit of researching data from trend periods involving many years of change. In these incredible growth spurts we see the snowball effect in full bloom, so to speak, occurring right at the point where it appears that there is no chance of any forward momentum. Such points do not include peak repetitions that recur over time, but often follow a saucer-shaped concave low or valley. My intuition tells me that these points are the periods to look for that precede such sudden vacillations. As such they can forecast a future rich with incredible potential, or on the other hand, coming periods of famine and depression.

Heal the Land – Heal the Man

Forecasting can prevent these great vacillations in peaks and valleys and swift accelerations into chaos. As a matter of fact there were many indications before the depression set in during the twenties, even though they were overlooked. The going illusion was that because stocks could be purchased at 10% of actual cost, investors believe they would be richer than they were, when in fact a distinct void was forming beneath the impressions of false growth. Plus, there was a repressed feeling of impending doom during the Roaring Twenties though consciously, most people behaved as only blue skies were smiling at them, to refer to a popular song of the times. This kind of feeling often comes right before you get the impression that you've hit the ceiling of good times and sense that a down cycle is just around the corner. Part of the reason it came at that time was that regulation of buying and selling stocks were deregulated, just like the period just before the accountability days of the late 1990's and early 2000's.

When it came, tipped by a few simple warnings from forecasters, its potential left-handed, negative acceleration took very little pressure to get it rolling. In those times people had gotten out of touch with the land and with themselves, which means, in a very real sense, that their connection with the greater whole was totally out of sync. There were countless floods, droughts, erosion, spiritual indicators like those prior to our current problems. Proof of humanities coming punishment by the world spirit was the forlorn Dust Bowl days. This occurred because humans sought to take what they could without giving back. Right afterwards came the Great Depression when the value of stocks fell as much as 90% in a few days. Cocky bulls who had believed they were imperious to poverty, thinking they lived on easy street because they had so much money, awakened to the sad reality that in a matter of hours they were homeless and destitute. It is no wonder that many threw themselves from buildings or committed suicide by whatever means available.

For what seemed like an eternity the socio-economic climate fell to its lowest frequencies, but the thing that helped the economy regain its momentum to move upward to higher frequencies was Franklin D. Roosevelt's CCC or Civilian Conservation program to fight land erosion by replanting trees, irrigating, terracing and other methods of restoration. A leading motto prevalent was "Heal the Man – Heal the Land." Correspondingly, the same could be said to be true: "Heal the Land – Heal the Human." Our first environmentalist, Roosevelt launched a campaign to restore the land, putting millions of young men back to work in labor camps where they were given three square meals a day, recreation facilities, showers and a place to sleep, plus 25.00 dollars a month. Once paid, twenty dollars of it was immediately sent back to the wives and families of these hard-working laborers, which subsequently were recycled into the economy, much in the same sense that Barrack Obama's subsidy checks helped restore our economy during the most recent depression.

To get a jump start on radical changes in frequencies that lead to major changes, one should get acquainted with psychologist David Watkins who produces frequency charts on emotions. One can even learn to apply Fourier analysis to frequencies patterns to convert them into wave patterns to discern the outcome of future time increments. Such charts could conceivably make it easy to get an idea of how direct and quick your focus is on your movement toward your future goals. A big portion of the secret to how and why time unfolds as it does lies hidden in the simple formula of knowing self in terms of your emotional composition, since it is these unconscious or hidden factors built into your patterns that influence your choice of stock investments and divert your energy toward what you might consider to be future oriented plans. Often, like a detour of labyrinthine mazes, most of the vital energy to get to your goals is siphoned off though your conscious intent and may be perfectly sincere. Couple this crippling inner data with the barriers built into time increments produced from the affect of the emotional climate from the bigger picture and you will get a broader panorama of why your future is either destined to success or shocking failure.

MEDITATIONS

1. Go to the library, the internet online, or to your favorite bookstore. Study books, articles, magazines or blogs detailing the national and world economic market.

2. Research diverse and competitive views of the economic market to get a broader picture of the conflicting views which make it up.

3. Strive to make a determination of the nature of the world market as it compares to your own outlook emotionally on life.

4. Realize that the choices you have made up to this point reflect emotional elements hidden in your lower limbic system.

5. Outline the many aspects of your emotions and make a map depicting the structure of the emotional waves which best describe how you feel deep down.

6. Make a list of things you want and why you want them and compare these items to where you are at in life. In this list you will discover, when compared to the items in number five, exactly who you really are. Often this will shock you.

7. Determining who you really are deep down with where you're really at will give you a picture of the path you've taken to get there. From the picture that arises, note how many detours you've taken.

8. Ask yourself this question: If I didn't detour at these different points, where would I be?

9. 9, The peaks and troughs in these patterns determine a) how well you used your energy, b) what blocked your paths, and c) what now stands between you and your desired goal.

10. Study David Watkins emotional frequencies charts and apply that information to composing a personal emotions chart.

11. Note that the variables such as the emotional climate and your own personal emotional make-up, coupled with the general trends in media and world economic and political atmosphere, should represent time increments determining the rate at which your desired goals can come into fruition.

12. PS: Classes for spiral charting that integrate your personal data into the sum of the variables affecting your snowball; will be available in the future. For the time being, you are requested to experiment with the ideas for a chart based on the suggestion presented in this chapter.

8

OPTIMIZE YOUR ENERGY:
TAP THE CONTINUUM

"Vladimir: That passed the time.
Estragon: It would have passed in any case.
Vladimir: Yes, but not so rapidly."
Samuel Becket – Waiting for Godot

Reality and the Psychic Input of the Observer

All movement toward our goals is determined by the amount of energy we commandeer to get to them. Whether the flow of current is weak and diverted or strong and channeled is vitally important to the accuracy of your aim and the time it takes you to get there. In short, optimizing energy is all about channeling body by mind, that is, 'focusing self-image' and directing it optimally into matter. Hence, it is correct to say that achieving your goals is all about how well you know yourself and integrate these details into your psychological aim and manipulate its physical outcome in matter. This means that at the core of everything we do or think about, is a logistical step in the direction of energy potential. Unless one learns to optimize the channeling of mind into matter, achieving one's ultimate dreams will be detoured and the power needed to get there drained. Down deep in the very core of this book is my desire to teach you how to optimize your energy flow to achieve your goals in record time by learning to rapidly shift the space-time matrix. Though this may sound difficult it isn't. In fact, it simply means learning to direct your energy to alter the continuum and it is something we unconsciously do all the time on a hyper-dimensional level.

However, full, conscious manipulation requires diligent training and focused application. But first and foremost, the steps leading to this level of control requires an understanding of the 3rd dimension we live in and its relationship to the 4th dimensional continuum. To properly interact with this somewhat mystical 4th dimension, we must refresh our memories of the differences between what comprises the 3rd and 4th dimension. Firstly, the 3rd is the everyday reality you encounter of cause and effect while the 4th dimension is a holistic, invisible, curved space that encloses it. Ironically, though the 4th dimension permeates the 3rd dimension it is intrinsically divided from it. This occurs because everything in the macro is continuously undergoing a revolution from the lowest to the highest energy potential. It turns on a revolving hub of a creative generator that pivots around the hub of the spiral wheel. The wheel undulates like serpent between the hub and its periphery in a piston like compression of up and down strokes.

The up stroke represents the peak energy potential state and its movement downward the bottom the lowest. Like a car engine, the highest stroke intakes energy from the 4th dimension and it explodes sending it into the creative cycle throughout the 3rd dimension. In the 3rd dimension is gradually returns to its lowest energy state – that's entropy in the physical plane. However, the energy doesn't stop there it completes the cycle of the rotation depositing its remaining portion in the 4th dimension. In this way the cycle is completed between 3rd and 4th dimension. However, there is more to this decompression cycle. Once it reaches its lowest point on the down stroke it goes through the singular point again at the hub of the template into a paradoxical infinite but finite space below the Planck length where it continues to compound, rebuild, expand and rebound. After entering the 4th dimension, it returns to its original high energy state to produce continual pressure that once again seeks to burst forth.

When it blows anything can happen – usually another universe is formed and what's incredibly beautiful and profound about this creation is that it takes place right in the very center of your being. Depending upon the way it is funneled or channeled that incredibly power energy dynamo can produce all the wonders of the physical plane and more. At its core the dynamo is generating enormous potential energy and once it begins to be released its unlimited force can transform your life into any dream. However, bear in mind that there is an order to its process that is built into the specifications of its creations – **everything tends to cluster and/or network so that any individual creative Part unfolds into a larger Whole**. Thus, individual creation only works at its optimum when everything and everyone works together. Creations focused solely on individual aggrandizement only blunt the capacity to do wonders. Therefore, keep in mind that what you do for self-blunts the magnanimity of the resultant action. Thinking back on what the earlier chapters in this book taught us about homeostasis and the healthy order of Parts within Wholes - anything works best when it works together with everything else.

The central purpose of the dynamo of the spiral is to bring form to chaos. To do so and maintain it properly involves the interaction of many parts in an ongoing Whole. *Knowledge of these fundamental prerequisites of the template to bring form to chaos through networking is the perennial secret of bringing about dynamic success from the creative cycle.* Those who strive to work outside these specifications will find that the dynamo's output will be proportional to their adherence to this rule. Its creativity when invoked accordance to the rule, on the other hand, will lead to a contagion of unbridled proportions. Once started it cannot be stopped because the cooperative unity between Whole and Part is the most powerful force in all creation. The only process that can properly handle and/or successfully channel such stupendous power is the spiral dynamo for it is the channel of energy flow that turns the wheel of creation that births the HOLOVERSE.

But to understand it one must begin with the fundamentals of the dynamics between 3rd and 4th dimension. Look for it, the 4th dimension is pretty much invisible except for those who aren't accustomed to its nature. Virtual and wispy it is nonetheless palpable; therefore, it does have a tangible presence, but *not* to our outer senses as they are configured from fleshly sensory limitations. Not easily discernible but there, on another level, we do possess inner senses that can make the 4th dimension figuratively tangible to us. In truth, sensing with them is how we orient between two dimensions which are so different in structure and context. To an earthling bound in 3-d reality the 4th dimensions presence appears paradoxical and enigmatic, the stuff of whimsy and supposition, but to the awakened, it has just another kind of substantiality to it. For instance, while the 4th dimension is the concentric point that encapsulates the whole of the physical plane, its true nature has no limits in itself. While being a

Whole, its boundaries are not as limited as the order that is promulgated into form in the physical world. Plus, while the Whole of the 4th dimension contains all times, it is in itself not limited to timely order as we know it in this world.

Let us say for wont of a better description, that its Whole is composed of an infinite number of probabilities, each separate yet united through frequency and synchrony. Furthermore, the 4th dimension acts as an energy source for the 3rd, which means that all the energy in the 3rd originated in the 4th. In fact, the template acts as a channel for the 4th dimensions infinite potential energy. Its energies are the force furnishes the power which pushes the wheel of creation about through the heavens of the macrocosm. The template directs the flow of energy into order in much the same way as a river bed acts as a conductor for water. All energy in the 4th dimension is in a free or chaos state, meaning it is raw and undirected. Without the template to act as a channel through which 4th dimensional energy can flow, the raw energy of the 4th dimension would lie untapped and useless. Knowing how to tap these raw energies, which have unlimited power to create, is the secret to making the 4th dimension an incredibly dynamic energy source in your life.

Therefore, the complete study of these two dimensions and how they operate is designed to extend your power to take charge of your life and change your personal reality. It will also help you channel more of its infinite energy to navigate life's changes and create the perfect life you always dreamed of making here in the 3rd. Without a deeper sense of connectedness between your relative self in this dimension and that 'greater' Whole, your efforts to make these creative changes in your lives would remain measurably weaker because they would be insufficiently based. Thus, in this chapter we will delve into the space-time mechanics that operate at a deep integrated level of transformation where our outer lives here in the 3rd dimension become unified with the 4th dimensional continuum.

Compared to frustrating, slow, everyday efforts to manipulate physical reality, space-time shifts in awareness will lead to perceptions and experiences in personal reality many parapsychologists might think of as paranormal. You'll learn how to shift dimensions and in so doing, consciously bend the continuum in your favor, so that events separated by the causal barrier will be available to you in a much shorter period of time. Eventually, when you learn to focus correctly you will begin to shift your reality back and forth effortlessly between the two dimensions. Some shifts will incur physically dramatic trips into other realities, defiant of the appearances of the principles of matter. Though some of the changes that will occur may be spectacular compared to what is normally taken as reality, in truth, these shifts do not defy the laws of physics, per se, but actually apply them consciously and in a focused way. However, seen from a hyper-dimensional level, they tap into principles that transcend, shall we say, what is normally considered possible. For example, because the 4th dimension is a continuum, all time (s) and spaces are contained within it, which means time travel is possible into every era in our history and many probable histories, in addition to parallel universes and their histories. You will be able to travel to these other worlds via alteration of frequencies both by the power of mind and physically. In those terms, yes, the 4th dimension is palpable and readily available for your exploration.

When you journey there you may have encounters with alternate modes of space and time, bizarre at times and counter to the known, and in all probability will expose deeper truths which have remained opaque to your senses. Expect your experiences and/or awareness to be enlightening because these journeys will expose the limitations in the way you've learned to accept and relate to your everyday world. In that regard, the experiences will be more than normal – they will be paranormal and represent shifts or alterations in the way you: a) experience reality, or b) perceive it to be and c) operate within it.

Primarily, these alterations may either come about slowly but in some cases quite dramatically. When they do you may be amazed with your discoveries and changes, but when you become proficient in recognizing and executing time/space shifts that awed you at first will, of course, appear to be relatively mundane. Don't expect to understand all your travels. Many shifts may be obscured, as it were, in dreamlike vagaries and what appears to be chance associations, but don't let that fool you – that is the way of the 4th dimension. Others may slip by totally without your awareness until upon looking in retrospect you will marvel at how incredible the experiences really were you took for granted. And finally, some will pass you by as if you didn't exist at all. When that happens you will get a vague sense like a ship passing in the night that something ominous is about, but as to what it is you will be left in wonder.

Hopefully, this section will raise your percentage of personal control to as near maximum as possible. Attentive students can become psycho-cosmonauts of intra-dimensional space-time. Personally, your experiences will include vivid encounters with subjective emotional content, such as feeling frightened, disoriented or confused, or like a person suddenly bowled over by a Tsunami wave of vibrations. Unquestionably, many time slips will involve deliberately, or quite spontaneously stepping from one particular framework, i.e. place and time, into an alternate probability. Initially, time shifts may take place in small increments, or at least slide by as commonplace events, or in fragments that will excite and amaze. On an everyday level you may go from feeling success is stacked against you to being baffled by how things just suddenly seem to fall into place. This is a time slip whether you realize it or not. You have simply walked into a different reality and a new you. Eventually, these shifts will begin to happen all the time, like riding a rubber raft through forks in a plunging stream, hanging on as the current changes. Sometimes it may be like driving a swift vehicle up or down a hill that sharply inclines, dips, or curves with abrupt twists and turns or even stops abruptly.

You will also incur sensory alterations that come with these shifts in awareness. Sometimes impressions will only involve limited sensory awareness such as visual or audio with a tactile sense of contact. Sights and sounds, for instance, may become flat or sharp in contrast similar to the need to adjust the color or contrast on your television set or turn the audio up or down. You may move from multi-hues with unearthly highlights or into grayscale. Sounds may become acutely pronounced, irritating, faint, piercing or you may only be aware of slight static-like changes in audio frequency or everything may suddenly dim and become totally inaudible. Some shifts may start with startling synchronicities that will shock you right out of your habitual frameworks of reference by blending mind and matter into a narrative with a revelation that is awesome. Other synchronicities may be subtle, unspectacular and so blended into everyday events that they go relatively unnoticed except by the most scrutinizing eye.

You may also experience shifts that involve the sense of déjà vu during semi-conscious reveries that occur when you're watching television and drift off to some psychic port you've been to, oh so many times, in some strange, exotic space-time rendezvous lying hidden in the outskirts of your memories. Dreams may become startlingly dramatic and poignant, obviously pointing you in a direction that you've overlooked, sensed or felt but never acted on before. For instance, you might find yourself not sleeping well, tossing and turning, recalling experiences from tattered pieces of dreams that seem connected somehow with everyday events. Such fragmented déjà vu slices are deliberately aimed by the 'higher' mind at waking you up to the Whole operating beyond the Part. These types of dreams may seem tempting you in some way, often connecting you, it seems, to trivial but impressive presentiments. Ironically, they are often connected to movies you will see the next day or people you coincidentally are going to meet on the street, decisions you think you are making on the spur of the moment. You may get telephone calls from someone you knew in a dream or find yourself thinking of them then make meaningful communication or contact moments or hours later. When events like this occur, pay close attention to the content and context of the associations. How you respond is interconnected to a grand plan outside your ken. Encounters with relatives or friends you haven't seen for a while that drive you to call them because of the eerie connection you feel toward them, despite the fact that you can't decide what prompts your decision to call.

Once these presentiments occur, stay in touch by compiling a record with data, time-place, etc. This interaction will pump up the energetic volume of the channeled flow between dimensions. If you wish to make deeper contact with the hidden whole operating outside the scope of your awareness, look for the connective factors that link 3rd and 4th dimensional events. Reinforcement is helpful. This means you must check out every minor detail that links what you might, superficially, think of as everyday data and dream encounters. Do research and deliberately seek to follow every angle in the curve toward unification of mind and matter that can integrate everything together. Most importantly: disregard your spouses or friends' negations or your own tendency to belittle your discoveries. *Trust your intuition* and above all - to one's own self be true/honest. In that way you develop a track record your psyche can rely on for details.

Mind is connected to matter through everyday events. Unique connections will abound and unusual associations arise. Often these apperceptions are deliberately dampened by unconscious memory failures calibrated to obscure the deeper, meaningful connection. It is a ploy by the 3rd dimensional self to keep you focused in the physical. When your sense of intuition says it was different despite what your conscious mind rationalizes as silly or ridiculous, deliberately pay attention to these events. FYI: **Anomalous perceptions often fly under the radar of consciousness simply because the process of observation is governed by mechanisms designed to see only a specific portion of what we term 'reality'.**. Such events are normally swept under the carpet of awareness where they are disregarded, discarded and soon forgotten. In that way the conscious mind keeps the reality game tidied up – made to fit in with the causality trip. The conscious mind will label such experiences to an over-active imagination, fantasies or silly mind slip. This is the job psychiatrists, psychologists, doctors and professors of Euclidian physics employ to keep the reality clones functioning and on course for the REALITY GAME. Take note, unusual apperceptions are all important.

Later on, as you become more proficient at side-stepping the REALITY GAME, you will begin to recognize when time is shifting. Moments like these occur sharply when falling off into a deeper level of sleep, which by the way, is just another state of awareness where the structure of what we term reality is not so fixed temporally, shall we say. Bear in mind that illusion is a sensory REALITY GAME that you can master, but you have to stay lucid on the playing field. Eventually, you may perform controlled shifts which can entail deliberate visions or the impression of physically walking into or traveling to other worlds. Don't be surprised if you find yourself communicating with someone thousands of miles away within what you might think as your 'mind's eye'. You will also have clear precognitions of the future, sudden journeys into the past or direct awareness of people surrounding you.

Overall, you will experience a decidedly stirring rearrangement of space-time into segments or fractions, experience gravitational anomalies such as a feeling of levitation or to the converse: gaining or having the sense of taking on excessive weight. Ladies, often, in these experiences, you are not actually increasing your physical girth or size, it's just a secondary illusion created by a shift in psychological framework. At times movement can become suddenly difficult even impossible. You might feel glued to your chair or rooted to the center of the earth. Rest assured you are in an altered state. Strange feelings could also be experienced in the limbs, similar to phantom limb phenomena. An old, stiff, cantankerous body may begin operating suddenly in youthful ways or a young one, awkward. You might undergo the impression of your limbs or body stretching to unusual lengths or shrinking its proportions. You may experience flexibility that is sudden and impressive.

Depending on how good you get in employing these mental states or abilities, you will nonetheless eventually learn to control them. At times some people get a feeling as though under stress or become phenomenally strong or weak, depending on your state of mind. Expect miraculous healings to transpire, or on the other hand, there are times when some people spontaneously display stigmata, like exuding blood in the middle of the hands as did Christ. If you're sense of touch is enhanced, you may find yourself drawn to suddenly extend healing hands for someone who is injured or in pain. Memory enhancement is common, intelligence can be affected or dramatically altered in terms of dilated or contracted. Changes in personality take place. Where a person who was unusually reticent and introverted, they may suddenly or even slowly become ambitious, outgoing and commanding. Totally new personalities may dramatically emerge, following abruptly by a movement from one area to another. Even amnesia and the development of secondary personalities are common.

Though strange or unusual in contrast to everyday life, these abilities or changes are not far-fetched or beyond your reach, neither do you need the aide of drugs, psychedelics or advanced meditation to experience them. In fact, they are just the results of alterations of consciousness when you reach certain states of mind. It is then that you will see definite changes reflecting frequency alterations that attract you to remain locally or to become a global traveler. REMEMBER THIS: Change the mind and you change yourself – maybe not altogether at first (some cases may be sudden) but as you go on and practice, the results become dramatically more spectacular.

Consider this perspective closely: you have psychic dreams all the time but you probably don't recognize them or know what is going on. You travel to distant worlds and fail to realize you've been there before, even when everything in your mind is reminding you that you have. Mind is like that – it can wake you up or deliberately put you back to sleep, depending on what you're telling it from a hyper-dimensional level. Keep this foremost in mind: the mind you put so much trust in to take care of you, your so-called conscious mind, is pretty much unconscious at work doing such a great job fooling you into believing that the dreams you've experienced are just part of your active imagination.

One thing for sure, in contrast to the everyday world about you – consciousness will give great support to the dictates of Maya as it struggles to keep the obvious from your attention. It will tell you teleportation is impossible and furnish you all the data to prove it. It will assure you that these things are too spectacular for humans to achieve. But the truth is, you teleport all the time and never realize it. For one thing, rest assured despite your detachment and your immersion in the delusion of reality, the spiral force is taking your body apart and putting it back together as you walk about. What a quick-change act! Yet you know it not nor think anything unusual has transpired. And what of levitation, you might ask? The fact is we never touch the ground but hover above it, the molecules floating as if on a sea of waves. And that gravitation we struggle to cope with, you might be surprised to know your own bodies put out their own fields, pushing us away from the earth. None of these abilities are any more unique than the everyday achievements produced by the Spiral Template that brought about all order and furthermore, maintained it despite the incredible odds it had to deal with. If you learn to tune fully into this force, in time you too can learn to master these abilities too.

Where and When the Shifts Occur

In this book I have sought to describe points where the everyday flow of events are linear, cause-effect bound. It will also describe what is known as bifurcations, tributary points between dimensions where alterations in the flow of events break through the linearity of the norm. Looking back, you'll recall that bifurcations erupt at crisis points and form forks. These event points represent growth spurts that occur when cycles or waves suddenly change frequency as space and time adjusts to a different configuration (CPS). Normally, when such changes occur, the transition in space and time is noticeable. These changes may be visible as either a mental shift in perspective or as a physical shift where you sense yourself entering an alternate reality dramatic enough to be noticeable.

As I have mentioned, each chapter is designed in some unique way to alter individual perspective, which essentially involves shifting the space-time continuum. For some people all the examples that show before this chapter may not be enough to ignite the awareness necessary to make awaken consciousness on how to shift the matrix with deliberate intent. That is why I am including these additional chapters explaining the process more in-depth. Think of the following pages as personal tutoring for those wishing to comprehend the psycho-physics of space-time alteration. This section will be divided into three parts: 1) Einstein's Special Theory of Relativity and Space-Time, 2) Psychological Aspects of Perspective and Space-Time, and 3) Studies from a 4th Dimensional Perspective. All three will be grounded in the underlying geometry of the spiral principle.

Primarily, I've endeavored to teach throughout this book that time and space is shaped by the spiral dynamo. The spiral is based on an information template existing, for the most part, outside the scope of 3-d sensory awareness. What we witness as its spiral form throughout nature is the effect of the presence of the underlying template. Its presence gives birth to the wavelike appearance of the spiral shape which can be seen above us in the galaxy-like clusters of matter. In fact, the template is the origin of the process by which order arises. The process of the spiral is, for the most part, a simple, inherent principle that when applied correctly not only can unravel the origin of order in terms of biogenic shape and function, it also provides enough data that you can learn to apply its principles to socio-economics, psychology, social psychology, the evolution of self-organization and society as an organic Whole. It can also be used as a homeport for practical time travelers moving throughout the continuum.

Essentially, I have also sought to demonstrate how the presence of the spiral force leads to our notions of order and symmetry throughout the natural universe. Ostensibly, knowing how that principal works is hoped to lead you to expanded awareness when coupled with the meditations at the end of the chapters. Used correctly, this knowledge will help an individual alter their consciousness and thereby shift the space-time matrix. In each chapter I have striven to give examples of how this principle, some may call God or all-that-is, operates according to a simple set of rules that govern the underlying process which produces all-natural order. The intent is to demonstrate that reality is physically alterable by mind or individual perspective. Mind is seen as the representing a higher or extra-dimensional space encapsulating physical space.

Think in terms of the Russian Matryoshka doll analogy where one space and/or doll is nested in another. To demonstrate the preponderance of this state a chapter has been provided that describes reality as a 'standing wave' comprises what is termed matter or organic natural order. This in turn is meant to help you understand that the structure of matter is the outcome of the frequency and/or periodicity or frequency of the wave pattern. Thus changing the frequency, as we've seen in chaos theory, and as relative motion in Einstein's Special Relativity Theory, changes the shape of the wave and therefore the appearance and hence structure of matter.

In a simultaneous manner we also learned that when space is altered so also is time. This is the whole point of Einstein's Special Theory of Relativity, i.e. to demonstrate that when a) all points of reference are valid reference planes for examining physics, and, b) that when we change the relationship between points of reference the appearance of object reality according to an individual point of observation changes our apprehension of the event in terms of time and place, in accordance to the speed of light. The reason it changes in accordance to the speed of light, in terms of relativity theory, is because it takes information a certain time to travel from point A to point B. that time difference determines our relative appreciation of what took place in terms of cause and effect. For instance, observers in the same frame of reference might see an event as happening at 9:00 Monday in Massachusetts, but the information transmitted about that event to a receiver on Mars would take approximately 11 minutes to arrive, thus the receivers on Mars would experience a time lag when that event took place. So relative to the position of the observers and their own speed or velocity, what they observe in relationship to observers standing still is altogether different.

These points of reference mark alterations in the space-time matrix where space and time appear to be reshuffled. Although the clocks in all frames of reference keep the same time the points of relative observation of the events by viewers at rest or in motion are different. In terms of relativity all frames of reference are valid hence a person could as easily be born 11 minutes later as well as 11 minutes earlier regardless of time-place settings of each independent viewer, because all frames of reference are valid. So what we learn is that according to the perspective of the observer, the arrangement of the flow of time is different depending on the a) the speed of information traveling at C (light speed), and the b) relative position of the observer, and c) relative motion of the observer. Thus, time could be seen as flowing from past to future in the same frames of reference or it can appear to flow from future to past when viewed in terms of light speed or relative velocity.

This means information, in terms of relativity, is limited to the speed of light. Thus, information traveling within the physical plane can only be measured according to speed C and movement in space dependent upon the position of observers in motion or rest. There are other ways of observing these same space and time alterations without depending on information traveling at the finite speed of C, or through verification by observers in different frames of reference. The limiting factor here in terms of the event, or what physicist describe as 'causality' is the time and place of the event – meaning if it refers to your birth, you were no doubt born, as to when it happened it depends upon the frame of reference of the observers according to whether they were at rest or in motion.

The question that remains to be answered is: which frame of reference is valid and the physicists tell us that 'all' frames are valid. If that is so, then no one frame could be more valid. Most people would agree that this fact nullifies the assumption of causality because the speed of light is finite, that is, information takes a specified period of time to travel from point a) to point b). Thus if you were born on Andromeda forty five years ago, light traveling through space would take 45 light years to arrive on Earth, because no information can travel faster than light. But how about altered states of consciousness or the presence of a higher dimension impinging on physical space?

Time-Space and Frequency Patterns

Studies of the brain waves and sleep states of individual subjects have provided much insight into the nature of time and space in terms of both brain wave frequencies and a subject's personal experiences. With relativity theory we discovered that all frames of references are valid places to do physics, in much the same way individual perception can demonstrate the same notion of space and time to be valid for all observers during altered states. For example, keeping relativity in mind, it could be said that all perspectives are valid, that is, each subjective perception represents some individual point of order though it may be radically different than our own. Yet, it contains something of our own perspective in it, whether we see it or not.

For example, often we think of a state of consciousness that varies from what is considered an agreed-upon perspective of reality as an altered or trance state, suggesting that these alternate angles of observation are invalid or distorted points of view. But in terms of Einstein's relativity theory, we must reevaluate that old notion when we discover that each individual perspective or frame of reference is valid, depending on whether the individual is in a similar state of consciousness. Bear in mind that frames of references depend on whether an individual is in motion or at rest. If the individual is in motion relative to an observer at rest, then distortions of observation occur such as time dilation. This is the appearance of time being stretched out so that many things can occur within that span.

Time dilation takes place when two observers are in relative motion or rest – that is, one observer is at rest and the other one is in motion. This means all states of consciousness are alternate trance states (perceptual frames of reference) regardless of the point of view of the observer – except in terms of acceleration. Frequency and motion or velocity and acceleration equate to one and the same thing. The only exception is that velocity is usually a term used to refer to uniform motion, whereas acceleration means to speed up. The point I wish to make in this regard, is that motion, whether it includes speeding up, slowing down, changing speeds suddenly or the frequency of a wave; or simply maintaining a steady speed -- all are examples of relative movement. The point being, when an observer views an object traveling past them at an alternate speed, then the relative time experienced by the observer will vary in relationship to the time experienced by the other object in motion. The factor that causes this time distortion between the two is the observer's relative motion or frame of reference.

Black holes and time dilation can give us a workable example for explaining this aspect of the bending of time and space so that alternate events normally 'outside' the flow of relative time can be observed. A light cone, for example, approaching the vicinity of a massive black hole, or body, for that matter, is bent by its gravitational presence and the field around it is reshaped. Thus, light carrying information from future or past flows according to the preponderance of the curvature of the black hole's field. Think in terms of a river which acts as a channel to carry water toward a lake destined to be in its future. In a like manner, imagine streams of light being pulled, like objects floating on the surface of this river being dragged along by this hidden current. As the shape of this *field* or *bed* of the river changes its course, the current follows suit, like a cork bobbing along on a river. It appears to be pulled along by the rivers current when in fact, it is flowing along the curvature of the field following information provided by its hidden form.

As I've mentioned, light is information, it tells us what kind of events are taking place and why. Remember: we must have a *time and a place* for an event to take place. This means that information contains vertexes or lines which are directions to and from a central loci or point demarcating the juncture of an approaching event. Because it is an event, it has an order. All order, or information cascading into the 3rd dimensional plane becomes filtered by the senses into a cause-effect classification, and in that manner, it adapts a relative time and a place. Thus, time and place already are implicit in the sensate equation.

To review our black hole analogy: light traveling into the proximity of its field (event plane or horizon) is pulled, like our cork upon the waters current, according to the underlying structure of space. Therefore, the farther away from the field, the less the curvature while the closer we approach it the greater is the angle of incidence where our involvement by its effects become more evident. As the light cone approaches very near the horizon of the field the more it bends space into a 90° angle. If you apply this reasoning to division of time into increments, you began to realize that changes in the shape of the field are likewise changing the shape of time, so that it flows into new patterns or arrangements. One might say that the worldline or arrow of time, as it is known, has been bent so that the flow has been rerouted or turned around, even skewed. Some Russian scientists would agree that at this ninety-degree angle time and therefore space would be experienced as frozen momentarily at this point.

To observers falling toward the black hole, movement would appear normal, but other people watching from outside would appear to move slower and slower. Thus, observers traveling in a spacecraft in orbit around the black hole might experience time dilation. In fact, it is this bending or curvature of space-time in extreme gravitational fields that are responsible for the continuum, a point where all times converge to form the NOW. For instance, a mere hour might never seem to past while a year or a century passes quickly when measured by an observer from the outside. Travel outside the orbit in the vicinity of the black hole and returning would be experienced as the future. This is exactly what has happened to people who have traveled into areas where the curvature of space-time has been bent, or the frequency of their awareness has been altered. The factor that influences these changes in the flow of time or in perception can, therefore, be explained as warps, that is, geometrical changes in the curvatures that shape the flow of information within the field

Accelerate or reduce the frequency of the brain wave of the observer relative to the observer and that individual's subjective perceptual experience will change. Thus, the observation of the event not only is subjectively experienced different, it is encountered in a totally different space-time arrangement. What has happened is that the matrix uniting the observer and the observed has been shifted because of a) a change in relative velocity, or b) a shift in brain wave frequency. For instance, we think of ourselves as experiencing when awake a physically-oriented beta wave state, the state of consciousness s said to be predominant when we are awake. However, in truth, the beta wave state is just another trance relative to a person experiencing say, for instance, alpha. That is why awakening from the beta state is referred to as 'enlightenment' by practitioners of eastern religions and students of altered states of perception. Enlightenment then essentially means to awaken from a fixed angle of perspective, or a particular way of viewing what is collectively called reality. Once we are awakened, if we are fortunate enough to be shaken from that fixation, the world appears totally different because the frequency, our new trance state or point of reference, is different. This can be experienced especially in the way we interrelate to each other and the world. Individual awakening is the aim and intent of the spiral dynamo. Once awakened the student will never experience what was formerly termed reality in the same way again. Hence, the world appears different because the individual state of awareness has changed frequencies or relative motion. Ergo, their perspective is different because the angle of their individual perspective has been changed because of a frequency alteration in the brain wave pattern.

Another name for a change in the state of awareness, seen from a different frame of reference, is 'altered,' which, when viewed by psychologists who are locked into the beta framework of perspective, is mislabeled a 'distortion'. Such distortions can and do include totally different perceptual experiences of both space and time. Not only does one perceive space differently, but they also perceive their movement in time from a totally different perspective. Events that might have seemed to whiz by in beta under the influence of alpha may appear inflated, slowed down and involve a sense of déjà vu, which is the feeling that you've been here before. Remember the person born on Andromeda relative to the time it takes for information traveling in light waves to reach earth? Forty-five years have passed in their life because it takes 45 light years for the information to travel to earth.

In actuality, there isn't any such a thing as a distortion in consciousness unless there are some pathological lesions of lobes in the brain, just different frequencies of perceiving the order of time relative to its perception by someone traveling in a different frame of reference. In a two-dimensional universe, the general flow of time is said to be from past into future based on Newton's application of Euclidian geometry, which we have discovered is flat plane, or possessing two dimensions. However, on the other hand, we have also discovered that observation of the same object-reality when viewed from Einstein's relativistic geometry which is spherically measured versus the Euclidian two-dimensional flat plane, automatically produces a totally different perspective as to the experience of time. Keeping the conclusions of these two different frames of reference in mind as we proceed, you will quickly be able to comprehend how such changes in geometrical reference frameworks determine our ability to perceive the temporal of what is 'real' in terms of space and time.

Again, bear in mind, according to the special theory of relativity, all frames of reference are equally valid points of reference to do physics, depending on our relative acceleration and/or frequency. Thus, as I see it, altered states of consciousness and frames of reference are just two different ways of saying or viewing the same thing. Changes in perspective or frames of reference and alterations some psychologists term 'distortions' produced by brain wave frequencies, reduces to a form of subjective acceleration. Relative frameworks of observation and altered states i.e., changes in frequencies, can also be viewed as different ways of appraising what it is we think we experience in terms of time or space. For example, as the mind speeds up time is perceived as slowing down and as the brain slows down time accelerates. Thus, relative frames of reference appear to expand or contract the shape of space in which we experience physical reality. It appears this way because the motion of the wave disturbs the angle or ripple 'shape' of the wave. This change in shape can be seen as an acute alteration in the Bell Curve. When the curve is changed, as at the edge of the black hole event horizon, light carrying information within these frameworks assume a different order and appearance in terms of how space and time are aligned. In short, changes in the wave produce changes in the structure of space which in turn rearranges the perception of the flow of time.

Prior to these changes certain subjective perceptual signals are sensed. Maybe a person might become nervous, apprehensive, irritable, even experience headaches or nausea. This can also happen directly afterwards depending on the abruptness of the bifurcation and its nature. At, sometimes slightly before and directly thereafter the subjective experience of a bifurcation there are also specific physical signals such as encounters with people, places, events or phenomena of different kinds, especially in the texture of the experience – how it feels or appears to you that signal you are in an alternate reality other than the one you experienced moments before.

Thus, the scenes that are viewed and/or experienced appear different. If the brain waves are oscillating at a high frequency, you have a lot more time to experience in-depth everyday objects and situations as they travel through the scope of your subjective perception of temporal space-time. You might have the feeling that things are a little 'weird,' even 'bizarre,' unusually slowed down or speeded up, flat, strange, misty, dark, unusually bright. You might even have the feeling of irritability and edginess or feel slightly paranoid. That is why people who are entering altered states via chemicals or pharmaceuticals, pot, hallucinogens in general undergo a feeling of panic, as if they are out-of-control at first, but later have the feeling that they've got it together. What they are experiencing is being locked in to a framework that sedates the transition experienced in everyday reality. Thus things which went by us during alpha were perceived not only to flow in relationship to that wave, but our perception of the world about us included only the sensorial range associated with that framework.

During the frequency accelerations in consciousness we associate with alpha the feeling of having more time to examine and interpret temporal or everyday reality is experienced, hence perception is often keenly enhanced. Yet there might be a sense of unreality or detachment from direct involvement with the experience, and 'unreality' which signifies both the altered state and the frame of reference, like an 'outside' observer. Again, this takes place because objects and our appreciation of them are experienced in a different time-space framework. For instance, strange sensations and apperception will include unusual colors, odd patterns. A person's subjective sensitivities to the experiences and phenomena, contrary to a feeling of detachment, can on the other hand, include acute and detailed perceptions. Feelings can be enhanced, magnified to the point where they take on a life of their own, like a cinema with scenarios acted out on the stage of perception, or they can remain detached as has been mentioned. If on the other hand, brain waves are decelerated inner perceptions may include anomalous or even bizarre encounters with people, aliens, sights and sounds, the structure and shape of order may seem to blend or take on unusual patterns. Dali has a sense of these deep, internal states when he produced many of his surreal paintings which were thought to depict temporal reality under the influenced of an altered state of perception.

To give you an idea of these type of perceptual and physical 'distortions' experienced by people who have undergone actual changes in time due to frequencies changes, the Philadelphia Experiment, conducted by the Navy in the Brooklyn Navy Yard to test an invisibility radar shield in 1943. As a refresher on that event in the reshaping of physical time and space let us momentarily review it. Originally the PE was conducted by scientists Dr. John Hutchinson Sr., Dean of the University of Chicago, Nikola Tesla, Albert Einstein and led by Dr. John Erich Von Neumann, an Austrian physicist on staff at the university. A Thomas T. Brown joined the project because of his expertise in electro-gravity effects. Suffice it to say, following intensive study beginning in 1936, the group of scientists decided to test the results of their research. Under laboratory conditions they achieved partial invisibility. Encouraged by these results, the Navy elected to continue the work and allocated unlimited funds for additional research.

The drive power for producing the invisibility shield was supplied by two Tesla coils. A test was conducted in 1940 proved fruitful. However, there were no people aboard the ship so there weren't any tests to describe the effect powerful electromagnetic fields have on humans. This was important because of what happened later on. Differences between Von Neumann and Tesla led to Tesla's resignation due because of his concern about the potential negative effects of electro-gravity on personnel aboard the new test ship, *The Eldridge*, which was chosen for the experiment.

Nonetheless the project, supported by unlimited funds by the Navy Department, decided to go ahead with the project. Using four massive generator banks and modified Tesla coils to convert direct-current electricity to alternating current, they amplified high gauss frequencies. The stepping up (amplifying) of wave frequencies is particularly significant because, as I have said, amplifying, as well as slowing down EM frequencies, can produce alterations in subjective perception causing a shift in the structure of space-time. Remember that alterations, such as amplifications or decelerations in wave patterns, produce a change in the shape of field. Changing the shape of the spiral field is at the heart of shifting the space-time continuum.

On July 22, 1943, they conducted their first test. The test was a complete success. This time the whole ship became totally invisible, and now we see the alterations in subjective state of those who experienced changes in frequencies. Researchers in charge of the experiment noted major perceptual changes in the crew. Some individuals became very disoriented while others suffered from unknown illnesses. Medical personnel could give no thorough account as to the nature or origin of the ailments or the distortions in perception. Disregarding these negative personal experiences, the Navy still wanted to go ahead with final tests, pursuant of total radar invisibility and not just optical invisibility. One word on optical invisibility – if you recall our commiserated brain subjects in the sub-chapter on blind spots in perceptions – essentially optical invisibility has a lot in common with both the subjective as well as the so-called objective nature of the field.

As subjective perception shifts from one frequency to another, the appearance of objective reality undergoes a change in its apparent order. Frequency shifts can not only make objective reality appear different because it can also literally change its space-time structure. Shifts can cause object-reality to become invisible or they can make what was invisible suddenly visible. Thus, scenes from other dimensions, times or universes may suddenly either *appear* to merge with ours, or they can manifest providing a channel by which we can walk into them. Sometimes this happens automatically, apparently by chance. When this happens people suddenly encounter strange objects, artifacts, visions, worlds, ancient or future periods of time.

Psychologists are quite familiar with what they think of as illusions, delusions or disturbances in perception. This takes place when neurological changes in brain wave frequency alter awareness and the individual experiences what is termed *perceptual blindness*. Subsequently, objects that are right in front of them may suddenly disappear, fade or reappear in a new shape, context, color, and to the right or left of where they stand. At such times one experiences not only physical alterations in the shape and context of space and time, but also perceptual changes where, so far as personal reality is concerned, events do not happen even though others may see them clear as day. For the perceptually blind, it is as if these events have not taken place. Think in terms of hypnosis. So far as the hypnotized subject is concerned, appearances are filled in, so to speak, with the subjective suggestions implanted within their minds by the hypnotist. A bucket of ice on naked feet may be made to feel like a soothingly, warm blanket, or a hot pepper becomes free of searing pain when the subject is told that it is a candy bar. Put simply: perception under the influence of frequency alterations fills in the information dots or patterns where it encounters empty space or asymmetry with what it assumes to be there.

On another note, relative motion may change. When the brain speeds up or accelerates, objective time appears to slow down, and when brain waves slow down, objective time may speed up. Many times not only does the individual subjectively experience an alteration of perceived reality, for example, where the passage of events seem to slow down or speed up, the mind may be influenced by the outward state so that the subject in turn experiences an actual change in their behavior, such as acceleration or deceleration. One time during a 100 meter race I suddenly felt out of it and noticed that regardless of how hard I tried to run, my body seemed to be going in slow motion, while the other runners raced by me effortlessly.

A Space-Time Shift Wins the Race!

Recently, in an article on slips in time, I found a fascinating account garnered from the 1983 Fate Magazine of an outstanding teen runner by the name of V. Fred Rayser who during an 800-sprint experienced what by all accounts was an alternate time framework. One of the main reasons it is recorded here, is to make note of a few details that are crucial in understanding the subjective psychological impressions prior to going into a 'time slip' or alternate framework.

According to Rayser, on the day of the race in Spring Valley, New York, the weather was good, bright and sunny but not overly hot. The race was a handicap, meaning slower runners were given a head start so that as the race progresses the finish should bring about a dead heat. As it turned out Rayser got his handicap and when they lined up, he ended up the last man in the trail of runners and from the start of the race, most of them quickly raced ahead out of sight. By his account all 15 runners were pretty much on the opposite side of the track. From his perspective the probability of winning the race looked bleak and if it wasn't for his cheering section in the bleachers, he said he'd probably would have given up right away and walked off the field.

But Rayser had a plan. His strategy was to move past as many of the runners as he could on the straight-aways and catch as many as he could on the final stretch. However, things didn't look too good when nearing the 100-yard point near to the end of the race. There were still seven runners ahead of him so he realized he'd have to run wide around the "U" turn for half the distance to pass. At this point in the description of the race details it is necessary to illustrate a few fine facts related to the Special Theory of Relativity and its relationship to the spiral pattern.

Bear in mind that the "U" point on the track is very auspicious in terms of a fork or bifurcation in the space-time field because of its curvature. Tracks aren't perfectly symmetrical they're closer to elliptical, narrow at either ends and long in the centers. At these points the structure of the gravitational field is on the side of the runners who run closest to the hub which is the inside track, not only because it is the closest distance between two points, but because of its acute curvature.

"Then it happened," said Rayser. "*As I started around the curve, the light appeared to change from bright sunshine to a muted glow. It was as if I had suddenly entered into a translucent tunnel. I was conscious only of the runners ahead of me. Their legs were churning and their arms flailing but they seemed to be moving in slow motion.*" What we observe here is a change the 'frame of reference.' This is highly significant because it signifies an alteration in the frequencies of both Rayser and the other runners in the space-time field. Prior to this perception there was the feeling of entering a glowing tunnel, something curiously similar to what many people see during near-death encounters and other so-called altered states prior to unusual changes in perception.

Another fascinating space-time effect described in the words of Rayser was, "*Not only that, but they were **scattered all over the field** instead of being grouped at the pole as is normal. Never before, or since, have I seen runners so dispersed.*" Let us stop for a moment and take note of this interesting observation. "…they were scattered all over the field instead of being grouped at the pole as normal," from Rayser. Here is another peculiar detail that when first encountered might easily be overlooked as insignificant; but on the contrary, it is extremely important, especially when coupled with the fact that, as he put it: "*…I began to weave my way through them and…I passed them on the inside instead of having to run around them.*" That the runner appeared to be scattered about and that he was able to easily move through them is exactly what would be expected if there was an alteration in space-time. In addition, the slowing down of relative time contracted Rayser personal space, shrinking him so to speak, thus allowing him to move through his slow-moving opponents as if there was a great deal of space between them.

The phenomenon of a framework alteration is familiar to studies in relativity of what is termed "bullet-time." Bullet time is the framework difference experienced by a person when either a) they're brain wave frequencies have been significantly increased, or b) when the framework between a speeding bullet is noted with an outside observer. Two perspectives are encountered, a) the speed of the bullet in terms of its time as compared to, b) the time experienced by the outside observer. In terms of The Special Theory of Relativity this variation is referred to as 'time dilation.'

Time dilation, in the theory of relativity, is the actual difference of elapsed time between two events as measured by observers either moving relative to each other or differently situated from gravitational masses. The elapsed time between the two observers is the unaccounted period or 'in-between space' between specific points. For instance, the elsewhere space can represent the period between one observer who sends a message and the relative time it is received by the observer moving at his own relative speed. In wave signaling this period or time differential between the two points is known as the "*elsewhere.*" For example: when a message is sent between Earth and Mars at the speed of light, the time difference between sending it and its reception would be eleven minutes because it takes light eleven light minutes to reach Mars. In this case the time distortion could be described as the psychological 'elsewhere' space between Rayson and his perception of the other runners since they are moving at relative speeds to his perception. This difference in relative motion may account for their apparent slowness in relationship to the velocity of Rayson.

Relativity mathematicians tell us that both frames of reference are valid in which to do physics *until* encountering a frame of reference where there is a difference in motion between the two. It is this variation in the speed of opposing reference frames that lend themselves to the observation of time distortions. In the case of a speeding bullet, it travels so swiftly that when viewed from a clock reference framework, basic time would appear to be going by slowly or even to stand still. Of course, time is actually passing at it normal rate, so to speak, but to an observer from the accelerated point of view, the passage of real time would appear to be slowed down. It is at this critical juncture point formed by an acute curvature of the field between the two frames of reference where the order of time and space is altered. At that point or bifurcation, standard space and time would appear to branch off into an alternate energy flow. This juncture is like the forking of a river where a placid, slow-moving current forks off into fast swiftly plunging white water. Should the white-water loop around and pass the slow-moving original flow it would appear to a person in canoe as barely moving.

Reduced to essentials, when this analogy is applied to bullet time, the relative gap between the velocity of the moving projectile and another reference framework would give the appearance of a lapse or break in the relative passage of time from the standpoint of the observer. Hence, events taking place within that space, for all accounts, would appear to decelerate or stop. Thus, the dilation of time and space between the two events provides a window in time for viewing reality from an 'outside' framework.

When Rayser reached the final lap, the point where the final 100 meters starts, he felt there was no hope. I am familiar with the layout of fields because of my own personal experiences in running track loops and in reaching the final 100-meter point. That point closest to inside track is acute in the outcome of the race. For runners in the 880 it is representing a critical point to propel them the final increments of the race when stress is at a crucial limit. Needless to say, head runners at these points usually win the race because they have gravity on their side, contrary to the runner on the outside who are moving counter to the flow of the current. To kick at this point and win after having been in the rear of the pack the whole way would have been a phenomenal achievement, something nearly impossible even for a thoroughbred in the Preakness.

On a positive note being the acutest angle providing maximum stress, it has it parallels in natural processes such as phyllotaxis points where the plant aids in the creation of a new branch or leaf at critical limits by putting out a dose of growth-catalyzing auxin, an enzyme aiding in the perpetuation of growth and survival. Physicists and rocket propulsion designers, as I've mentioned earlier in this volume, recognize the benefits of these junctures. These are points where the curvature in the gravitational fields provides the impetus in a slingshot effect to boost a rocket, with a small amount of jettisoned fuel for launching it into outer space, onward to its destination on the moon or nearby plants. That same point in the curve represents a point of stress, of acute curvature and the bifurcation the result of a catalyst into a parallel world.

Suffice it to say, Rayser passed the other runners feeling as he did so that he was coming out of a tunnel off the curve into bright sunshine. He hit the tape running full speed, continuing to lap the track afterwards. In fact, he seemed to have more energy than ever had, which is quite understandable since he was actually tapping 4th dimensional energies where the current is greatest and the power unlimited. This is exactly what happened to Tesla when he rolled the snowball down the most acute grade and it terminated in an incredible show of force and power. Tesla, like Rayser, had connected with the continuum, uniting intent with target thereby tapping the maximum curvature of the field. This equates to channeling more of the infinite potential of the 4th dimension into the 3rd.

The Nature of Space-time Slips or Shifts

What we see in both the time slip example of The Philadelphia Experiment aboard the *Eldridge*, and the case of the young runner named Rayser, are evidence that at certain junctures we fork into alternate realities. The processes governing these shifts in space-time, therefore, are wave frequency alternations. In the case of the Philadelphia time shift, sudden amplification of high gauss frequency waves disturbed the molecular structure of matter causing it to become rearranged and in this case *'spaced out'* or separating into fragments. More specifically, the space between the atoms was widened so that the structure of its appearance so far as outside observers disappeared. Forced apart by high gauss frequencies, the physically structure of the ship vanished. This means our sensory were not privy to its presence, yet to another life form, such as a dog whose senses were not so limited, it might seem quite present. I mention this because in many UFO sightings, which I feel are extra-dimensional visitations in nature, only dogs were aware of them. This also was reported of visitors from another dimension who happened to pop into our space-time coordinates. In one case a woman walked through a window that vibrated open between times and encountered a couple intimately disposed in a park setting. Not wanting to interrupt their special moment together, she hovered in the background for a moment wanting desperately to ask them what year and place this was. As she was about to step forward, a small dog ran up towards her and began barking fiercely. The man stopped momentarily embracing his girlfriend and shouted, "Now, you stop that boy, you know there's no one there." Startled, the woman who had walked through the window in time realized that the people were unaware of her presence, yet the small dog was looking right at her. There are many cases such as these. I mentioned them to make note of the fact, stepping through doorways in time doesn't always make you visible to those around you, though it may obviously make them quite visible to you.

In terms of the *Eldridge's* physical reality, that space no longer was visually occupied by its huge bulk, which in itself might seem phenomenal. Yet, in reality we discover that the ship was merely outside our sensory/frequency range, hovering in an extra-dimensional space. What was changed is the relative frequency of the reference frame between 'outside' observers and the *Eldridge*. This reduces to altering the curvature of the field, just as a sharp 45° curve on a street inhibits the viewpoint of an observer coming down the road. Once the electromagnetic oscillations or frequency of the ship was reduced or turned off, it slowly returned into view, thus in terms of the observer, the curvature of the field returned to normal. This indicates that one can either step through these naturally occurring doorways or return via the same route that you came. In fact, these doorways often act like wormholes allowing one to move freely between times and spaces with comparative ease, once you get the knack of shifting.

Perhaps the size and structure of the ship required especially high gauss electromagnetic frequency waves to move its bulk back and forth through time; at least that is the indication of this example. However, people have driven vehicles down roads in current space-time that opened up into other times without the same kind of effects.

Clearly, the high gauss EM frequencies are not necessary, but examples of an overdose and what it can do to those who dabble with these fields without knowledge of their consequences. We can only judge these indiscretions by the results which were apparently recorded in this instance, which appear to have had a strong effect on individuals caught in its field. Tesla understood this, and that is why he opted not to go through with the experiments to produce invisibility. Clearly, experiments with various biogenic subjects should have been conducted before proceeding. The effects described to personnel aboard the ship such as personality changes, or reports that some were actually impaled in the walls or deck, indicate that they and the ships frequency synchronized. This is a naturally occurring phenomenon. For instance, two randomly swinging clock pendulums set close together will eventually synchronize or swing harmoniously together. In a similar way the molecular structures of the afflicted personnel became synchronized to the frequency of the EM field and the ship. Thus, when the frequency was turned back down they became embedded in the structure.

This means both the ship and the personnel were vibrating at the same oscillations. Thus, if this experiment is a true account, these individuals could have become permanently stuck. The problem with high gauss frequencies it forces time and space apart, like tearing an object into pieces rather than smooth transition from one dimension to another. The spiral template accomplishes the task of reordering space and time by applying a principle that is in line with natural processing. The body, for instance, is constantly adjusting to change while maintaining a continuity that is impossible to notice, yet this goes on all the time as millions of cells die and is replaced daily. Think of this process as a vacillation between dimensions something life the synchrony of millions of firefly lights winking on and off in the darkness of the night.

In a like manner, people who experiences time slips encounter a frequency in the field which synchronizes a so-called distant future or past point in time. This doesn't mean you're automatically going to become lost in the space between these cycles of another world. Our bodies change frequency and time zones all the time and they aren't locked in any one state. In fact, the logarithmic spiral is an ongoing living process. It constantly moves ever onward, never static or fixed, continuously dipping into the infinite power of the 4th dimension and recharging the 3rd. At the same time it conserves order by constantly rebuilding it, just as our systems do when you go to sleep at night. During rest we recharge our batteries, replenishing cells with energy garnered from distant times and spaces. In fact, there is a constant ebb and flow between parallel worlds; a constant recycling that involves the tearing down of one level and rebuilding on another. When people walk into these distant times or worlds, they are experiencing in the macrocosm, an automatic process that takes place everyday on a micro level. For that moment then, people who have walked into other times are simply beginning to vibrate at the frequency of the time window.

As mentioned earlier in this text, when our frequency resonates with the window or time portal, it opens the channel between worlds so that a person is free to come and go. When the body refreshes its energies, for instance, during sleep, napping, dreaming they are, in effect, slipping between times. Understanding and putting to use the psycho-geometry of the spiral template naturally opens and closes these doors, thus reducing energy loss and accomplishing tasks with greater ease. Time slips rather than negative experiences, for the most part, can be beneficial, energy conserving and stress relieving simply because they provide alternate avenues of self-development quite outside the linear line of time. The spiral geometry achieves this energy conservation and transformation process by eliminating linear time and contracting its space.

Changes in brain wave frequencies are another thing to take into consideration, because not only do physical frequencies affect us, brain waves undergo alterations too. In unusual circumstances, extreme alterations in brain wave frequencies give rise to psychotic episodes or maladies when individual brain wave remain synchronized to alternate time zones. The reality of this condition is not as far-fetched as it may seem. Using another example: when a person refuses to change as they adjust to the responsibilities of adulthood, they have, in fact, become locked into another time-space. Such people become trance-fixed, so to speak. They are emotionally clinging with uncertainty at transformation forks and refuse to bifurcate or move on. In psychological jargon, they become fixated, regressed. Fixation is a time disorder caused by fear of transitioning beyond a certain emotional juncture where a person needs to undergo some form of growth. In a word, the energy which comprises the gestalt of their personalities stagnates and thus appears out of context with their chronological age.

Looked at in terms of what the spiral force teaches us, personality is a byproduct of frequency states synchronized with the dictates of certain space-time forks. Sometimes, to facilitate adaptation to changes in frequency points RNA catalysts are released which prompt the generation of a new growth spurt. In the case of a) organic damage to the central hemispheres or to specific lobes, b) individuals suffering from dysfunction resulting from injury, c) malfunction, d) chemical poisoning by drugs, e) lesions brought on by malignancies – these individuals may find themselves caught, so to speak, between alternate dimensions. So for those who can't or won't change when prompted at these forks, they are figuratively locked in time. *Time lag adjustment difficulties*, therefore, and *being locked in time* have much in common because the two represent fixations at certain resonance frequencies. Keep this in mind: all frequencies can be changed, just as access to any 'intervals' or increments of time are accessible at any point in the continuum.

To break free from these frequency fixations, think on this: have you ever found yourself faced with a need to adjust to a situation that you found somewhat unappealing? At first you put up strong resistance, but as time (which is fixated frequency) went on, little by little you found yourself giving in, despite your will power? What has happened is that your brain waves gradually synchronized to the medium. Thereafter, from the appearance of an obvious 'outsider' or newbie, you gradually blended in and became one of the gang. In essence, you have picked up on and adjusted to the time-space resonance of the continuum of intervals that comprise the order. Like a movie (which remember, is composed of a series of separately filmed segments) you had become fixated, or locked into the flow of images associated with a certain segment of the drama in which you play either an indirect or a direct role at some point. When that happens, step back and improvise a new scenario, AND DON'T WORRY – EVENTUALLY YOU WILL SYNCHRONIZE TO A NEW REALITY!

MEDITATIONS

1. To begin these meditations, it is important to purchase a special journal just for taking notes on shifting the continuum.
2. Make notes of any audio, visual, even tonal changes you sense, see or hear.
3. Decide what frame of mind you were in during the moment and write that down too.
4. Along with the sensory notes be sure to detail your emotional state and your focus or expectations. The reason

that this is important is because these things will provide clues into the event.

5. Again- be sure to listen especially for tonal changes. Tonal changes reveal frequency states, especially when you are near a window between dimensions. Tonal changes are those tones that you hear or sense which give you the impression of a shift or change in the pressure in your ear or around you.

6. When and if you feel a tonal change, breathe deeply, open your mind's eye and strive to sense where you're at and what is going on. You could be entering into either an altered state, or you could be approaching or be actually in a time window.

7. Deliberately look for a record any synchronicities you encounter around the clock, because they specifically reveal that you are tapping the continuum, or 4th dimensional field. That's where mind and body connect as a Whole and space contracts and time dilates.

8. One of the most important things within your mental state to look for, especially when you are relaxed, watching television or reading a book, drifting off to sleep is subtle to dramatic changes in information content. These impressions can be a feeling of familiarity about some foreign turf, a bizarre image, a sense of soaring, out-of-body impression, or any number of odd déjà vu like impressions. When they occur, your mind has clicked into some alternate dimension and the arrangement of the cluster has suddenly taken on new significance.

9. Stay alert while driving, running or walking to any shifts in consciousness, such as feelings of disorientation, spaciness, sudden manifestations of unusual events, behavior in animals, people, etc. All of these items reveal alterations in consciousness or in the field.

10. Listen for high-pitched hums when you are near power lines and watch out for unusual phenomena taking place. Frequency changes are quite noticeable near high voltage electro-magnetic fields and you could witness (see) objects moving in or out of our dimension.

11. If you find you have any unusual fixations, fantasies or dreams, write them down and study them because they may be things that are limiting your energy flow and/or your ability to move well between dimensions.

9

CONNECTING ISLANDS OF TIME

"Birds of a feather flock together." Old Saying.

Resonance and Intra-Dimensional Travel

When physicists talk about *synchrony,* they are referring to the capacity of two systems to oscillate together in unison. Synchrony occurs when two systems begin to behave the same, i.e. to blend frequencies. This means each of these space-time systems behave as if they are ONE. Quantum physicists describe such states as coherent, or resonating as one, or decoherent, or separate. When two time-space systems oscillate in synchrony it suggests that they have become unified in a higher dimensional field, such as the 4th dimensional continuum. Should you begin to oscillate, for instance, in synchrony with another person you have begun to take on their traits and share some of your own traits with them so that you and the other person begin to meld. In other words, two individuals have become ONE with each other in what was apparently an outside space. This is not necessarily a 4th dimensional example; however it does give you an idea of the oneness possible when many parts of a system are in synchrony.

Though organisms on earth began as independent life forms they in time began to blend and take on each other traits and qualities until they formed a holistic, e.g., multicellular organism. Organisms sharing a common space have reached a state of symbiosis, a cooperative oneness whereby each life form overcame their individual quest for space and working with other resolved potential danger by learning to share space with another. Indeed, instead of quarreling over limited space they circumvented the problem of competing for it by sharing it thereby exponentially increasing their mutual longevity. It could accurately be said that they acquired space by sharing energy and in the exchange became more than what they were. In addition, they reduced the problem of burning up more energy through fragmentation and alienation. From a position of repulsion, they entered into an attraction, or increased their cohesiveness as a Whole. In an indirect manner this attraction to absorption and synchrony appears closely to mimic Malcolm Gladwell's *stickiness factor* simply because from islands of existence with independent space and time, they began to cohere together – to stick together. Again – they have moved from linear to curved space or from 3rd to 4th dimensional awareness.

Even to this day there is a constant give and take between individual and group behavior. The individual representing, as if in a 'relic organism' way, traits that were like the prototypal organisms that once made up the bulk of primeval life. But as I've mentioned, life tended to give up the isolationist way, in time melding into wholes quite reminiscent of spiral galaxies, and for that matter spiral systems of sorts. But as is the spirals way, its nature is to be driven into clusters which become clusters within clusters, ad infinitum. Eventually, all of space and time become relegated to Wholeness, as if it capitulates to expanding, nay, retrogressing to its primal state of Unity. Expansion a kind of absorbing process in itself because as Parts gather together, they compound their own space exponentially, thus through networking they absorb other life forms that co-habit the space around them so that the two in this way become ONE mega-cluster.

In this way absorption or stickiness, a natural corollary of frequency synchrony, which is the tendency of things to begin to vibe as ONE, leads toward the continuum where it obtains its complementary components Remember our primary law that the greater the curvature of the space, the stronger the field of attraction. Thus, the ability to draw from the surrounding space and make use of independent 'islands of time' is greater. Let me explain what 'islands of time' means. Space isn't occupied simply by linear parallel universes, per se, but consists of individual islands of information composed of frequency patterns, each representing increment fragments of time-space. Like islands in the sea, these free-floating segments of time, like pieces of puzzle from a handful of slides in a movie, can be drawn into the vortical field of individual perspective. Driven together through the process of spiral convergence, order is brought about. Subsequently, the pieces are merged into what scientists often term parallel universes, subjective stories that are pieced together by a subjective observer complete with a plot that moves along toward a target climax composed of past-present-future. The stickiness factor is at work here, pulling meaningful sequences out of space splicing them together through the glue of memory. In other words, the islands are gravitating into subjective field of the observer, or being absorbed into Wholes. The completed puzzle is composed from segmented time islands to create a hypothetical linear timeline with a dramatized Past-Present-Future or 3-d flow. As I have intimated, subjective timelines or Wholes are literally drawn from a vast sea of free-floating time islands, each containing a fragment of order related to a specific flow of time and space. When we create our personal reality, we are in fact, drawing from these free-floating islands of time-space, and we do it automatically, following the clustering effect of the spiral force.

Synchronizing Time Lines

We examined the phenomenon of synchronicity earlier in this book – that's discovering correlations between thoughts (usually memories with strong emotional content isolating unique moments in your childhood) and spontaneous, associated mind-body actual incidents which seem to defy the boundaries of what is termed 'real' time and space. Reflecting on his contemporary mindset, Carl Jung referred to these time and space-jumping incidents as an 'acausal connective principle'. F. David Peat's research has focused on 'subtle' or non-visible but palpable points where matter and energy merge as wave unite. This theory is quite similar in context to the template's spiral which is in context a connective wave principle. The main differences we will reflect on in this sub-chapter are the intricacies of synchronizing space-time qualities.

So far as the reality of such observations they are without question far too numerous to dispute. The next step, which David Peat has undertaken so valiantly, is the problem of how to describe them properly. One thing that does stand out quite saliently is the similarity between the uniformity of the patterns of what was in the mind and the corresponding physical events. As such, these correlations could be called *symmetric or coherent*. Looked at in terms of symmetry, what one is remembering or thinking about within the mind and the following encounter in the physical world presents a holistic pattern of similarity. Seen in physics terms, this corresponding similarity in context and content would be said to have 'parity;' e.g. a pattern cut from the same cookie cutter. Because of the synchrony in the two events, a) the one in the mind of the observer and b) the corresponding physical event, they could be described as having the earmarks of synchronized timelines. They are two different but similar events that occur in separate timelines. The one in the mind moments before, and the following events minute (s) later. Synchronous 'timelines' refers to dual events brought together by frequency correlations. Dual frequency patterns correlate because of their pattern of similarity in resonance.

What we are witnessing is a convergence of time streams, i.e. a correlative resonance or bearing 'core' similarity in a harmonic whole. The underlying subtlety of the whole which binds the two events together, mind and matter, in that sense, *jumps* the 3rd dimensional framework to reveal a unifying whole. This is the bifurcation point between 3rd and 4th dimension. It is the synchrony in the resonance, "the stickiness factor" that draws them together. One might say they have collateral appeal, or qualities that make them cohere.

One immediately is drawn to ask the obvious question what this collateral appeal could be. As I have said, the glue that binds the mind-matter synchrony together is emotion. The word 'appeal' derives, if you recall, from the root 'peal' to ring or simply resonate with a certain quality. In this regard they 'appeal' in nature and quality to each other through vibrational content. Therefore, from a 'subtle level of energy,' in Peat's terms, emotions could be said to be the glue that unites the non-visible with the visible, thereby creating colorful dramatizations of events, like music and color make a movie entertaining. Why we feel and to which we are drawn have a corresponding resonance. Thus emotions bend the field, as it were, removing the apparent division. They cause the curve in the matrix of linear space and time, uniting them in the continuum. Looked at in terms of subtle levels of matter and energy, remove the sensory experience and impose the continuum and you have a continuum linked by the emotional content and you have an underlying Whole.

In fact, our emotional connection to the illusion of the physical is so commonplace that its non-physical qualities are overlooked.

People simply get sucked in by the illusion, fooled by the convincing magic act of what is taken to be the 'causal' plane. In a sense the world of flesh and matter has 'appeal' and we're *stuck like glue* to it through our feelings. What we don't see, until we have synchronistic events, is how emotions bend what is actually two timelines into one phenomenon. The senses do such a good job of filtering out the inconsistencies so that the slight-of-hand act begins to look like the real thing. By 'real' here I am referring to the actual unstable or oscillatory nature of the physical plane. Interestingly, what makes it appear or 'feel' real is the ability of the screening mechanism of the cerebral cortex aided by the filters of the senses to establish what appears to be a fixed or static picture. In a word, feeling gets into the equation in more ways than one. It is feelings that produce the appealing quality of experience, bind it together into a meaningful whole. The clever job these processes have accomplished of masking the uncertainty behind the temporality of order has effectively obscured the fact that time and space aren't the two separate states they appear to be. In the continuum these two states are actually one, the division comes about through the transformation into matter and flesh. Correspondingly, the reunion takes place when they reunite as ONE.

To reinforce the illusion of distinctly different times, i.e., the division between 3rd and 4th dimensional space and time, we humans employ mechanical data processes like the old-time piece on the wall, or rely on cycles we take to be persistent evidence that while things appear to change (just a little bit), they actually stay pretty much the same. We strive as a race to maintain self-similarity in all things, that sense of consistency, perhaps as a throw-back to our former non-separateness in the continuum. None-the-less, behind the temporality picture, time plays a game of dodge ball with our awareness. Hidden by the curtain of continuity, time slips, or synchronizing time-lines are occuring all the time. In short, we move in and out of time streams like a seal diving in and climbing out of pools of water.

At this very moment or lack of it, you are connecting to increments of time outside clock order, but you probably aren't aware of it and if you are, you're probably the unfortunate person who has trouble snoozing while sitting up. Increments or pockets of time are all around us and we are being drawn to them as much as they are being drawn to us. Once the blinders, so to speak, are taken off people's minds then they become aware that the illusion of linear order or its appearance in a past-present-future order is an illusion created by a closed or limited temporal perspective. Reality is plastic and can be remodeled like clay in the potter's hands. As the emotional or meaningful connection to the moment changes so also changes the space-time increments. Hence, to create an authentic version of the reality you want, you must learn to draw these islands of time to you. Remember first and foremost: it is your resonance which attracts the information you need. You shift the information to bring about an alteration in the field, rather than the continuum, per se, since the 4th dimension can't actually be changed. What you are doing is interrupting the flow of information into the field by superimposing new bits from a different perspective. For instance, a simple form of time traveling and its alteration occurs when you remember an incident from your childhood and embellish it with new information.

Memories form around energy constellations, patterns of intense emotional charges. The charges bend the space-time field so that the continuum is infringed upon. In a sense, you are going to the continuum when you do what we call 'remembering,' but you see it simply as activity within certain lobes of the brain. In actuality, you are time traveling and each time you do you take the so-called present experience with you and impose it upon the original experience. In that way you are constantly building and reassembling clusters within clusters of memories, although you have little realization of what you are doing. You simply think that your journey 'down memory lane,' is as it originally occurred, when it is actually altered by the content of your present experiences, so much so that it is an entirely different experience every time.

What has happened is that memory, in bending space-time, has gathered around it spaces and times with similar resonances. With every change in perspective there is a corresponding change in arrangement of the patterns. This is why when you dream you may suddenly find yourself transported to exotic places suddenly such as the past or into the future. The bend in space caused by the emotional content (like marbles of different colors rolling around the curved center of a flat plane to form Rubic Cube like patterns) has attracted those elements with the strongest binding force to them. The predominant fields form observable clusters to the restless mind's eye, constantly emerging or submerging with each rearrangement with new fractal-like mosaics. As in synchronicity where the bending of the field by elements of like mind match up to strong emotional, recurring emotional patterns spark the spontaneous emergence of corresponding fields of order to surface. Each time, they unite mind and matter in different yet hauntingly similar ways.

What you are actually experiencing in these journeys is practical alteration of content within islands of time. For example, let us say, that you are creating continents which is, essentially, extending small content into larger and larger accumulations – stirring the cauldron, in alchemical terms. You can reduce or enlarge in accordance with your expectations the whole of the trip into that time zone, it's up to you. Your impression about what you are doing when you travel there is responding according to the lensing effect we've talked about before, so keep that omnipresent in your mind. An interesting and helpful thing to do to test your time traveling against the current linear backdrop of space and time, is to take some information intentionally back by memorizing so aspect. Think of it as a time-space prop from its present.

You might say it's impossible without a time machine to take a prop (such as a modern firearm, for example) back into the past. This is true in terms of materiality but remember - reality is plastic and therefore can be manipulated. Like the brain, time is affected as much by the illusion as it is by the so-called 'real' thing, because at a deep level of awareness, everything is One; which means that it is all waves and hence what is real and what is figurative reduces to the same. So when you go take a mental image, that good enough, and implant that image into a specific time period and I guarantee you, that if you look carefully enough you will see evidence in some form in your near future of your presence in that time period. In fact, if the visitation is significant enough, it will visibly alter something about your life. Expect it to happen. It may appear in any form: communication from someone, in a book, on television, in a movie, something that occurs spontaneously during an outing, a discovery that appears odd or unique.

REMEMBER: REALITY IS PLASTIC. THEREFORE, ANYTHING AND EVERYTHING CAN OCCUR IN ANY CONTEXT OR CONTENT.

So be careful how you describe your subjective reality because the very act of description can have temporary binding qualities. Of course, being malleable it can be changed at will, so not to worry, yet not knowing or acting on that realization does influence imposed temporary structural limitations. This is what happens when we share social memes – we accept restrictions and impose boundaries both on ourselves and upon others according to the depth of our emotional immersion into the information shared. Thus stay abreast of your emotional state of mind – know yourself has great importance here, because if you don't recognize your own susceptibility to certain emotional influences you open your mind and hence, physicality to invasive presences.

Please be aware of what you receive and what you leave at these dual sites. Also, be sure when you make these trips that you do your meditations first, relaxed, deep breathing with focus and inner vocalization. Say specifically what you want to do and visualize yourself doing it. Your thoughts and especially your emotions have great impact on the dream experience that will occur. Totally give up the idea that dreams are things that take place in your head because they, like memories, take place with the continuum. Every emotion you've experience is stored in that field. Irwin Laszlo has done a lot of seminal work in describing the effects of this field commonly known in mysticism as the Akashic. What they're really referring to is the continuum which is the main storage bank for the information that comprising the HOLOVERSE.

Several things occur in these exchanges: a) we give energy through our emotional output and b) we receive energy by our empathy with others. Thus, during the search for islands of time, subjectively meaningful frequencies are exchanged so that there is an ebb and flow of energy. Thus, when someone is in synchrony with us, there is an exchange – that is, a conjugation of reciprocal fields. Love, for instance, is such a field of wholeness, in terms of synchrony. It ebbs and flows according to the strength of the exchange. You receive as you give, thus the greater the giving the greater is the energy received. That is why strong emotional content produces reciprocal reactions, and this can apply to all forms of emotional energy exchanges. Thoughts are like an adhesive and the quality of the stickiness of the emotions we share binds our time-lines together.

One might say, like a powerful glue (because we're in love) I'm stuck on you, or like birds of a feather we stick together no matter what the weather. Feelings continue to draw us together though we're far apart, eventually we must reunite. It's impossible, some might say for two lovers to be held apart, and if you try, it can even cause death. Some people are bonded so strongly they are willing to and do die together rather than part. Though you may be unaware of it, you and someone else are already sharing islands or intervals of time. Marriage, family, friends are all everyday examples of synchronizing time-lines. It is the feeling content that imbues the 'e' (the intent) into creating the vibrational correlation or 'motion' of the field.

Quite simply, you have exchanged and are exchanging energies at this very moment with others unaware. You might notice the time-lines converging when you get that sudden *synchronistic* phone call just when you are thinking of that certain someone. In this resonating we are drawn together to create the cluster of materialization that builds matter. In fact, you are helping each other to create the 'space-timeline,' of your collective lives. If you wish to test this fact just focus intentionally on someone or something that is important to you and watch how it manifests in a very short time. Be aware that your emotions bend the field so that your beliefs draw or repel your desires according to the degree of your self-investment in the activity. Remember that you are interacting with other people when you send out these feelings and/or thoughts, so watch your 'intent,' sometimes negative intent lurking in the bottom of your emotional pool can ripple back on you. That's what they call karma in its rawest, time-traveling form.

In a hyper-dimensional sense, we network to bridge and/or build the matrix of space and time. This takes on both a psychic as well as molecular/chemical and biological components. We, in effect, are exchanging information as we oscillate together to manufacture a plasmodial energy web or gestalt. If you could see yourself from a hyper-dimensional perspective, you would appear to be a rotating, vortical, luminescent energy field. In fact, this is what people are seeing when they view UFOs – they are projections of collective energy. Their defiance of 3rd dimensional fields belies the fact that they operate outside its domain nearer to the continuum. In short, they bend the field because of the large amount of accumulated mass in its amoebic like structure. With this power over 3rd dimensional gravitational forces surrounding the mega-cluster (like flying cities of energy) they are able to move with impunity throughout time. Seen in a literal sense, UFOs are hyper-dimensional spiral fields or "islands of time/information." They could be seen as literal time-traveling vehicles in terms of 3rd dimensional concepts of space and time. Bear in mind that when I speak of an 'island of time' these segments do not contain definitive linear timelines. It is the subjective observer(s) who create(s) and/or projects the constellation of order seen in the physical world and experienced as segments of past-present-future time. In fact, the whole phenomenon of synchronicity is part of the materialization process, even though that when they appear, the *meaningful* quality appears to the conscious mind as quite mystical in its synchronicity nature. **IMPORTANT NOTE:** Bohm's fascination with the 'intelligence' lurking in electrons in synchrony, i.e., plasmas, was an intuitive epiphany of the energy bridge spanning mind and matter.

All of relative or linear order is related to perspective which is partially a creation of individual perception in accordance to the subjective/objective angle produced by the optic principle. If you recall, the optic principle reflects your self-image within the framework of the 3rd dimension. However, its extensions involve processes that are multidimensional. Islands of time have no specific order but represent random or temporary information spaces. They can, however, while not being a part of a greater stream such as an era or epoch in terms of linear time, contain incremental slices of space-time within the periods. Thus, encountering an island of time and experiencing it as a literal encounter with another century, for instance, is often like time traveling, since you will experience a sense of being there, though you are encountering only a segment of the whole era in which it occurred. In effect, these islands of time are creative force in its rawest state; hence, the imposition of structure is subjectively related to the act of observation. On a different, but related note, recently, engineers filmed a UFO spotted near a copper refinement mine in a remote location in the Andes, (see: Huffington Post article for July 4, 2014 – Chile Releases Official Study on UFO photo) that appeared as an intelligently controlled object which emanated its own interior light source.

What they spotted, in my opinion, was one of these creative centers or islands of energy. Yes, they are intelligent, and yes, they are mobile, and yes they are centers of immense activities, and yes, they are attracted to information relevant to their presence in that area. Hence, the activity they are attracted to is important in terms of its content to them, since they (like ourselves) are interactive with resonant frequency fields. The frequency content says a lot about their presence, therefore, the activity going on there is important in terms of its ability to draw similar 'birds of a feather' together. Perhaps the Chilean government is using that energy source in a highly confidential or classified manner. Thus, the raw energy accumulating there is building up. Whether retreating, approaching or simply hovering, the fact that it paused overhead and moved in semi-circles speaks volumes about the nature of the plasmodial objects presence.

Whenever you see energy accumulations like these in the rawest of states it means time traveling energy is flowing into a field, something like an orgone accumulator. If you have read my first book or Wilhelm Reich's (see: Serge King) works on orgone accumulators, you'll recall that energy forms cones or spirals when there is a lot of input from various sources – that's when data is being exchanged. The activity creates accumulations, clusters as it were which can appear as independent entities that possess the mobility to travel forward or backward in time at will from the creative center of their point in the continuum.

Thus, in that sense, these energy vimanas (Hindu) or Tulpas (in Tibetan mysticism), if you will, are centers or ports at which other worlds of energy exchange data with individual psyche; which is crucial in the forming of bridges between dimensions. In other words, outside of the time-traveling aspects, their work is of a much higher level. Think of these energy plasmas as life in its rawest and most creative form, displaying its plastic qualities which aren't normally observable at a 3rd dimensional level. As such these life forms act as cosmic engineers of sorts that are involved in networking on an energetic level of creation.

The important thing to remember here is that the memory of time as an arrow from past into future, such as being born on a certain date and so on, is the portion of time you remember, so to speak. They represent points of order along a hypothetical line. But those points do not contain the whole story. They are your own *conscious* timeline sense of order which you have purposely strung together, like specific beads chosen to adorn a necklace. Going deeper, as when a person enlists a hypnotist to help recollect various specific events, etc., exposes more of the complete story that was experienced, but even then, the whole story it is still not complete.

In fact, without the hypnotists or your own awareness, subliminal prompts are guiding the evocation of the event. What surface's is actually a cleverly concocted tale told as if from an 'outside' observers place. It therefore, contains data that more often than not is unconsciously perceived by the person who is hypnotized, but not consciously understood. You can reach these others levels from the 'outside observers' standpoint, or you can simply deconstruct the images and replace them with an expanded view. By 'expanded' view I am not inferring a fabricated one, per se, but a reconstruction according to a deeper and richer creative take of what took place at a specific time and place. Thus, what you are achieving here is accessing more of the infinite creative potential of the spiral principle to produce a more clearly defined image of your self while moving forward.

Reality: A Patchwork of Time Streams

Seen from the panorama of the 4th dimension reality is a patchwork of time streams derived from a sea of incremental periods held together in clusters. Thus, when a person experiences them, they often get the impression they are experiencing a 'whole' era or epoch in which the events occurred. In a sense, they are, but not completely as it might be portrayed by a chronographer or historian of the times. This is true even then the storyline reflects more of the perspective of the writer than its does these so-called extended periods of time. Such a person is merely taking carefree jaunts into islands of time and plucking from them that which fits their own subjective storyline. In a similar manner this is what takes place during time-slips, or for that matter, any creative and imaginative journey in the production of a new self. A person's frequency is simply resonating or merging with incremental islands of time. The islands length or durability in space depends upon the size of the cluster that makes up the segment. Time clusters are segments of time that can correspond to seconds, minutes, hours, days, weeks, months, years and so on. Seen this way, it is easy to understand that practical time traveling to recreate one's self, rather than an extended journey through a specified space, is actually done via incremental 'hops' from island to island.

Encounters with islands of time occur spontaneously, especially when you travel either in so-called out-of-body trips or during actual physical travel. That's when you suddenly find yourself encountering another time, so to speak. During these experiences people get an impression, for example, of walking, driving, awakening to another time, which they might very well have. I have had this experience's more than once, and the encounter while shocking and disorienting, leaves you realizing that this physical reality we see about isn't as fixed and static, e.g. deterministic as it appears. Journeys like these can also occur in unusual sleep states and we often assume these experiences to be just fascinating dreams. In these kinds of dreams people suddenly discover they are in another day and age. Usually, they feel quite comfortable and aligned, like it is a memory of a distant life, or they may, on the other hand, become frightened and panic.

When this occurs they have entered abruptly, like walking through a vortex or doorway without recollection of how they've gotten there or why. It's like coming home only to find yourself in a totally different place, which leaves you wondering if you're going mad. Without doubt, spontaneous encounters can be quite shocking and disorienting. Imagine yourself traveling down a road, for example and suddenly encountering a person driving a car that is obviously from another time period. Now imagine how that experience would be as equally disturbing for the driver in that other car, especially if they are fully aware of you passing. If you recognize someone in a dream from another era or time, they probably recognize you too, which has happened many times to numerous individuals. Sometimes these meetings are greetings, like inter-dimensional postcards from another world, another age or another time from old friends who meet and refresh their associations on subliminal levels, but have forgotten on the conscious.

Other types of encounters, such as seeing our so-called 'future selves' can be quite awesome, and they usually leave us wondering, enigmatically questioning what time and space self that is and why we are meeting it. The reasons can be understood, while sometimes the deeper purpose may escape our conscious selves much as a déjà vu leaves us puzzled and curious. Encounters with other selves are so strange from our perspective, in the illusion called the present, that at the moment it may seem as though you temporarily inhabit the body of another person. When I as a young man in my twenties encountered my elder self from the future, I thought that I was inside another person's body; which can and does happen sometimes. It's difficult at these moments of dissociation to accept that the person seen in the altered consciousness state is one's own future self, though aged and different looking. These moments tell us that a definite probable self is out there you can pull in. But when you do, if it's from the future, there is often that shocking recognition that it is none other than you. Again, if that self becomes conscious at the same time you encounter him/her in the future, the impact is magnified exponentially. On the point of sexual identity – any of these selves can be either sex, regardless of what sex you identify with in the present.

Often events of this sort emerge or submerge so quickly that there is little time for you to fully adjust to the reality of what just happened. However, if you sense that time is missing or elapsed and you realize you've become submerged in a time stream it may become difficult to discern which information is which. This occurs because after even a short time lapse you will begin to resonate so much with the encountered island of time that in a mimicry way, you become it at some level. A frequency exchange has occurred. What happens, as I've intimated, you adapt according to your own frequency CPS; cycles per second. The islands of time you've encountered have been attracted to you because a person begins oscillating in synchrony to their current frequency interval of time.

This phenomenon is universal and takes place spontaneously every time you adjust or rearrange your self-image to get in tune with information frequencies around you.

To get a clear idea of what that is all about, take musicians who are jamming, for example, they are great at mimicry and get in tune quickly to the music patterns spontaneously and begin playing a song or beating a rhythm in synchrony. A mina-bird and parrots are two creatures that specialize in mimicking the sounds around them to blend into or camouflage themselves from the creatures sharing their surrounding habitat. In a word they take advantage of the gullibility of other birds or animals. This versatility at mimicry can be extended to the imitation of voices or adopting general physical characteristics such as clothing, locomotion, gestures. Mimicry is an art and actors consider it a necessary part of the repertoire the need to accomplish skill at acting.

Think on this: the actor who wins an academy award is the one who has the ability to fool you into believing in their character the most. I think of them as 'frequency hacks,' people who are good at resonating both in terms of giving and receiving vibes. They literally pull you into their strong fields and before you know it you're trying to be like them. In fact, that's how they add to their popularity and magnetism, as it is known – by accumulating clones. Sometimes uniquely skilled actors are so good at faking the frequencies of villains that they have been attacked because people were unable to separate them from the characters they played. In a practical sense, people often use this skill to become a part of a group or blend with the crowd. We are all unconsciously frequency hacks and automatically utilize resonance when we want to slip through certain sociological turfs when we find ourselves on the wrong side of town. Such people are said to 'blend into the woodwork,' or become a part of it. In a sense they render themselves *invisible* to the 'alien' detection radar of people, even if they are totally of another race and don't speak the language. They are capable of 'masking' their presence, just as a Stealth bomber masks its presence from the sweep of radars when passing overhead or Ninja assassins sneaking up on enemy encampments. As mentioned earlier - the purpose of the Philadelphia Project was aimed at creating a radar cloak of invisibility which was carried out electromagnetically to bring about the reconstruction of the frequency patterns of the ship. In that way it could slip out of our space-time.

Energetically, during these frequency reconstructions something happens at both ends of the receiver and transmitter - an exchange of energies takes place. Descriptively, one might think of this exchanging of energies or what I am wont to call 'cross-masking,' or getting in sync with the vibratory field of another person, place or thing. It truly is a holistic process, like the blending of Yin and Yang. Being in-sync with our environment or being in a symbiotic situation is actually resonating at its frequencies so that the exchange is mutual. Together the cross-masking creates illusion of changing your molecular structure, like teleportation or psychokinesis. On the negative fringes, being out-of-sync or inharmonious with your environment makes you easy to spot by its inhabitants. They're like prey out of their environment who make easy targets for predators, Part of the whole art of camouflage is fooling the predator or the pray into not seeing you coming, depending upon your perspective. For example, an outsider, at first, is clearly off-tune like an unschooled person who is tone deft in a choir. He/she sticks out like a sore thumb.

Cross-Over's and Time Builders

When people cross-over into a time cluster without being conscious of what they are doing and feel 'strange' or out-of-sorts, they have been spontaneously drawn in accordance with their own aura or synchrony. However, the realization of the frequency change hasn't crossed the threshold of their cortex into consciousness at that moment, so they still retain a feeling of alienation or weirdness. At that point they are still 'tone deft' or out-of-tune, meaning they haven't as of yet acquired an 'ear' for the cluster or Whole in which they find themselves. Unconsciously, we are always listening on a hyper-dimensional level to incoming vibrational patterns, whether we're aware of it or not. Even if we're not conscious of it, we feel 'drawn' as it were, to gather into groups with specific types of people with whom we resonate. This attraction signals 'cluster attunement'. We are drawn by these attunements without understanding why and keep a 'cluster attunement ear' out for similarities. It's somewhat like the gathering of people at different kinds of musical events; there is a common resonance in the vibration that they are all cohering to – think of the stickiness factor. Cluster listening is like firing an arrow from a deeper level of consciousness outside the periphery of awareness and sensing it hitting its distant target down line, even though your conscious self may not have any realization of where that target is and why it is there.

Another phrase that describes this cross-over process is 'time building.' Time building is an extension of crossing over. We cross a bridge in space-time to get to a specific point on the other side. When we get there, we link up with its vibration and in this way pull its influence into our present lives. Quite literally, what we are doing is either de-constructing or reconstructing segments of time that we wish to encounter as our future. It's somewhat like renting 'time shares' since we are in fact, rubbing psychic elbows, so to speak, with other people with similar vibrations who share that space-time point of resonance. We probably won't stay; we are just dabbling creatively in the production of a new self. In this way we acquire islands or segments of time and figuratively place them in an ideal linear order through the manipulation of an altered perspective. Some people are artisans of time. These individuals have the ability to manipulate their optical lenses to bring information in or block it out at will. All the senses can be attuned using the optical lens metaphor, hearing, touch, smell and taste, or they can all be integrated like synesthesia, the admixing of sensor input where you can taste color, hear color, smell form, feel sound, etc. The way we experience reality through the censorship of the senses reveals a barrier erected by the mechanism of the physical self-occupied with fragmental periods of time we deal with in the physical world. But the truth is, senses can behave in any manner, there is no set order for the senses other than the way you have grown to experience them. You can experience your senses as you have become accustomed to, or each one differently, or you can experience them as ONE. The process of sensory focus is part of the trick to make reality appear as it does so that you can believe in it more. Without this process of obscuration, you would mix sensory input, fail to orient properly in the physical, or see through the illusion altogether. The truth is that's where you're headed anyway, only this time you'll do it consciously!

Within the Whole, which is outside the linearity of consciousness, the unconscious is already attuning or orienting itself through resonance, that feeling you have for knowing where you're going without knowing exactly why. What you are doing unconsciously is organizing your time line. A time line is that order you arbitrarily decide upon as past-present-future, none of which have any meaning other than the order that you give them simply because physical time is determined by your angle of perspective. Change that and you arbitrarily alter any predetermined angle of time. In a literal sense that's what practical time travel is all about.

Trust Your Resonance Radar

To get down to essentials the vital part of the whole process of practical time traveling is recognizing the importance of resonance. Resonance is an unconscious yet vital sensory organ for assessing the vibrational context of energy environments; it tells you what feels right and what doesn't. If it feels wrong it is generally because a) it doesn't fully fit your conscious resonance, or b) you aren't in synchrony with the new vibration yet. If it feels right, it's c) because you are moving right onto target, or d) you are synchronizing with a new vibration. So if you're feeling out of sorts with your new environment, you haven't acquired a resonance ear and are simply out of tune because you're out-of-conscious sync with the greater whole. On the hand if you're feeling good, it's because you're developing a feeling for following your resonance radar.

Out-of-tune individuals are usually entrenched in their own inner frequency voice, that part of yourself that constantly tells you who you are. If fixed strongly to the inner voice, such individual can be thought of as focused concavely or introverted. Extremists in terms of introverted focus, they are often socially autistic or insensitive to information outside themselves, cut-off, refusing to open up their feelings to the myriad vibrations around them. One might say they can't fully adjust the receptivity of their resonance radar and are still at the level where they are using their perceptual optics as interferences cloaks to create their own special space to block out the world. This – by the way, isn't going to happen anytime soon because we're all part of a bigger network and frankly there's isn't any such place as a corner in the resonance game.

A simple trick for altering suffocating space-time fields where your resonance is out-of-sync is to practice opening and closing your optical focus referred to in chapter three. Visualize altering the focus, like a telescope, from concave to convex. Think of yourself as crossing over from self to other, future to past and back. Play with the order of time. Imagine yourself in any number of settings with your own kind of creative changes in terms of past-present-future timelines. Once you get the hang of it you will also notice that you become aware of a super-fluidness of the psychic medium you are in and begin to have encounters with islands of time. This may occur in the form of slips in time or déjà vu's and even clear presentiments of the future. Entering into and moving out of these frequency fields is easy once you learn to allow room for flexibility in your self-image. Individuals, groups, companies, cities, states and countries all can be autistic, this means - fixed on their inner space. Hence, their ability to grow and change is stagnated causing them to shrivel up and dissolve.

The good news, once a person, out-of-tune with their environment, learns how to resonate with their surroundings, they begin to blend better with it. In that way they become an intricate part of it, rather than remain alienated, standing out like a sore thumb. They move from a singular cluster at this point and become a part of a greater cluster, or part of that larger cluster bearing many clusters. Thus, people who could easily identify you when you first arrived in town will soon have difficulty discerning where the personality you came in with ends and the new one begins. In fact, unconsciously you will discover yourself taking on a whole new appearance to blend in with the locals, plus developing the ability to identify and become part of any living whole.

Always bear in mind that when you change your identity space you also change time. Thus, this change includes both a subjective as well as an objective change, but not altogether, Although there may be some vestige of subjective perceptual alteration in your attunement or awareness to new vibrational turf, it doesn't always mean that the whole of the self-changes. If this happens, become part of the picture, but feel out of tune or sync with it, your sensitivity distorted, off-center. However, all perceptual changes in awareness do include a change in your brain waves or you wouldn't be privy to any vestige of attunement. Hence, changes in perception involve a change in personal perspective. Now you see things different because you are feeling different in your self-image. That's a focal phenomenon and it works forward or backward. Self-image determines your perspective and as such reflects a change in your attunement or resonance to objective reality.

As I have said, this may include full awareness or it may not, meaning you might be conscious of having changed and identify with a new group, environment, idea, philosophy or be drawn to a specific part of the country. What has happened is that on a subliminal level you have begun to mirror the vibrations around you so that you and your surroundings have begun to come into synchrony – that is, *mirror each other*. This mirroring effect has a lot to do with mimicry, which I've already mentioned and camouflage. A poorly camouflaged jungle cat is sure to starve in his natural habitat, unless his coat dramatically changes. Correspondingly, when the frequency of the environment is absorbed, one becomes conjoined with its time and space frequencies.

Blending vibrations may sometimes come quickly, so smoothly in fact, that there may appear to be little if any differences between the two space-times. When the differences are acute, it becomes obvious shortly after entering the field something is amiss. A traveler, for example in one account, passing through a bifurcation point between his home and a store five miles away didn't really notice anything except a fog-like atmosphere at first. Shortly thereafter, he felt a sharp bump as his cruise control came on when he went up an unexpected hill. This disturbance alerted him that he was suddenly ascending an incline. The individual had taken the route many times and never noticed any grade inclines between the store and home, which was the scant distance of five miles. Then, just as quickly as he'd entered the fog and ascended the hill and became suddenly aware of the change in the structure of the field, he found himself again on the same route he'd always taken.

This man's encounter with a time slip was impressive but not altogether shocking and his transition back into physical reality quite seamless, except for being shaken out of it by the kicking-in of the cruise control. Stay aware – you may be going through time slips and without being aware of it, unless at some bifurcation points where reality unexpectedly branches into alternate time zones, frequency adjustments are difficult, particularly if one is fixated at certain frequencies and hence, inflexible to changing vibrations.

Time Slips and Time Lags

Difficulty handling changes in frequency zones are generally referred to as 'time lags'. When you travel aboard a jet airliner speeding between time zones at 600 to 1200 miles per hour, difficulty in adjusting are called 'jet lags'. Adjustment may incur headaches, restlessness, sleep problems, unusual dreams, disorientation, even depression and anxiety. Such problems in readjusting to these changes occur when altering frequencies varying from subjective to objective reference frameworks. Very few people put this together, assuming that these maladies are simply sleep cycle deprivations or changes in schedules. Obvious difficulty in readjusting is especially noticeable for people who have to pass through as many as three or more time zones in continuous or long term transatlantic flying or for a person traveling back and forth from east to west coast.

Regaining one's equilibrium, shall we say, involves becoming familiar with   new time-space zones you will be flying to in terms of the local culture, food, geography, jargon and psychology of the people. When a person takes some time to become immersed or acquainted with local culture and habit patterns, even speech and historical content, an adjustment in resonance is more likely and less troublesome. This same reasoning applies to crossing over to the bridge between time zones and readjusting to the vibrations. Let's face it, it's like a trip you've chosen to take, which in a limited sense perhaps, you prepared for; except the shock of getting there hasn't occurred yet. Once the reality sets in, if you're not ready for it, the adjustment can be difficult, so proper preparation is essential.

As I have mentioned earlier in this volume, crossing into or changing time zones involves learning to readjust to frequencies that are often quite different than what we are familiar with. However, should you be able to make that transition smoothly the pay offs are quite worth the trouble of doing the home work of attunement before starting out. Think about it: if you're going out to dance Latin music, wouldn't it pay off to get acquainted with the patterns? See what I'm talking about? It's all a matter of getting attuned if you don't want to experience time lags adjustments.

Memory, Order and Time

When a person experiences a time slip they also experience a perceptual disorder in terms of sequencing of time intervals. Time sequence is the order in which memory is formulated. For instance, an increment of time includes past-present-future reference points on a grid. Think in terms of a group of slides in a film. When the separately filmed sequences are spliced together and run in a straight line, with a given order, they make what we call 'sense,' that is, they have a recognizable correlation. Our memory is like that. It could be compared to a string of incremental resonances (given events) arbitrarily strung together as in the movie analogy.

Essentially, this is what the big 'ta'do' about 'string theory' is all about, i.e. increments of space-time strung together according to their vibratory content; like beads on a necklace. This is the nature of the space-time grid, that is, a series of incremental resonances strung together in sequences, like a movie. As such they represent a given topography of order, incremental segments, dates with related to cycles of a clock. This is the nature of place and time, the order in which particular events arise within the framework of your subjective vortex of perspective. The order was pieced together through resonant association. Until the whole picture is recognized it may remain somewhat piecemeal or poorly strung together, without direction or clear order. So we see that memory is actually a form of comparative order, a somewhat cinematically dramatized illusion, colored with the emotional and sensory content for effects that highlight its sequential appeal. Like a movie with color, lights, action, it rolls through our mind like a freight train so fast we don't see the linkages that hold the spliced slides together. When it fits together nicely, this way, we say it makes a formal pattern of order. From this cleverly orchestrated production we build our memories.

Seen another way, stringing incremental events or resonances of time together could be compared to going to a mall to shop. At one store you may have stopped to look at clothes and found something you liked but didn't decide on buying yet, so you continued on to another to look at other things and new stores to shop. Should you decide that the first store with the interesting piece of merchandise that you saw was what you wanted after comparing it to others in terms of price, color, quality was what you wanted, you would have to check the time-space events in your memory to retrace your steps to compare. If your memory or sense of incremental observation about the order of events was accurate, such as to specific details about shape, size, color, pattern, when you first dropped in there at 1:00, you might buy it. These elements represent space-time resonance markers, points where subjective and objective frequency converge to create the order, that is, the cinematic dramatization of your memory. That order you perceive was determined by the incremental events, i.e. their importance dependent upon your powers of resonant observation. Outside of the order that you assume, they could have fallen together in any sequence ALIGNED TO THE IMPORTANCE YOU PLACE ON SPECIFIC RESONANCES OR INCREMENTAL ASSOCIATIONS.

So, we see that memory involves time – distance – frequency – order divided by the power of SUBJECTIVE observation, which is somewhat redundant simply because all of these factors reduce to you the mirror you use, its angle (whether convex or concave) that determine the powers of subjective observation. From observation, which is the accumulated results of space-time increments (what drew you to stop at the store) and frequency (how observant you were during that time) distance, how much time elapsed and subjective angle of order, the flow of information into the sequences governing the whole production. It is important to always bear in mind that the *sequence of the production is a byproduct of the flow of time in terms of relative acceleration or frequency into the angle of observation.* The angle of observation is governed by the curvature of the wave; that is, how the frequencies flowing from an event converge or flow into your subjective framework of reference,

We've already examined frequency enough to know that it is the cyclic revolution of the cycles between trough and crest within a given time. So far as the subjective observer is concerned the curvature in the framework of their mirror determines the order in which it is remembered and/or perceived. For instance, if you were passing through the store very quickly, your relative frequency of observation equals the amount of time within a given space through which you traveled at a given speed. If you went through the area quickly, your memory probably was pretty sketchy, so there wasn't much time to gain a deep impression of what it was you observed. Here frequency equals speed of observation.

An interesting factor here is that if you change any element of this equation, you automatically change all the rest. Change speed and you change time or the sequence in which you observe and remember what it is you encountered. Thus, the order of your memory is not quite clear. Later on, you might find yourself wondering did I go to that store where the pretty shirt was that I liked first, or was it later on. If so which store did I frequent first? The problem in order here is a byproduct of the frequency or acceleration, your movement through the store and your attentiveness to detail as you passed. Should you find that your memory of that order is lacking, it is no doubt a result of both time and velocity or acceleration. Here your reference framework was affected by the sequences or patterns of order you established in your memory as you past.

If you discover that your sense of memory is bad, then it is linked to your powers of observation and your sense of order in terms of time. Should you desire to increase your memory then, you would have to slow down and make note of events taking place within your framework of reference. So framework of reference involves the frequency of time within the increments provided by your control over order. Should you find that your life is disordered then it is clear that the disorder reveals your framework of references. You are moving through the increments of time without focusing upon what it is that you are experiencing.

Thus, for people who have stepped 'outside' of time means in part that they have passed through frequency changes, bifurcation portals where the increments or fragments of association between past and future were poorly assessed. This is quite common with time slips, along with the jet lags that have a way of accumulating sequences without awareness that leave a person feeling disoriented. Knowing where you're going requires having a sense, then of where you are coming from. It involves a sequence of order, that is, two points in a reference system that correlates with the experience and the time/velocity you experienced it in. When you find yourself in a time slip, fear not, then because what it is telling you is that you have merely undergone an alteration of consciousness. An alteration of consciousness is a slip in time or change in frequency. Unless your subjective consciousness was attuned to the change in relative velocity, or framework of reference, your observation of where you're at is going to be distorted. So it is important, then, to recognize a) that you've undergone a frequency change, and b) realize that you have moved into another space-time zone. Adjusting to these changes in reference systems requires acceptance that your powers of observation were skewed by your relative speed of movement.

If you want to make a close study of order and its relationship to frequency, simply take note of your dreams. Try to establish order within a dream and you will quickly discover that most of your sense of order will be a projection of what you 'think' took place rather than actually what went on. Trying to connect the dots between events will only lead to frustrating suppositions that in turn produce a picture that is line with your expectations. To gain a full sense of order in dreams, you would have to move to an 'outsiders' position of observation so you could watch the segments which occurred and even then, what you would come up with is a supposition about its supposed order. Getting a perspective on an order by studying dreams gives your insight into how expectation or anticipation brings about a gestalt. In other words, what you anticipate connects the dots so that they appear to be completed in a gestalt of order.

In a dream, if you think you've traveled along a certain course such as from your house, along a street upon which you walked to get to a certain location at the end of the block – stop for a moment and look again. You will quickly discover that the order is related to what you assume took place rather than what actually took place. In fact, you will notice a number of blind spots that will stick out, places where voids exist. In these voids you may discover other dreams with totally different themes imposed upon them. For example, you might see yourself walking down the street to the house at the end, but in the voids at different intervals, there will be other dreams taking places, like a flash back of going into a house on the way and meeting with a certain person. When that occurs, you will find yourself amazed that turning into the house in between took place, when all your treasured outer memory follows a false course that takes you from your house to another house at the end of the street. Dreams expand exponentially like clusters within clusters, parallel universes with universe. Outer memory doesn't function well here, and when it does it tends to impose order where there is none, or at least that is what we do to escape the inconsistencies which leave us anxious and wondering about our sanity. A good memory leads to the voids where another memory jumps across from island-to-island states. These states include other dreams within dreams, and some of them may turn out to be quite lengthy, convoluted and bizarre.

As I've indicated, in the voids where you assumed things took place instead you will have projected an imagined sequence of intervals connecting what you take to be the original journey from your house, a walk down a street and the encounter of the house at the end. These details are crucial because the contemporary version of contraction or dilation often includes a manipulation of time, as if it is stretched out or contracted, when in fact, to have contraction and dilation there would have to be a beginning and ending, when there is none. So here, in dreams, which reflect the 4th dimensional nature of the spiral, there is no order except the order that you project into the sequences we take for granted in the 3rd dimension. Knowing this tells us that since there is no order other than the order we impose, than the intervals which make up segments of time is by product of the observer after-the-fact.

Manipulating Time Waves

So, we learn that time equates to intervals of order and that the order encapsulated in an interval depends upon how much our awareness as we transitioned through an event was focused. Put together in a string of moments, similar to individually filmed movie episodes reconstituted on a movie reel, the sum of these intervals as a movie, representing a Whole, are fitted together sequentially. Once arranged, like beads on a pearl necklace, the order of the sequences is aligned with a specific point of origin, or beginning aimed toward an eventual end. Thus, the fixity of the order determined by the observer is the implied or imagined chain of events. The element that rules the observer of these sequels of intervals arranged along a linear course is the focal impression of the observer. Hence an astute observer, in the final dictum, must exercise a modicum of control over the process of perception by determining the velocity or frequency of the intervals connecting the continuum of time. This implies that the observer must, if they wish to manipulate time waves, remain versatile in terms of their subjective perception. However, a brief note on time intervals and their frequency model is in order.

A useful illustration of time within fixed intervals of seconds, minutes, hours and days and their eventual compilation, can be visualized with a Fourier wave set against a backdrop of a common clock. Think of the waves as emanating outward from the face the clock. The waves emanating from the clock in terms of amplitude and periodicity would reflect the clockworks increment of time. The largest amplitude or propagated hourly wage would complete its cycle in approximately sixty minutes or within 360 seconds. In terms of amplitude, just inside the hourly interval minutes would be nested and within the increments of a minute, a second interval wave. The sine wave representing the periodic frequency of the hour would be extend into a deep 90° wave, the wave completing the whole cycle in 180°. Inside the hour hand wave would be a smaller, shorter wave representing the minute hand and inside the 45° minute wave an even smaller incremental interval known as a second. Thus, what we see is waves within waves nested in time intervals; or simply intervals within intervals. In this way we get a picture of time as a series of interval waves of specific frequencies. Each specific wave containing data moving at specific space-time velocities locked in incremental crests and troughs accessing at specific brain wave frequencies. Remember that these waves comprise a matrix of conjugating energies converging into patterns of wholeness, each bifurcating or joining at specific points of impact sensed by our proprioceptive system which regulates our homeostatic relationship to the cosmos.

Once you have this image firmly in mind, it is much easier to imagine moving back and forth with these intervals or space and time waves, like the runner Rayser moving around each competitor in the 800-sprint moving within their separate time zones. In the above clockwork illustration, we can easily see then, that each frequency moves along on its own momentum or amplitude governed by its periodicity or relative velocity. Time viewed this way appear as cycles within cycles containing pattern data or order, quite similar to the galactic clusters within clusters or the Matryoshka doll analogy. Here one space-time is nested within another all governed by the spiral template, like the hard drive in a computer which provides the governor by which order comes about. The governor is the ruling template or proxy pattern from which all other patterns of order are cut.

Therefore, all the other patterns emanate in the way they are initially structured and the order by which they unfold according to the curve of the wave, or interval nested within a given pattern. Intervals bifurcate then according to an inherent pattern of order provided by the spiral template much like a pulsating light that blinks off and on at given intervals. These intervals reflect rhythms of perception that correspond to states of consciousness, i.e. brain wave patterns. I bring your attention back to the original spiral model to let you know that, like a caring parent, the template is built in to your system to guide and direct you. It does this by automatically sending signals at precise bifurcation points where converging space and time merge into new order.

Thus, there are obvious cues that take place when one nears a bifurcation point, such as a general energy change. A general energy change may and often does include a stillness that is unusual, fog, a feeling of anxiety, sometimes depression, a feeling of foreboding as if something unsettling is about to take place. One may suddenly hear loud explosions, bird calls that are startling, voices, be seized by trembling or panic, fear of moving forward, strange odors like ozone, see something at or near to peripheral vision like a wing or movement that sends off an alarm. Going forward one may even encounter a deep sense of familiarity, as if they know right where they are going and why.

As I have mentioned, intervals of order and the cues that accompany them are, for the most part arbitrary, meaning they may follow a general or even 'familiar' structure, just as we instantly recognize the correct protruding edges of a puzzle piece, sense that it will fit perfectly and none other. The same sense of presence, shall we say, or *knowing* often accompanies predilections that are about to take place. In giving readings the sense of sureness or what we call a 'positive' feeling reinforces the realization that not only something integral is taking place in this shift of time, but that it fits a pattern.

One example that comes to mind is once I went to the horse races with twenty dollars to make some wagers. Sure it wasn't much money for placing bets, but the conservative investment was the limit of my wager on things of this nature, with the intent that the less I took with me, the better my chances of following the right 'hunches' and placing the best bets. As was my habit when gambling on horses, I bet on the stable and the jockey, for the most part, and the horse last, knowing that a good rider would be placed on the best horses, and so on. As the races went on I won and lost over three hundred dollars off that initial twenty dollar bill and finally coming down the final race and only six dollars left, I called my wife and told her to come and get me, that it was time to throw in the towel. Going back to the viewing screen to watch the final race, I got interested in a Trifecta because, when reading about the stable and jockey I got a strong rush of excitement that filled me with elation. It was telling me to put my remaining money on that race. By the time my wife arrived to pick me up I was standing at the ticket office with 350 dollars in my hand. I had followed the energy and won. Turned out it was exactly the balance we needed our rent.

Thus, manipulating time waves begins by learning how to contract and expand perspective, which we have described. It is also about recognizing changing reference frames and switching your awareness from one increment of time to another. Switching awareness enhances your availability to wider panorama of choices. This can be achieved by fine-tuning your intuitive discernment to hone into anticipative cues. Anticipative cues are guided by that inner sensor guiding your target arrow into a specific future. Following the hardwired organizational foundation of the spiral template, it draws from an infinite number of probable choices, (time intervals) reducing them down to one specific path. Learning to trust your inner guidance system, you will not err in your course regardless of how small the size of your snowball of choice or its course down the destination mountain, accelerating as its moves swiftly to its destined target. Your inner sensor is a vital part of a healthy perspective and is guided to the exact interval of time you choose. The greater whole outside from which this information is derived drives this process by a connectedness requiring a total trusting investment in the processes bequeathed to us by the spiral template.

As you expand your parameter of receptivity you automatically become more aware of a wider range of frequency choices. It's like choosing from a much larger banquet of probable futures rather than from the one you think is straight ahead. Your frequency rate attracts the time interval. This is important because it means that your brain waves are acclimating to specified patterns of order reflective of the frequency of the wave pattern feedback within your memories. Memories are information pads situated in neurological frameworks that are receptive to certain frequency time intervals. Hence, you find yourself attracted to certain frequency environments. Examples of attraction to frequency environments are your friends or associates, the area of town you live in, your choices in moving to a specific area of the country, educational preferences or the lack thereof, and so on.

Therefore, it is vital for you to recognize your frequency attractions, if you wish to reconsider your path in life and achieve your goals with the least energy dissipation and maximum focus. To begin you must learn to recognize your attractions, they represent your frequency perspective. Your sensors of direction are keyed into these frameworks and what you see in your future is unconsciously pulling you toward the future with or without your awareness. The function of a direction sensor could be compared to a gunnery sergeant on a howitzer range firing shells toward targets far off in the distance they cannot see. The howitzer is guided by a computer hardwired to make automatic adjustments to a moving target scanned by a radar determining the speed of the object. If the calculations are accurate, he fires just ahead to hit bull's eye. Guided by this automatic system, the sergeant must trust that its accuracy is finely tuned to hit an invisible target miles away in the future.

In much the same way as the automatic adjustments to a moving target in a probably future, a person makes constant readjustments to hit a target not visible in the present that exists somewhere in a probable future. To hit the target, one relies on the frequency of their subjective perception, knowing at some level far outside the range of their conscious mind exists a co-frequency target in the future. What is even more tedious about targets of time is that if one were to depend upon consciousness alone to hit the target, by the time they made the necessary adjustments the anticipated target would already have moved outside their range. Thus, the probability of making plans in the present, which quickly becomes the past, is highly improbable without relying upon a process that automatically makes adjustments in frequency in the past for changes that may be occurring in a probable future.

What is truly frustrating for the individual without consciousness of this principle the future target will never be hit unless the individual recognizes the fact that frequency creates the rate of acceleration which controls linear time. Frequency patterns can and do constantly change. Because one's subjective frequency creates the future it is imperative that you make a sincere effort to become acquainted with a) your self-image patterns, b) the frequency patterns of your subjective islands of time, c) your expectations. Getting in touch with these patterns and recognizing which frequencies you're creating and why, gives you control over your anticipated materializations in successfully reaching that probable future you're shooting for. If you haven't made an effort to gain control of optical lensing in your creativity focal point, you may simply be pulling in realities that are the net result of habitually lazy habits of introspection. It is time to improve your focal awareness.

Your Focal IQ

Research demonstrates that as little as 200 milligrams of coffee can accelerate focal awareness, proving that the frequency or speed of FIQ (focal IQ) is the rate or velocity at which your consciousness operates in response to a) your habitual patterns of focus, and b) adjusting to changes in your proprioceptive flow with data arriving from your environment, c) your willingness to adapt and change. To improve your Focal IQ you need to practice Perspective Targeting. Perspective Targeting requires quick responses, so be on your psychological toes. Allow yourself plenty of room to be honest about what you feel, and additionally, be willing to make adjustments to change where it is necessary.

Like the spontaneous focus I gained by playing the *Zen of Basketball*, increasing your focal IQ requires repetitive practice such as checking out your inner ambitions and beliefs, then aiming and directing your focus with as little hesitation time as possible and firing away toward that invisible target in the future. Actually, to be totally clear, the target in the future is the frequency model in your memory. If you're aware of your subjective model then the problem of firing away at an invisible target isn't half as difficult, mainly because you know right where it's at, i.e., it's in your self-image – if you know where that's at; if not, you better get familiar with who you are.

Gaining insight in this way rapidly up's your frequency game, so that you quickly become an expert in sensing modulating adjustments between your own subjective frequencies, incoming data and that moving target somewhere in your future. When you do, it's all about responding attentively to the incoming data, sensing self, knowing the direction and following through as if the process were one complete Whole from beginning to end. Your ability to know a) what, where and why your target is at, b) to make rapid adjustments to changes between the point of the present and the future, and c) to fire spontaneously toward that somewhat invisible destination in the future. When you act spontaneously in these three steps you let that predestination snowball or FIQ, ascend to a marksman level. Reaching that level predetermines the rate of your ability to succeed in an impressively reduced time. When you reach this level there is a maximum reduction of entropy or energy lost with a minimum amount of effort. Reducing the focal aiming time unerringly locks you into that precise arch which connects you between present and future islands of time. In this way you rise to the highest degree of accuracy needed for that predictive future snowball to gain optimum magnification to manifest. Once holistically focused and released properly, the exponential momentum needed to produce optimum results is easily achieved.

Focal IQ equates to sharpened awareness of the observer's subjective mindset, coupled with the ability to sense increments of time. Looked at in terms of our frames of reference, examine this amusing but significant comment by the master of perspective, Albert Einstein. He once quipped, *"If you want to understand relativity, it is like the difference between sitting down next to a pretty girl and experiencing an hour as though it were a couple minutes, or sitting on a hot stove for a few minutes and thinking it was an hour."* The insight gained from this analogy is quite provocative because it illustrates that the rate of acceleration of the observer is directly proportional to the perception of the event. Looking more deeply into this realization we understand that what Einstein implied was quite in line with our contractive/expansive lens concept. From that we can conclude that expansion or contraction of our experience with time is proportional to our FOCAL IQ. Put simply: energy is either conserved or dissipated *in the interval* between observing and hitting our target. Our expenditure, therefore, is proportional to the degree of our focal lensing. Control the interval and you control the dissipation of energy and enhance the probability of hitting a constantly changing future target.

Applied to perception, it is easy to see that *'slips into and out of time'* is actually a byproduct of our framework of reference. It takes frequency pattern consciousness or focal guidance to hit time-traveling targets. The curvature in space between present and future is a result of the amplification/frequency of the wave compounded by subjective interest and response. Are you on the ball, adaptable to change and sensitive to your subjective frequency state? If so, by this definition, focus and interest are synonymous. Please be aware that order arises from the duration of a frequency pattern and the promptness of our response. Seen holistically, order reflects the gestalt of interference waves shared by both observer and that which is observed. If a person finds that they are experiencing serious amounts of missing time, as when a person passes through a topographical time zone in an hour and but experiences only minutes, then there is a good chance their perception was clouded by unconscious brain wave frequencies specifically designed by the self to obscure their awareness.

In summation, learning to change your patterns of focus is the key to maximum energy conservation and maximum bull's eye target hitting. Be sure to make careful note to your awareness of changing time zones. Be hyper-vigilant in following cues that activate awareness. Cues come in the form of psychic prompts, namely because they arise spontaneously from outside the censorship of your conscious mind. Because this is true, they will come to you in the form of premonitory insights, hypnogogic data, déjà vu's, dreaming and so on. They will also often arrive via alpha waves which is those just outside the beta flow afflicting our attention to our everyday flow.

MEDITATIONS

1. Make a habit of noticing what kind of events, people, lifestyles and situations you re drawn toward. Also notice what kinds repulse you, because in these two extremes you will discover a lot about your own negative-positive frequency fields.
2. Vibration isn't just another exotic New Age term, it says a lot about the state of mind of people, the field you're encountering, or the outcome you can expect from a situation.
3. Remember that you are a frequency field moving into or out of surrounding fields. How you 'vibe' with your surroundings tells a lot about how you see yourself and into what circumstances you will most likely find yourself drawn.
4. Learn to recognize and trust your intuitive powers, that's the almost 'common sense' part of yourself that tells whether to stay or to go when you find yourself in what could be the wrong side of town.
5. Make a list of how accurate your intuition was in telling you what to do and how you responded to it.
6. Find a quiet place and lie down. Study the state of your own mind. Is it quiet and relaxed? Do you feel anxious and emotional? Why?
7. Make a habit of seeking to calm yourself by taking deep, rhythmic breaths and watching how as you do what goes on in your mind.

8. Seek to know your course in life. What is your timeline like? Where is it going? Are you satisfied with it and if not, would you like to change it?
9. Imagine yourself changing your life course. See yourself rearranging the timeline. Insert any kind of potential scenario in the outcome.
10. Make a conscious habit of speeding up or slowing down your vibrations. Then totally calm them. Note what kind of thoughts, impressions or events take place either within your mind's eye or nearby in the so-called real world. You are at the initial stages of practical time traveling.

10

TIME TRAVEL TO CHANGE YOUR REALITY

"The only reason for time is so everything doesn't happen at once." Albert Einstein

Perceptual Frequencies and Time

Let us review for a moment: If you recall, we arrived at the conclusion that all-that-is chose a template or pattern for establishing biogenic order from an infinite number of probable patterns. The template furnished a cookie cutter pattern from which all order was generated. Hence, even though the components of order are changed, the template itself remains the same. The reason this is possible is because the spiral template is like the hard wiring in a computer – it sets a prerequisite for the software programs that can be used on the computer. For instance, you can't use Microsoft software in a Macintosh computer because the programs contain different algorithmic patterns. Algorithmic patterns are encodes, an encrypted language usable only by certain programs. Try talking Russian to a Spanish speaking person and the words sound like gobbly- gook –

nonsensical, meaningless prattle. Lack of comprehension of the language which conveys the collective symbols in cryptic frequency patterns effectively blocks receptivity and communication. In a similar manner the underlying template sets the pattern or encode for basic order in the 3rd dimension. In other words, it has created a data language for directing the process of organization throughout the physical universe. It is from this inbuilt template for order that all the energy flowing into the physical world finds a channel. Thus, the template serves as a pattern for channeling energy flowing into the 3rd dimension; and I might also mention, it acts as a border for energy flowing 'out' of the physical world as through entropic dissipation.

A simple visualization for comprehending energy flowing from the 4th dimension into the 3rd dimension is to imagine a stream made up of droplets of water. Think of the droplets of water (4th dimension) as individual frequency patterns. See them being channeled by a river's bed (the spiral template) into the 3rd dimension; i.e., the river. If you were to suddenly blow up the channel of the river, for instance, all the water molecules would cease to exist as a directed flow. In short, the whole-forming ability of the river bed would disappear and in place of it would be innumerous separate or isolated water puddles filled with innumerous molecules. Without a channel and/or pattern to direct their flow, there wouldn't be the Whole known as a river, nor would there be any order we call the 3rd dimension. All you would be left with is innumerous, free-floating islands or time without a central organizational force to direct their flow. That's what the spiral template does – it directs the flow of information or islands of space-time, incremental frequency patterns representing separate phase periodicities.

Periodicities are rhythmic increments of 'wild' time. Wild time is like domestic animals without an owner or a field. They are free roaming, almost like rogue lions. Rogue lions are single males that want to be a part of a pride but lack solidarity with a group. So they roam around trying to interlope on a pride when the dominant male is away, sleeping, sick, weak or aged; if they are lucky they take over. In the similar manner wild time is time without order, without a direction, plan or purpose. It can contain incremental periods from given 3-d time, but without a specific connection to a given flow or arrow of time. In other words, they are like the molecules of water without a channel. Waves with patterns are organized, meaning they have a purpose and a direction hence they can be called channeled or 'in-phase.'

Patterns are in-phase waves within waves, meaning they are connected or interlocked like pieces of a puzzle that form a picture. Each in-phase piece reflects a state of focus connected to a generalized Whole or over-arching pattern. In terms of order, a period of time is a specific number of cycles within a given interval. The more intense the focus, the greater are the number of revolutions or cycles within each incremental focal period. Brain waves oscillate at varying frequencies; thus, they have variable access to corresponding increments of time-space, meaning they both fit into a given Whole. Again, think of the puzzle with pieces that interlock together to form a picture.

Because brain waves for each individual can oscillate at different frequencies, either slower or faster cycles, the way that they phase-into certain periods (pictures) of time can vary. So when a person tells you they *walked into or saw* another period of time from say, the 15th century, what they mean is they phased into a given wave (resonated) unique to their brain frequencies, which was more than likely, not the whole century. However, some people can become locked (temporarily) into longer periods, depending on their brain wave or vibrational response to patterns. Longer, wider, broader amplitude waves can contain shorter, faster frequency waves within abundantly rich in varying increments of time. To the converse, some can simply be restricted to slower, broader periods of time, without the necessary detail as shorter, faster waves. Thus, with greater amplitude detail is often excluded while with the shorter wave greater detail is possible but with shorter increments of time. For instance, one second of time compared to one minute, or one minute to an hour and so. Change the CPS (cycles per second) and you automatically change accessibility to varying increments of time because in truth all time exists in increments, whether shorter or longer depends upon the periodicity of the patterns, that is, CPS per second. The shorter the wave or faster the CPS, the greater the curvature and therefore, the stronger the clustering capacity

Beta waves (and gamma) contain the greatest cycles per second (7-14 CPS) and rule the outer consciousness that orient us in the 3rd dimensional plane where the fabled increment of the 'present' is said to reside. Perhaps the greater frequencies affect the formation of matter at a quantum level, because the well-known 'observation principle' is at the heart of materialization. It is a natural lens component of focus which involves expansion and contraction of space-time. In terms of spherical space, increments such as past-present-future do not exist per se, and if they do they include much greater periods of time and space. Hence the more beta waves the greater is your immediate focal consciousness in a 3rd dimensional or 'linear' flat plane. Two dimensional planes are best illustrated in Euclidian geometry by a piece of paper – pretty much dimensionless except for length and width. All of Isaac Newton's physics were based on flat plane analysis, whereas Einstein's view of reality was totally hyperboloid or spherical. In such a world the term perspective has totally different connotations than in the Euclidian. For example, in Euclidian geometry distance would be divided into incremental periods representing points on a straight line between the past and the so-called future. In Riemannian math a hyperboloid is a perspective from the vantage point of a sphere. In such a reality object normally separated by distance or have a future and past would tend to merge do its curving structure. Therefore, to make things easy to comprehend, think of the hyperboloid perspectives as four dimensional and Euclidian as two or if you choose, three-dimensional. See the difference? Time viewed this way is all a matter of angular perspective. That's the essence of Special Relativity.

Now, the greater the frequency the less you see because the higher frequencies limit our perspective to the two-dimensional plane. They are the CPS of brain waves in the beta range. Thus, we are back to our problem with wave amplitude and frequency where our view is diminished by the CPS. For example, if an individual has little memory of an event such as the transition from one time zone into another, then there is a greater chance that the brain waves employed in the perception of those increments of time were not those needed to view the interval. Therefore, it would behoove you to become acquainted with the description of waves emanating from a flat plane time.

In other words, time slips represent alterations in perspective and perspective equal's focus; the more memory loss the greater the chance of missing time. Regardless of your attempts, by the way, to memorize every detail, some things will be lost, at least temporarily until you move to a deeper level where their significance is united into a more meaningful field. Focus is a great quality to develop, yet it tends, like concentration to increase your perceptual attentiveness to specific detail and thereby obfuscating your awareness to things transpiring outside the sphere of your attention. Remember: attention is a curvature in the field. Thus everything which has like resonance is attracted to its bend in space-time, isolating some details and eliminating others. When these details are obfuscated or blotted out, we experience an attention deficit, meaning many blanks spots exist in the detail. Thus, within every field there are many empty spaces, whether we are aware of it or not, where there are time slips occuring without notice. Research on the brain using CAT scans has revealed that people who have done a lot of drugs, drinking, and suffered from different neurological disorders, have large holes in the lobes of their brain. When that occurs, whole sections of the brain instrumental in bringing clear pictures/frequency patterns together are minus pieces in the puzzle of perception. Such individuals lack holistic trans-ception centers for decoding neurological data; hence, they miss much of the detail and sometimes the entire picture. On an up-side, (and this may sound puzzling) we don't need the brain specifically to perceive, but it does serve as an information central related to details concerning the physical world.

As an example, we leave our body and take psychic journeys to the far reaches of the Holoverse and most of the time this occurs without us being wholly conscious. Such journeys are often labeled OOBe's, (out-of-body travel. NDEs, (near death experiences) are sudden awakenings to the reality that we don't need the brain to perceive since many people have watched their own operations, or been cognizant during intense bi-locations in meditative states. But as to decoding data related to functioning in the flat plane, deeper coherence or conjugation with converging time streams is needed to avoid the negative effects of sudden time slips or blocks and the problems of time barriers with a decrease of *energy, irritability, disorientation*. These three elements 'EID's', (energy, irritability, disorientation) are the results of the inability to maintain stability while converging or diverging from energy streams. In short, such occurrences reflect energy blocks or resistance in the organism to abrupt time alterations. Keep these signs in mind if you find yourself experiencing one or all of these symptoms; you could have just passed through a time zone, an alteration of consciousness, or an actual time slip.

When there is an exchange of energy from one state or frequency to another that swiftly takes place, little will be consciously noticed, except perhaps one or all of the foregoing signs. To correct the balance between incoming and actual perceived order, requires speeding up the relative perceptual frequency. Speeding it up, as you recall orients your concentration or focus of 2nd and 3rd dimensional space. Changes in time awareness then is related to two things, a) the brain wave frequency experienced by the observer whether conscious or unconscious when they pass through a time portal or zone, and b) the frequency of the time zone encountered. Continuously flowing alpha, theta, and delta waves operating at slower, broader frequencies could possibly act as an amplitude boundary for assembling varying time zones into clusters.

Hypothetically, this could possibly explain journeys into other time periods during altered or sleep states. Dream time travel occurs almost nightly, since most of the dreams you have are transitions into other dimensions or into the future or past. The freedom of unbridled traveling in dreams occurs because the conscious ego is relatively subdued. If and when you do become conscious (or even wake up) during time travel in dreams, the texture and quality of the experience is modified by your psyche in line with everyday reality. In place of the actual experience of time travel, for instance, symbols that you can relate to readily are exchanged for actual journeys. The mind does this quick shift spontaneously as part of the 3rd dimensional charade.

However, not all dream journeys fade automatically. Some people adapt to them and consciously become involved in the energy exchanges, especially those who have done a lot of consciousness expansion, meditation or introspective work over a long period of time. Sometimes conscious dream journeys and intra-dimensional information exchanges continue during more than one life; which by the way can be many, many lives as we constantly bifurcate into alternate universes of being.

Frankly, knowing what it is you perceived tells everything about the way or manner you perceived it, or your 'state' of mind. If the frequency between your brain waves and the time zones conjugates or match up, the transition will be smooth and effortless. However, should the subjective frequency of the would-be observer be grossly out-of-sync, then the observer could run into some adjustment problems, not to mention disorienting time slip readjustments.

Thus, the ideal subjective state for an observer, in any case, is learning to achieve frequency flexibility while changing brain wave states. If this is achieved then free access and awareness to multiple time streams is highly possible. Actually, individuals who are short on patience with people or situations, energy, receptivity to scheduling changes, adjusting to patterns of any sorts, suffer from rigid frequency pattern syndrome which the inability to change frequencies readily. Breathing meditation is helpful. Adopt the peaceful mantra of chanting - let go and let flow. Afflicted individuals should also avoid stimulants such as caffeine, uppers of any kind such as white sugar, downers, pot, cigarettes; things that affect or stimulate their cortico-steroid cycle. To avoid the pitfalls of unexpected irritation due to time lapse adjustment syndrome and its side-effects, make a habit of maintaining a serene mental state.

Data Molecules and Time Streams

In reality we run into frequency changes all every day as we transition from one time zone to another, and I don't mean zones in terms of major time zones such as encounter when we fly or accelerate suddenly. Instead, in this case, I'm referring to the zones or intervals between emotional or highly energetic personal scenes, so to speak. During those increments you are actually slipping into or out of frequency intervals. They are a form of data molecule or a time streams. Think of diving into a stream as you walk across a field and getting out on the other side. The stream only takes up a given increment space, but during the moment that you spend in it, everything is different. Another example is the analogy I've given you of life as a series of separately filmed intervals connected by a pattern of wholeness, like a movie, comparable to the order-inducing whole of the spiral principle. Without the spirals pattern of wholeness to arrange the intervals into a matrix, you would experience slips in time like those people who suddenly find themselves in another day and age and possibly stay locked into it. The spiral pattern pulls you out because it furnishes an order-generating barrier that surrounds those stray data molecules, or rogue frequency patterns, enclosing them within a given boundary.

For the most, people who have had sudden psychic bursts into alternate space and time - rarely if ever remain there, because in truth, they don't experience the entire actual century, more than likely they only encounter periods encapsulating specific events. Entries into these alternate streams follow frequency changes going on within the brains or in the surroundings whether remembered or not by the individual who perceives these other times. Like an episode in a television series, they are just getting peeks into select sequences stitched together by resonance that comprise short vignettes, subjective movies of that era that resonate to their personal frequency. They might stay like that for a given period of time; as long as the resonance occurs, then slip out. It's something like getting a sudden audio tone that is different in your ear or a visual glimpse from a different angle, or a vague sense of something that you don't fully perceive. Hypnogogic states are temporary attunements to altered brain wave states. In these eerie halves conscious dreams, a person is temporarily in sync with an alternate time zone. Therefore, they might see objects or identify people perhaps they've seen before, but upon wakening fail to recall clearly who it was or where they were. Thus these events, tonal fade-outs or fade-ins, get relegated to the realm of odd experiences or fuzzy-brained fantasies. Without the convergence properties of the spiral to create order, you would be encountering segments/incremental events without the linkage of memory to identity time and place.

Following the channel that the template dictates, the spiral automatically governs the propagation of frequency intervals into a meaningful pattern of order. To visualize this process, go back to our example of the stream found in chapter one. The template is the rivers channel that directs the disparate molecules of water, each singular, isolated droplets, complete unto themselves, into the mold of the spiral. Until the template organizes the isolated molecules of water droplets into a concentrated stream, each conjugating into the puzzle of the flowing stream, they remain independent and chaotic. Once under the controlling channel of the template, they fall together and form one coherent Whole image like water flowing in a river bed.

In a like manner time exists in isolated increments of space, somewhat like molecules in the same sense as an ocean is formed by billions of separate drops of water. Under the organizational emergence of neurological order, dictated by the underlying spiral pattern, the independent intervals replete with packets of information are drawn together into a stream of sequential order known as the arrow of time. Looking at this picture from an outside perspective, it is clear that without the organizational pattern of the spiral to create the arrangement of these isolated molecules of time-space into a coherent stream, they would simply bounce around in the chaos of the 4th dimension. It is the subjectivity of individual perspective that sends out the wave that corresponds in terms of synchrony with the probable linear line of order that makes meaningful Wholes of disparate Parts. What we see is waves within waves with waves.

Thus, when our ever alert proprioceptive system sends out waves it encounters waves coming from each disparate molecule (bit of information) existing in light packets, quanta, and spontaneously (in accordance with the organisms subjective needs to adapt to a changing environment) creates the order of direction we call the arrow of time. It is from these data streams that we receive orders that are translated by the DNA into responsive traits, patterns of behavior, that help us to evolve, i.e., intelligently adjust to the dictates of the planet and cosmos in general.

Revisit the Past and Side-Step Hindsight

You can revisit the past and when you do it changes things in the present. As I have mentioned, reality is malleable, change any Part of it and you change the Whole of its manifestation. The Whole is a network of interactive players all contributing to the harmonious unity of the matrix in which they are a part. You cannot shift any aspect of it, without causing a ripple or wave to travel out and reverberate throughout its core. Going back to revisit past situations, as we have discovered, is an illusion created by the way we view the present, yet it is a viable journey that has its effects upon the present. Think on it and you change something of its structure. You are your memories and adding or subtracting by the infusion of new ideas, feelings or impressions has its long-range effects...

Change the present and you change the past. The same thing applies to the future – sending energy into your so-called future-planning regardless of how far ahead you may look, automatically alters not only the structure of your goals in terms of the future target but the structure of your present as well and your relationship to any past associations. Thus, envisioning the Whole can bear enormously prodigious fruits because the matrix is interactive. It is the net sum of all the linked parts that make up your creative vision. With you at the helm of these visions, like a captain at sea aboard his ship traveling through the chaos of a tempest, you are directing your energy into the far corners of the matrix, following the wave that travels out from your hub. That wave is constantly reverberating, coming back to you, like children you have given birth to but forgotten bearing data you sent with them. Somewhere in space and time they return retaining vestiges of the 'you' that sent them and something more – they whole of what they have learned and/or accumulated in their spiral travels throughout the Holoverse. What they bring back affects you and what you learn through the assimilation and correlations of their synchrony constantly alters, intensifies and builds the snowball of associations leading to that virtual target somewhere in that virtual future.

Therefore, for the emergence of any one production, such as the manifestation of a project you might designate as a future target goal – the collective gestalt of that creative endeavor is the net whole of many participating players in the grand symphony called reality. What is most fascinating about that creation is much of its manifestation takes place from levels of subtle energy that is far outside the spectrum of your ken.

Hence, before we bring this book to a close, let us contemplate the importance of the contributory participation of all the players into the production of any future, past and present-oriented event. We will broach that subject by firstly interjecting interesting data related to the chaos factor. Bear in mind that when I use the term "chaos factor" in this section on time increments and travel, I am referring to the infinite time-space increments available in the continuum. Think of these random or free-floating increments of time-space (phase chaos-factors) by using the analogy of many separate individuals on a highway driving each at their own speed. As long as they all continue at their individual pace in an independent and comparatively disorganized way, there is little if no synchrony or order to their movement. But, according to chaos theory, if and when they suddenly began to all assume a uniform speed where they move as a group, we witness the emergence of sudden self-organization.

From our position in the pack, we cannot see where or why the pattern arose. IN other words, we are not privy from our angle or perspective of what triggered the sudden assemblage into meaningful order. To understand its origins we must rise to the position of an outside observer and when we do, the spark that triggered random movement to converge into order can be seen. What is most interesting about this self-organizing behavior is that it is like the collective movement of a swarm of bees, a school of fish, herds of cattle or a flock of birds. When they suddenly get up and move away as a group, fly, swim, walk - whatever their means of locomotion, they all suddenly converge and begin to move as a concerted force toward a central objective.

In other words, they snowball one-by-one toward a *predetermined*, collective destination. As they do they seem to follow the cues transmitted by waves to their senses, since there is no pheromone trail here to sniff out. Water molecules tend to do the same thing as a group when they flow under the guidance of a bed or channel/template as a river or stream. They are forced, as it were, by the presence of an unseen barrier, perhaps outside their perspective which forces them to converge together and merge. Remove the channel and the river disperses into myriads of individual droplets. Of course, even a droplet is a cluster of water molecules, so in that regards, the clustering affect is well underway that enlarges the bend in the space-time field which in turn induces mega- clustering that we in the macro tend to think of as *self-organizing* or *emergent behavior*.

What most people see is the stage of order that is closer to rain or the droplet state before it becomes a river. It's difficult to separate the states into stages of what is thought of as 'order or disorder.' A droplet is a whole bunch of molecules, just as a molecule is a whole bunch of atoms. Put a bunch of droplets together and you got a puddle, put a group of puddles together and you have a pond, lake, or if they have a central channel, they become a river. Keep this always foremost in mind: there isn't any distinct state of order or disorder, only *variable* states. Perhaps this is the reason that physics tends to describe a 'state' as a variable, meaning relative order on its way to becoming…. A great word for describing states is virtual, to indicate not order or disorder but something in-between. During these in-between stages/states there is a repositioning process going on as clusters change their order.

Returning to our flying friends on wing, the flock or herd, etc. is constantly in a virtual state of order and disorder, in other words, they are in a veritable state. The reason this is so is close examination tells us that there is a constant exchange of places between front runners and those further back in the group. What is taking place is the position of leadership is constantly being reordered so that in the end nearly every member has become a participating part, rather than just a number in the crowd. In that sense each one gets an opportunity to participate in the positioning of the group, i.e. the way that it assembles into time-space order.

Perhaps in a far-out sense, consciousness is like that – meaning that comparative positioning in the ordering of Wholes and Parts may play a big role. For instance, mega-clusters, like rivers and flocks and species with complex neuronal structures may get a 'feel' for being more awake or aware by this constant re-ordering. Compared to the positioning on the birds and bees in flight, changing positions changes the angle of awareness, hence, perception of where we are at in the scheme of things changes. What has changed most visibly is the relative phase or frequency factor, which perhaps gives us our sense of positioning in terms of 'time' in the line of order.

Here again we see a phenomenon which is arranged like a tonal or frequency pattern. Think back on the cymatics frequency patterns we talked about before in this book. Each pattern depicts a given tone, beat or rhythm. When the tone or beat is changed, the structure of the pattern is altered which in turn reflects the change in the frequency. Thus if the tone or frequency is constantly changed the pattern that emerges may appear to stick pretty much to the original order, but subtle variations arise from the introduction of the individual qualities of the new leaders as well as the convergence of the original leader into the group which rearranges the appearance of the Whole. Not only do these variations in leadership and position allow for renewal of energy at different energy crisis points, they break the collective pattern while vital processes are able to arise. At the crisis points, for example, where the need to change position suddenly arises, various biochemical reactions in individual participants demands a repositioning in pace, a respite if you will without which, the collective group would suffer in getting to their target destination. In other words, the collective health of the groups emerging and (let us not forget) submerging and re-emerging order would fail. Seen as a whole, the group, flock, school, herd, pack, etc, appears to interact and move in concert in a homeo-dynamic way with the Whole and with the environment at hand. Such adjustments are the group's way of transmitting and exchanging information in the group. Just as many of the cars that suddenly converge into a single group on the highway cannot see the road ahead, they get the 'message' that a convergence is crucial at this specific point, which can be compared to a crisis.

Thus, the reassembling of the group order is vital for the regeneration or safety of the Whole. It is also vital for its sustainability, which like any organic, viable creature, thrives on constantly restructuring and reviving its order to accommodate the demands of the changing Whole. So, we think of ourselves as individuals when we are, first of all, a cluster of independent, but collectively motivated cells, now all symbiotically working together. That group of cells makes up the individual, which is the first barrier or boundary to come together. That group of random but collectively ordered cells must than emerge as a cluster who act as a group by overcoming the boundaries in their own psycho-physical composition. This means, there is a 'taking charge' process going on which could be described as a self-re-ordering convergence. Subsequently, on a secondary level, the individual begins to move toward a collective participation with some specific group. These emergences from point to point or from order into ongoing order are bifurcations at crises points. That's when we change our lifestyle, which may seem suddenly but has been a much longer time in the making. This is an ongoing process, or one that continues to escalate into larger clusters.

At the social apex of collective order another bifurcation takes place. This one is the *crisis point* that leads to the social bifurcation or branching as everyone begins to move concertedly as a whole toward a group destination. Like the crisis in Egypt, the Ukraine or among gay people et al; people who en route move concertedly as a group. Diversity with a collective aim is the key here, and order that does not bifurcate but is stymied, blocked or detoured is energetically entropic. Therefore, emergence and re-ordering acts as a channel through which energy gathering below the surface, like the vortex, can rise to the surface and find expression. In short, bifurcating is another way of preserving order despite diversity by creating another organism whether social, economic, psychological or physical. We bifurcate or change into complex organisms while maintaining the integrity of the Whole, just as clustering in the galaxies is another way of maintaining the Whole while undergoing change. As far as the well-being and longevity of the group is concerned, 'changing synchrony' and or adjusting, synchronizing, melding into the whole, allows you to fit in with the group and adds to its collective well-being through diversity as well as your own.

Neurologically, the brain is always undergoing wave pattern alterations, particularly striking when we fall off to sleep. During this change or bifurcation from beta to alpha and on into theta, the transitions are marked by rearrangements in the order of the patterns. Have you ever had the sensation when nodding off to sleep of suddenly jerking awake? That's your inner radar telling you that you're bifurcating or slipping into a deeper stage of sleep. It's alerting you to the change in pattern. By learning to follow your brain wave patterns, that is, noting when you feel a change in a) interior imagery from common images to strange associations and fantasy-like patterns, or b) a feeling of being 'hooked up' to a greater network, you can actually discern when you are undergoing alterations. These are actually the clustering of waves within waves, and represent patterns of order that take you in or out of the body cosmos into greater wholes that can include yourself among groups of other selves existing as wave patterns. During in-between cluster states you are moving into greater patterns or possibly lesser patterns of order, depending on the nature of the changes, as you move back and forth in space-time. I experience these shifts between clusters all the time, particularly during meditative or breath-controlled states of lucid consciousness sleep. Awareness of these states doesn't always imply control because the mechanics of mind-wave phases are tricky. Try to force them and you'll find yourself awakening and losing control. The timing and interaction with them has to come with subtlety and skill, which takes practice.

What is going on inside goes on outside in 'so-called real time' where the awareness of the shifts is less obvious because of the gross veneer of time under causal effects and the radar monitoring feedback of beta. Let us say, that the cortex is doing a very effective job, hand-in-hand with the screening of the sensory data to promote the most 'distorted' picture of true reality that it can. This is to keep you oriented, like a boat on a stormy ocean, otherwise you'd become disoriented and find yourself unable to distinguish the so-called 'real' from the 'unreal' in your everyday life. In this way the individual moves through the miasma of the 'present' reality with the feeling that they are in charge or aware, following the signs like a car merging or de-verging at the forks in the road at the 'proper' detour points. What is going on here is that we are actually moving in and out of wave states, clusters within clusters as we exchange energy and move individually and simultaneously collectively toward our target goals.

So, we see that everyone exchanges or suspends individual goals for group goals, which occur at crisis points, marking alterations in consciousness and divergent frequency patterns. As participants in a group movement these changes appear to occur at spur of the moment demands to gather into greater clusters, but you/they aren't. Like cars moving down the highway, you/they are merely responding to information exchanged in the electro-magnetic quanta patterns. Seen in terms of information transfer, the demands of the ever-changing Whole transmit and receive data arriving from waves that are constantly merging and diverging from internal to external environment. In this way the inner or microcosm and the outer, or macrocosm maintain a homeo-static equilibrium that is mutually complementary.

Seen in terms of harmonics, the exchange of information could be viewed as a tonal adjustment between in the inner rhythms of the microcosm and outer rhythms of the world. Therefore, my use of chaos as an analogy should be seen as a harmonic guide for adjusting the focus of a given orientation toward a virtual target destination shared somewhere within a hypothetical and ever-changing future. It's just like dialing into a television station and choosing among the myriad channels which show you want to watch, while everyone else continues to do their own thing, and the broadcasting still goes on despite the changes among each individual choices.

In another example it's like matching up the tones or adjusting the FM, i.e., frequency modulation of the hologram. It's an adjustment of the collective image that is vital for the reorientation between the hub of the spiral and its periphery. Imagine the undulations of a wave in the surface of water after throwing a stone or the ripples or undulations a chord being struck. These points signify information is being exchanged and during these trans-ceptions the Whole is changed as well as the Part. A useful example comes to mind of the new science of teleportation where researchers are discovering that it's not so much the physical elements that are going to be exchanged during the apports between points, its information. We come from information and we return to it. The template of the spiral that acts as the original negative-feedback governor is a channel between dimensions through which information is being exchanged.

With this imagery in mind, let us approach the importance of renewal in the revisiting of the Whole Self as we move along life's path. In the convergence that reflects the self-organization or emergence of the individual vehicles moving along the highway, what we see is a transmission of information of information from the periphery, those cars which first encounter the obstacle in its path. That information is transmitted to individual vehicles which automatically send it to others, and in minutes the Whole is notified of the changes up ahead that they cannot see, but sense by the changes in the vehicles ahead of them.

Looked at as a safety procedure of the group, its destination is insured by a reliance upon the response to information from each individual member in the process at different points in the transmission of the crisis. Hence, the collective drama plays out as the socio-economics between order and disorder. Here, order can be seen as spontaneous group planning based on reformation according to the flow of information, that is, the feedback between the foremost transmitters at the periphery of the crisis and the hub - those at the center. The hub or central portion of the spiral cluster must in turn transmit the data to those individuals making up the rear, who must adjust their speed accordingly. Thus the information flows or gyrates back and forth like a wave that in turn keeps the group ergonomically centered as individuals and as a group. In this view we see an economics established between the constant resonance or oscillation between Whole and Part that insures the longevity of every participant as well as the herd, flock or swarm. The same thing would apply to the worker and the corporation, society and the individual, country and citizen.

Effective spiral economics based on the transmission of information between order and disorder to maintain the viability of a system depends upon the interactions to data flow from islands, pockets, or zones of time at various points as it nears the edge of crisis and transformation. Timely responsiveness at these points can be seen as adding to the rate/frequency and hence the longevity of its collective momentum; giving it a boost. Because these increments of order represent pockets or zones of potential outside our perspective, they may, because of our flat plane perspective of *the present*, be considered points or intervals of time (resonances) far outside our sensory range. But the truth is, regardless of how far outside the sensory range, there is a level at which information flow back and forth between these zones and a system.

Information, then, is the transmission and reception of resonances from outside perceptual ranges, accessible during growth spurts, which we in turn translate into action. The front runners gather data from the boundary and transfer it to the group, which act on it. The group translates the data into synchronous resonation to maintain the well-being of the Whole. So, in terms of viability and well-being it is very important that you develop sensitivity to resonances from outside the scope of individual perspective. Blocking incoming data could leave you out of tune with the ongoing Whole. Working with resonances can be done through appreciation of the arts or music. This may involve listening to a variety of music so as to expand one's resonance IQ and thereby improve Focal IQ. Seen this way, the ability to respond and to focus are essential features in the reception and transmission of viable data which mutually inclusive to the Whole.

Resonances, as I have intimated, are island pockets of time existing in a 4th dimensional space where collective order has little if no meaning to the Whole, since this dimension is featureless but, paradoxically contains all probable orders. Again: the 4th dimension can be looked upon as an archive in which all probable time-spaces exist as ordered increments and as a Whole has no order in itself. The way meaningful alignment, in terms of increments of order or time comes about, is by way of these pockets fitting together at branches between dimensions, those crisis points where reality emerges creatively into meaningful new orders. Meaningful order is relative reconstruction of disorder or even poorly constructed order into new order. As such it is order as we see it evolve from cause-effect in the physical world. We do not see the Whole of the emergence process going on outside the periphery of our sensory range; hence we are not privy to pockets of time. Pockets, data molecules, increments of time hovering in the 4th dimensional probability state arise and converge from an infinite variety of probable future or pasts. How they fit into the schemata of order depends upon the creativity of the spontaneous composition in the improvisational work trans-ceived by its main composer WHO IS YOU.

I am purposely avoiding the terms past-present-future when I refer to these islands of time because, in reality, they exist outside of order and fit in, like pieces in a puzzle, as the shape of the resonance dictates. Time-space designations such as arbitrary points on the worldline deemed P-P-F are all relative frameworks. Recall that relative frameworks relate to perspective from a flat plane illustrated by Euclidian geometry on a linear line. In other words, they are timely increments aligned on a flat plane grid and as such merely represent the gross byproduct of individual perspective in the illusionary Maya of the physical plane.

A far better way of viewing islands of time and their relationship to creation of order, is striving to view them simply as time-space intervals, i.e., frequencies available from the 'Akashic' archive of the 4th dimension through the FM radio of the extra-sensory self. The Frequency Modulator tunes into a specific range of frequencies existing in the extra-dimensional Self hovering just outside the limiting focus of the present. The frequency transmissions received by our FM radio is a wide band allowing free access to a broad range of probable periods of order. Again: probable periods of order are like individual tunes, musical compositions or a string of chords in a score, but in this case convey a rhythm of time. The rhythm as a Whole designates a probable order and as such follows the directive of the spiral's template. The template, an organizational ditty in itself, acts as a whole-inducing parameter or barrier that prods order to assemble just as the molecules of time form main chords in the orchestration that you or the group composes around a central beat.

Practical Time Traveling

Actual time traveling for instance into the future can be really exciting as well as profitable. Just think how far ahead you'd be if you knew what was coming around the bend before you got there? For one thing you wouldn't be making a lot of the mistakes you made because you would know ahead of time what was coming up. On a creative or inventive level, you'd be able to gain creative glimpses into the future for ideas or devices that were coming down the linear timeline pike before anyone else thought of them. For example, in several personal dreams of time traveling into the future I actually saw devices that could be built, if I had the right knowledge or mechanical background, I needed to produce them. Like for instance, one day I saw a bicycle run by stream turbine. On another, I saw a levitation device that worked off of duel, spinning electro-magnets. Recently, I encountered an interesting contraption ridden like a bike that involved a vibrating plate instead of wheels pumped by a chain. The plate appeared to be covered with a unique kind of crystal that when activated by a simple battery caused the gravitational field in front of the device to be bent so that it could move without resistance. There are an infinite number of things that can prove valuable about traveling into the future – who knows you might even locate that special someone that is meant for you and be led directly to where he/she can be found in the physical plane. The fun thing about practical time traveling is that it doesn't take a lot of hard work, since it is something, you do automatically when you sleep. The main thing you will want to bare in mind is to remind yourself when you go to sleep to remember or record your encounters no matter what they are.

Instead of striving to physical time travel into a probable past, which at best would be a hit and miss operation that would require complicated teleporting knowledge one can get there by consciously isolating time periods in which the events took place. By focusing on specific periods in history you need to read books, watch movies, visit museums, anything that builds up or synchronizes the resonance in your psyche. These methods came to me naturally by noting the kinds of dreams I had in response to the movies, museums or material read. That goes both ways – dream content can influence the kind of moves, museums and books you read because they reflect residual imagery associated with alternate choices you're about to make in the linear stream of the flat plane. When you become cognizant of your dreams imagery you awaken an integral, deep connection to these natural links plus you attract the frequency of the periods and thereby move into or out of the time zones.

Once we isolate a period and get the resonance or frequency in our minds, we slowly pull them, so to speak, from the sea of probabilities and begin to have conscious memories of traveling there. You won't recognize the destinations of most of your dream journeys, but there will often be a sense or feeling of recognition. That's because you're drawing the data molecules from an over-arching whole that organizes them into a meaningful order. In a sense you are inserting or transmitting these frequencies into and life. In a way you are actually recreating the vision of that time period so that your current time and the other correspond in many ways. When that occurs you might actually see people suddenly pass you with a piece or whole garment from the period, hear their speech patterns, see an event that reflects that you're pulling that energy to you. There are many different examples and facsimiles that can be drawn. In that exchange you are using frequency coherence and decoherence (adjusting and readjustment of the frequency lens) to time travel via your psyches to experience a perceived time retained, for the most part, in the virtual space of your imagination or memories.

If, on another note you return to the memory of an actual event, the residual perception is probably distorted because of interfering childhood perspective. The perceptual experience would be something like remembering our home and front yard from our youth as huge and returning to it as an adult to discover, with unsettling amazement, that it was quite different, perhaps small and insignificant. How did it get this way in our memory? Well, it got that way because of our perspective. That is why the real thing we must learn to manipulate or change to achieve effective time traveling is our *frame of reference*. When you began to recognize that you rearrange or reconstruct the event in the light of your new framework accordingly, which hopefully has changed for the better now that you're 'older' and have become, hopefully, more self-aware and definitive about what it is you are actually experiencing or what it is you wish to experience. Beware thought, this is a difficult state of mind to master and perhaps an assumption, because, in truth, we remain like children when it comes to our emotional 'ego I,' unless we diligently train ourselves to monitor our awareness and reign in our reactions.

Nonetheless, whether we change our selves, grow up and become emotionally in charge of our feelings, this form of time traveling to change the past, and hence, the future, is like mixing colored droplets of fluid in a clear liquid and watching it suffuse and blend, changing the pigmentation of the whole medium. Mixed together in this manner it creates something new from what it started out as, but it has subtly changed, so much so that it has been re-created, at least in part. Perhaps the original essence of which you are stays the same, like being born at a certain date, in a house on such-and-such street, etc., but everything else is often couched in the positive or negative perspective in which it hypothetically perceived to occur.

What transpires is a convergence and re-emergence that changes the Whole by its input. This idea applied to the experience of time and order will become clearer as we progress, because it is merely an extension of treating time as molecules or individual droplets of water. Seen as a timeline, our life for instance, is actually a series of molecules strung together in a hypothetical order. Around them cluster our emotional take of the event. For example, the conditions we faced at the moment of our birth, our initial impressions of life, etc. Your subconscious remembers these events and continues to react to them as if they were still originally still happening. In place of the present, they form so-called symbolic scenarios but slightly changed now with each current rehash of similar situations.

Then there are other events that contain meaningful clusters like becoming aware of our parents, talking, growing our first teeth, going to kindergarten or graduating from High School and getting married. Our memory carries the emotional content associated with these periods. In fact, emotions act as the river we learned about earlier in which the individual time molecules reside. Emotions carry the event in a medium relevant of our feelings during that period of our lives. The experience has enormous impact on our impressions of what we experienced. Hence, how you they appeared to you strongly influence not only how you react to present events, but our imagination creates even more fanciful interpretations of that experience. Thus, the original event, becomes changed, added to or detracted from according to what we think we originally experienced. Altogether, the factors of emotions, memory and imagination feedback in a time loop to constantly reconstruct the past and consequently, future events.

Thus, molecules of time seen as emotional energy clusters form concentric fields around which events constellate. As such, each pocket of experience represents the crux of our memories, the timeline story as we grow in the change of becoming. Looking back from our point of perspective in the present are comprised of incremental frequency patterns, like the period between crawling and walking when we were becoming acquainted with our bodies and adapting to growth patterns dictated by the organism. Our memories might also include negative recollections of falling and hurting ourselves as we tried to walk, which includes critical feedback from those around us such as siblings or parents. Thus we tend to mix these cluster-building feelings in with the events, sometimes getting locked into a bad experience associated with that period and wishing it could be changed but feeling bound by the pain and fear.

This is where practical time traveling comes in to save the day. It allows alteration because it encourages borrowing from alternate or parallel realities. These probable realities are composed of different emotional and visual takes on the primary experience as we relate to it in the present. It's all a sort of re-shuffling of content and context and the re-assemblage of a new perspective. In essence, it is a powerful tool for changing future's that might have been initially fixed by poor perspectives in the past. The great thing about the nature of time and space is its malleability; they can be re-shuffled too. Reality has a pliable plastic quality hence it is as alterable as is our responses to it. In fact, the inter-exchange of data between the subjective and objective content alters of each. As we change our subjective feelings and impressions, we see them different and in turn that changes how they affect us. For instance, if we see ourselves as being denied a happy childhood because we came from the wrong side of town and therefore feel rejected by life and people in general, we might look for data that reinterprets the situation. Thus, our effort to change how we respond to these memories by re-inventing or changing historical context, alters our feelings about the original events, at least as we remember them. In effect, it also changes how we relate to those who were a part of the original story, so much so that it sends out signals to the people responsible and affects them likewise. In turn they send vibes to us, even though they might not be aware of it except perhaps by sudden changes in their feelings toward us, or with other people who symbolically have something in common with those feelings.

The feelings that we get might become altered by our 'reaching out' into spacetime, the desire to open up and change, thus people who often feel maligned by fate and picked on by God who grew up on the wrong side of the tracks, so to speak, undergo a bifurcation and experience a life change. From growing up with poor self-esteem and the desire to avoid people because of those bad memories, they began to growing in feelings of self-worth and began working toward the common good of others, rather than taking out their pain and frustration on everyone around them. Instead of compounding problems with others by reacting to memories, they take a deeper look into themselves to discover a whole new person.

Again, it's the plasticity of spacetime that makes it possible to change and the presence of the spiral template that maintains the order while undergoing alteration. Thus any efforts to expand beyond the confines of our central hub can change those experiences into something different while maintaining something of the original order. This is an especially powerful visualization after coming into realization that reality is amenable to change, that nothing's fixed except the tendency toward order; it makes anything appear possible. That's clustering in itself. It builds momentum and acceleration into the movement toward future goals.

In terms of memory and altered self-image in pursuit of future targets, approach is everything, because it's the glue that keeps causing memories to be rebuilt. They cluster around feelings like bee a flower, because they get reenergized over and over. As I have mentioned before, any clusters are alterable, and the more you make an effort to borrow new increments to replace the old, the quicker is the transition for several reasons: a) your belief and effort brings in fresh energy which builds the momentum, and b) with fresh energy you add to the infinite potential of the dynamo to create. Energy is power! It makes the wheel go round. With it anything is possible; but it takes meditation and concentration to get it to spin really fast and most of all, the willingness to let go and let flow allows the energies to flow through the creative channel of the template.

In short, negative memories benefit by practical time traveling because as we revisit those periods and reassess who we are or *who we thought we were and reexamine why we got there and what we experienced*, we up the potential energy to make changes occur the way we want them in our future target destination. Like a monitored moon landing by a rover commandeered from earth, we assure the virtual success of future missions. Thus, each visit leaves an information track that we can recognize and easily follow and thereby come up with a totally new scenario without getting too far off of our target goal. In fact, after a while it will become fun, because once you're used to altering space-time and you get the knack of it there are space-time perks. For one thing you can start to insert altered pictures at will, for example in the past, and watch how they rearrange your adjustment to present situations. Each one will be complete with new emotional content as they shift back into the timeline from the continuum. What you will learn to accomplish is deconstruction of what is often thought of as a 'childhood self' in the light of 'a reassessed current self' albeit with a totally new subjective emotional scenario.

All of this you can achieve at will because of the plastic nature of space and time in confluence with the continuum. It is all funneled through the order-producing template of the spiral. Down here in the physical time appears to flow from past into future as if on a flat plane, like a piece of paper. However, from the perspective another perspective the straight-line order of time dissolves into individual fragments or cells. Bear in mind, that time cells are data molecules or frequency islands around which continents of information cluster. These molecules are synonymous with individual cells on their way to form multicellular clusters. A molecule forms around a central information point along a hypothetical straight line in two dimensional flat spaces. However, in terms of curved space you get a totally different picture. To get the broader panorama visualize a landscape from an airplane and you get a sense of the islands of time emerging into one big Whole. From the ground level it would be hard to get beyond the straight line due to the causal fragmentation of time which is somewhat like hills and bulging clusters that rise and fall like solitary vortices in an ocean of movement.

Continue changing perspective from one Whole to another and eventually the isolated data molecules began to emerge into mega clusters and galaxies of systems within systems are seen. If you expand your perspective even further you began to see that the multicellular creature is part of a symbiotic community and the community a country and so on. You can expand this perspective or shrink it as far as you like, what you see depends on your point of perspective. Before the change in perspective or frequency, they were all simply points, independent molecules of time or intervals on a string like pearls in a necklace. They can either be viewed as frequency periods, oscillating masses of information floating about in a void, drawing others like them by their self-similarity when the bugle of synchrony is sounded. Thereafter, they all tend cluster together, little snowballs forming a coherent file of order, gathered around a central hub of molecules if tune quivering with a common meaning and purpose. And so reality is formed out of this clustering; most of it which goes on from a hyper-dimensional level, yet all moving unerringly toward a singular target event in a virtual future.

As heretofore mentioned, the so-called river of time that is seen as flowing from past into future is actually composed of these multitudes of individual information centers that take the form of incremental frequency patterns. Each of these incremental orders represents different stages or points where the organism bifurcated or changed; in this way the matrix transforms into an organic whole. Gathered about a central theme as cells gather around an organic Whole, they contribute each according to their individual creativity and input in the improvisation that becomes the spirit of the composition.

Like snowflakes in a snowstorm, or droplets of water molecules in a rivers stream, or individual drivers on a thoroughfare, all, on the surface apparently going independently on their way, without coherent order until, suddenly, the seem to converge (self-organize) into a common symphony of Wholeness. Without the emergent properties of the spiral dynamo to channel order, these random islands of time would remain in a chaos of disarray, floating about as it were, in an endless void.

However once drawn by the convergence power of the swirling dynamo to bend the field, a synchrony of space-time bubbles become a powerful, cascading river of order, like the water molecules that transform into a stream. One caveat must be kept in mind: *eliminate the channel and the water molecules disperse into their own tonal zones as they dissipate into disarray.* When the direction of the field is reversed from centripetal to centrifugal, it can totally alter the flow from energy into order to order into energy. The template creates the field according to the direction of the flow, which can be seen in either right or left rotating helical systems.

So what we discover is that there is no true order to these centers of space-time except the modicum of order provided by the organizational properties of the spiral template. In the background of all order the spiral gathers random information bits into synchronized patterns of order that are then directed toward specific goals. Like lines of tin soldiers, it groups them into patterns, displaying the unifying qualities of their vibrations so that the pieces converge into the spontaneous picture we call order. In the final outcome the organizational properties of the underlying template directs all order like a temporal orchestral conductor the rhythms of space-time. Like a mirror of the template our psyches orchestrate our personal reality, miming shall we say the rhythms in the heavens in their oscillation from mind to brain. As each individual musician in their own world follow the tempo and direction of the conductor, all contribute spontaneously to the final musical composition. Such is the role of the individual to the collective ego.

From a subjective perspective the ego directs its lens toward goals that reflect the emotional curvature of their beliefs, while at the same time keeping an 'inner ear' out for the collective composition like an eye on a tempo-keeping conductor. In short, despite the convex or concave, contractive or expansive lens of the individual, the data undergoes a translation. It receives both a subjective and objective reconstruction that reflects the individual's interpretation of both angles. Imagine going to watch a movie that the audience could plug into and alter at will, to get an idea of how this spontaneous interaction might play out. For instance, an extroverted individual with a positive mind slant might like the whole production to play out in an uplifting or even lovable way, while a dreary introvert, emotionally burdened with suspicion borne of isolation would seek to annihilate the opposition and eliminate intrusions of all kinds from impinging on his privacy.

But this isn't all bad or all good, ideally, in some cases, a versatile individual views reality like an ambivert or from both angles simultaneously. Janus-faced, they see from dual directions without specific preference for order, thus they often lack clear boundaries. Like Janus or Mercury their true job is translator, or messenger – that's where some of their problems arise. Being a translator or interpreter, they are good at translating for others, but poor (because of the dualisms) at translating details for themselves. In fact, their subjective vision is poor because of the versatility which creates problems in being decisive rendering them over-compensating, wishy-washy and sometimes incapable of reacting or even acting. These individuals fail in reaching organizational depth, going with the flow or flowing with the go; unless of course they learn to utilize their gift. There are, of course, pluses and minuses with all personality types, such as adaptability and communication, but often they lack a cohesive center from which to begin anew. Hence, without a concrete central self an individual can come off wishy-washy or shallow, superficial or even conniving and opportunistic. Over sensitivity to influences, vibrations of all types in particular are the cause, such as found in a leader that lacks the courage of conviction to follow through with his decisions and looks or the world to tell him what he must do.

Not all introverts are agoraphobic or extroverts wholly outgoing, for instance, everyone is more likely than not to have an admixture of qualities. By the way, my interpretations of introverts or extroverts here are not meant to imply that this is an exact analysis of the personality type – they are merely probable examples. It is best with thine own self be true. Be objective and honest about who you are and what you feel and look for your subjective influences and above all NOTE THE EMOTIONAL CONNECTIONS.

Keep in mind that emotions rule the personality type and establish the hub around which their interests and associations constellate. Some people may need the outside help of a counselor to get an objective picture of where your self-image lies. Remember that that the terms introvert, extrovert or ambivert are psychological terms that refer to personality types in general. As such, in this book, they represent directions of energy flow, 'intro' for toward the self, or 'extra' or away from self, 'ambit' meaning both ways. In any case, one should seek some form of meditation technique to develop focus once finding one's emotional center or building an identity core.

Thus, learning to find a balance between the whole and the part can be assuaged with deepened insight into your general personality type and furnish keys to personal dream data. It can also alert you to general energy flows coming or going in your direction especially when examining déjà vu's or following through with precognitive hunches and feelings. Once integrated into conscious planning a certain modicum of versatility in focus is achievable providing it is modified by these intuitive tools. Moreover, if one wishes to make changes in their identity cones, *that inner, concentric spiral of self that forms the central locus of their focus*, they must learn to master the ego's control tower. Unless the central arena is commandeered, like the confluence of radars oscillating protracted path, then the important data contained in its bits will be obscured by the limitations of the trans-ciever. Hence, hitting target goals in a virtual future are nearly impossible to predict.

An excerpt from the following newspaper clipping provides mute testimony as to the outcome of the ego's control tower in the construction of potentially faulty trans-cieivers. Recently, I encountered an interesting article about Hillary Clinton featuring excerpts from her new book, *Hard Choices* which demonstrated how perspective influences target outcomes. In the book Hillary writes about revisiting past decisions and what she feels she's learned that might help her accomplish similar goals in what I would term another probable future. Clinton, a potential 2016 Democratic presidential candidate, points out that her four years tenure in the State Department under President Barrack Obama improved her sense of planning. Clinton states that it taught her much about the character of the United States, i.e., "*…its exceptional strengths and what it will take for us to complete and thrive at home and abroad.*" Interestingly, she got a brief look into some vain regrets, since she mentions 'hindsight, as it is often called, i.e., the facing of difficulties in predicting the outcome of decision making and the vain regrets of misjudging,

As is usually the case with the benefit of hindsight, I wish we could go back and revisit certain choices. But I'm proud of what we accomplished." And - "This century began traumatically for our country, with the terrorist attacks on 9/11, the long wars that followed, and the Great Recession. We needed to do better,   and I believe we did. Continuing in this vein, Clinton opines perceptively that, "*Our choices and how we handle them shape the people we become. For leaders and nations, they can mean the difference between war and peace, poverty and prosperity.*" Obviously sensing the importance of intuitive heuristics in the creative momentum of the snowball, she went on to say."…*the need to keep America safe, strong, and prosperous presents an endless set of choices many of which come with imperfect information and conflicting imperatives.*"[ψ] There it is then – '*imperfect information*', no doubt limited to distortion of a singular plane of perspective; information limited by vision and input. However, had its content been fed by a clustering of players in the grand opera, that is, from a community 'inside' and 'outside' or the time stream, rather than a single spotlight of subjectivity, it could have improved its potential to accomplish its mission and purpose of hitting that virtual target in the 'ideal' future.

For one thing, the theme and ideas were played reflected the limited input of one performer acting singly in a linear fashion, sans the advantage of an intuitive sense of being connected to an enhanced perspective. Clearly, her range of vision was stilted by a linear line of reasoning and lacked a holistic approach. In short, Clinton did not borrow readily from her resources, thus her creative self-organization shows the results of poor input and planning. There is no sense of a feedback between 'islands of time' and the target goal that comes with the precognitive feedback of time traveling which could have supplanted errors resulting from single line reasoning.

In short, the suggestion by Clinton that if she had '*known then what she knows now*', implies she felt locked into the present and didn't sense any *outside* options probabilities. She also shows poor decisions made because she was spending too much time fearing what the 'guys' would think; inhibited by fear of rejection because of criticism by a male-dominated profession. In short, she was afraid to venture forth and 'feel' outside-the-box, in fact, she bound by the limitations of a convex lens which directed the stream of information into too narrow of a perspective. This means she blocked her feminine stream of creative potential.

Interestingly, now she may become a better leader, to which I must concur, because she has possibly learned enough to know by looking back at her limitations in perspective through hindsight to make use of an expansive perspective in her viewing lens. Relax and let go would be the key words. If she could have stepped momentarily outside the present of the rigid dictates she projected upon her self – by first getting a good look outside her introversion, how she viewed reality and why, success in her future would come about much easier. But again, this is the problem with hind-sight based reasoning. When we employ, we are usually on the approach side of success and not vice versa. Thus we tend to see through our fears and expectations which are often clouded with fears of failure brought about by operating in new turf. As far as Clinton's expectations, it seems she expected (and hence acquiesced) to the idea of rejection and the struggle to be recognized or accepted as an equal, since these elements are clearly visible in her perspective. Following that baptism she underwent a male conversion persona, i.e., got harder, tougher, and more incisive – now she can afford to relax and let her feminine side to re-emerge which is auspicious in terms of potential success. Looking at her from a grander panorama it appears she was unconsciously striving to gain appeal by getting approval from those who meant to keep her back, thwart her success. Following this reasoning we discover a person who needs to fail a little to get ahead, (which has more of an ambivert quality to it) perhaps to make herself appear not to be too ambitious and hopefully heighten her appeal to conservatives. It is also a direct reflection of her feelings that America isn't ready for a woman to lead and that somehow, she had to go through this gauntlet of suffering to be accepted. With that in mind, I can't help but feel that her second time around should prove successful. Now, instead of putting down what a woman should capitalize on – her intuition, she is acting on these qualities demonstrating that she has grown up in self-esteem and is therefore accepting of her full powers as a complete person. This way she will avert a poor outcome engendered by being out-of-sync with who she is as a person in relationship to the collective ego. Instead of not trusting her aim or refusing to rely on collective advice she can now side-step disappointing hindsight. All these elements are former problems that contributed to impetuous decisions made from a linear perspective.

Bear in mind that a linear perspective, in this regard, could be seen as a 2-d flat plane which limits the magnitude of the incoming data to a single sliver of a track. Making use of the infinite potential of the expansive-contractive qualities of her lens, Hillary can now tap the infinite the islands of probable time increments while simultaneously increasing the power of her persona exponentially. Hence, the energy in potentia has greater probability to gain the momentum it needs to turn into an avalanche, if she employs what she learns and doesn't fall back on old habit patterns.

Looking back, this is how the snowball effect got going in the first place. It was manufactured by a basic pattern of anticipated order which built in increments, borrowing as it rolled from infinite probable time lines until it escalated into a mega-manifestation. Where it rolls in terms of its outcome depends upon the maker. Order will prevail regardless of how we manifest it, but its structure and momentum depends upon our focus. It is the pattern by which all patterns are created. Per usual, it is a pattern which builds around a predominant centralized theme, while borrowing from the probabilities of the "Greater Whole" what naturally adheres to it. Thus, it grows exponentially; size adding to momentum, and so on.

Again: by its *structuring effect* I mean its ability to build from a central model. This is the key to any form of emergence, which it - by the way - doesn't do by itself, but through the input of the joint creativity available in each separate island of probability. The big thing to keep in mind, the snowball can build into the desired effects at point in the game. Remember: reality is plastic, so continue to restructure as you go with the flow, adding or subtracting as the need arises, never giving into the fear of failure because there is no end except the end you choose.

Improvise to get all Your Ducks in a Row

And now to add one final thought about getting all your ducks in a row while appearing to be randomly innovative. A uniquely talented and creative friend of mine composed an interesting spiral emergence process centralized around the improvisational qualities of a progressive jazz band. The idea proves to have all the earmarks of a Tesla snowball that is certain to cascade into a major development, simply because its predictive qualities borrow from the individual spirit of its members. A bands potential to predict the success of its composition often lies dormant but palpable in the two major aspects; spontaneity and individuality. For the composition to channel its musical snowball into symphonic greatness it must: a) allow for the un-reined inspirational freedom latent in each player to emerge; and b) encourage that freedom to converge into the bands self-organization spontaneously. These two elements coupled together ensure that a *higher order* shall arise reflective of the convergence of the potential of the individual and the group. This is the nature of the clustering effect leading to a contagion.

The single most important element, the template of order, automatically guides the clustering effect, if we trust spontaneity and improvisation to run their course. Such freedom to express the unlimited potential within each individual turns an ordinary production into a magnificent production. Like the snowball rolling down the hill, the production progressively draws from energized activity of its own acceleration which in turn exacerbates its potential outcome. Like the snowball, the band has spontaneous taken a flight down a natural course beginning in the intent of the individual and leading to its ultimate cessation. Under the organizational force of the spiral dynamo, like Tesla's tiny snowball, the improvised production automatically gathers vast power as it builds, thus adding to its acceleration which in turn magnifies it far beyond a composition shrouded in the barriers of limited self-expression.

Thus, the jazz ensemble gathers musical 'volume' or mass from the ongoing input of an unlimited and continuously converging and interactive Whole. Connecting through synchrony modulated by the composition itself, each individual member contributes more energy as the Whole piece grows. In a word it snowballs through its inter-connectedness guided or held together by a self-same compositional synchrony moving like an unyielding arrow to hit the dead-center of its precognitive target. In this way the completed rendition is far more than the contribution of each singular contributor, yet contains that and more in the ostensive outcome. Wholeness as a virtual and always present target far outshines the linearity of any singular course; hence its virtual but sundry target is always but never the same. Improvised as it goes through the input of each individual, the snowball gathers about it a growing yet unifying synchrony while simultaneously moving toward one centralized goal. Thus, the group thrives and grows through the inspiration of its individuality compounding exponentially what is dormant in all within an emerging, self-organizing Whole.

Thinking back on Tesla's model for his poly-phase alternating current generators, this was his purpose, that is, to accelerate and/or exacerbate the potential of the Whole by kicking up the volume from coils or energy sources placed in a circle around its rotating center. Thus, the initial input of energy from the first coil is amplified by the second and so on until by the time it reaches the 9th one on its circumference, its total amps upped exponentially to millions of ergs. This same principle can easily be applied to any situation in which various players input their creative juices into the creation of a new product, rather than are controlled by a top-down CEO, for instance, who calls all the shots. This was the essential limitations of Edison's electrical generator model; its output was restricted because its motor rotated around only one central core to derive its energy source.

Thus, the total output only reflected whatever the input of that initial source turned out to be which wasn't much, especially because Edison feared harnessing the potential resources of huge contributing sources, sensing that his direct current carriers would break down in the process. So what we see is that far outside its awareness, every contributing group or process is directed by the spirals properties in the channeling of many resources into one creative endeavor. Hence, if the input is limited, the overall potential of a creation is stymied or maybe even destroyed before its inception with only one contributing source by which it can grow exponentially. In a word, the spiral provides the key that diversity unlocks in the creativity process by compounding the Many into the ONE. Symmetry and asymmetry or order and chaos work in creative harmony to bring into manifestation beauty and function.

Through it all, individual intent contributes by expanding the process in its momentum-gathering growth toward future goals as it builds by sheer numerical input; each part inversely receiving and transmitting according to the square of its vision. In that sense the power of individually motivated by the inherent infinite potential available through improvisation magnifies the whole of the composition as it is channeled toward a central goal.

Simply put: THE ONE WINS THROUGH THE WINNING OF THE MANY AND THE MANY BECAUSE OF THE ONE.

In a nutshell this is the essential deep truth of the spiral template. Taken as a complete process of emergence fed by the individual streams flowing into the oceanic vision, its far-ranging drive is essentially predictive, meaning possessing the ability to gather information from incremental, free-floating islands of time normally outside its visible goals. These increments of time or frequency molecules, draw from a vast well of probabilities which directionally are unlimited by the linear arrow of time. Thus, the vision of the greater Whole is the sum of the individual Parts *multiplied* by the square of the collective intent, albeit a palpable but hypothetically measurable number in terms of the dynamics of the output compared to the input. The whole draws its energy from the infinite potential islands of time beyond the main stream in accordance to their participation in any creative endeavor.

Hence when focused the contribution of these individual islands of creativity automatically contribute momentum to the snowball of improvisation, compelling increased potentiality for success by dint of their respective gravitational fields. In this way they eliminate the dam of the commonplace production which blocks the potential creativity of the average band playing strictly by rote. Groups such as those which deny the innovation or individual input through inspiration delineates great from mundane creations. Commonplace productions evolved from limitations wrought by the standard playing of a sundry piece sadly standing between its present and future composition possibilities.

Using the jazz ensemble as a working analogy for the creative process of the spiral dynamo we can deduce that working together like a wheel-within-a-wheel, life, like a musical spiral process of emergence - feeds off individuality to deftly sidestep the linearity of time and space to borrow from the island increments of time data that sidesteps the present to precog Nate and/or anticipate the future. However, should the band limit its potential energy to the collective production the singularity of one input such as the musical score, lacking access to improvisation it will have reduced the viability of its production to a mundane recitation within a limited scope so far as its future is concerned. It does this because it obscures the potential contribution of the input of its members, thus dampening the creative spirit of the Whole. The linearity of its parts could be compared to a causal or temporal route taken from point a to z along a road toward a goal hopelessly limited by a flat plane point of view. By accessing the curvature of the spiral, that deeper whole which guides unerringly the parts into order, it connects the unifying power of synchrony, or relative mass which in turn aids in the production and velocity of its actualization.

Have fun with these experimentations with your personal space-time travel port, and watch how quickly you accelerate once you get the hang of tuning into the continuum!

MEDITATIONS

1. You have already ventured into your so-called future to imagine yourself in different potential realities. This time while you're in these worlds, take time to look around and record what you see around you.

2. If you find yourself meeting people, try to communicate with them. If you find yourself walking, feel the earth beneath your feet, the sun on your face, or the wind in your hair. Make it a tactile encounter and employ as many of your senses as possible in the situation.

3. Lie down and reach out with your mind. What do you feel? If nothing or little at first, continue to feel around in the space about you. What do you feel? Do you sense anything? What does it feel like? Get use to recording your impressions. You are building your inner sensory experience.

4. Take time to notice how the visible world seems to pivot on miniscule or even totally invisible things.

5. Watch small almost microscopic things grow into large events. Strive to feel connected to these events.

6. When you listen to music, really listen, not just with your ears but with your heart and soul, so to speak. Get into music from within. Notice how you are affected by its vibration. Watch its effect upon others and realize that we are all moved by that which is invisible but felt.

7. Look for the holistic aspect of events, like synchronicities we've talked about. See events in the physical world as connected to non-visible aspects totally outside our sensory range.

8. Strive to do as many things spontaneously as you can and watch the outcome. What does it say about your greater self?

9. Notice how people are pulled together into collective productions. In these events take note of the fact that they are orchestrated by a larger whole far outside the present.

10. Reach out into your so-called future. Strive to imagine it. Feel for it. When you have a sense of it, write it down. Is it the reality you want to reach? If not, make an effort to interject totally new scenario's into it. Remember: you can change the future before it happens and therefore alter where you going in the so-called present.

11. Imagine yourself a time traveler and actively look for fellow travelers from other dimensions impinging on ours. Read Fortean Magazine and study Charles Fort. Allow yourself to take some risks and do things totally different then you would normally do.

12. Try out different selves. See how good of an actor you can be by switching your present personality while taking on a new one. This activity gives you greater flexibility in your self-identity and thereby allows you step outside your own time flow.

13. Check your dreams each day when you awake for evidence of time traveling. Look for unusual encounters, those that bring you in contact with inventions that you have never seen before, people who you get a sense of knowing but can't identify, feelings like you been there before many times.

14. Make a resolution to encourage contact with these places or their inhabitants. Check out any inventions, books, interesting scenarios that may suggest you've traveled into your own future or past. Ask your friends if they've had any unusual dreams – don't' be surprised if the two of you have met and traveled to other worlds during your dream time.

15. Buy a drum and join a drumming circle or get involved in a hip-hop dance class. Go to a concert and listen to music that is totally different than the genre your interested in. Expand your sensitivities. Be as spontaneous as possible and let rhythm and spontaneity become a vital part of your life in every way

BIBLIOGRAPHY

Bernoulli, Jacques. The Law of Large Numbers. 1654-1705.

Burger, Edward and Starbird, Michael. Coincidences, Chaos, and all that Math Jazz: Making Light of Weighty Ideas. 2006. W.W. Norton & Co. Reprint Ed.

Capra, Fritjof. The Web of Life: A New Scientific Understanding of Living Systems. 1996. New York Anchor Books.

Feynman, Richard P. 1985. QED: The Strange Theory of Light and Matter. Princeton Univ. Press P. 129.

Filippenko, Alex. Great Discourses on Tape. University of California at Berkeley.

Gladwell, Malcolm. The Tipping Point. 2000-2002. Little Brown & Company. 2000-2002.

Grof, Stanislaf M.D. The Holotropic Mind: The Three Levels of Human Consciousness and How they Shape our Lives. SF. California: 1993. Harper San Francisco. A division of Harper-Collins.

Haigh, John. Taking Chances: Winning with Probabilities. 2003. Oxford Univ. Press.

Holt, Ronald. The Spiral and the Holographic Matrix. Ascension Now website. Flow of Life research. Sacred Geometry.

Jaynes, Julian. The Origin of Consciousness. 1976. Page 141, The God-King.

Johnson, Steven. Emergence: The Connected Life of Ants, Brains, Cities and Software. 2002. Scribner Reprinted Edition.

Johnson, Steven. Future Perfect. 2012. Riverside Books. Penguin Group.

Krippendorff, Klaus. From: A Dictionary of Cybernetics. An updated report dated Feb 2. 1986.

Lawler, Robert. Sacred Geometry. 1989, Thames & Hudson. N.Y. N.Y.

Liddell, Henry George: Scott, Robert, A Greek-English Lexicon of the Perseus Project.

O'Neil, John. Prodigal Genius. The Life of Tesla. 1978. Angriff Press. Hollywood, Ca. 90078.

Peat, F. David. Synchronicity: The Bridge Between Matter and Mind, Bantam New Age Books.

Penguin Reference Dictionary of Biology. 11th. Edition -2004.

Prigogine, Illya. The End of Certainty. The Free Press. 1997.

Rose, Ronald. The Future of the Brain, Page 62. Chapter: From 1 to 100 Billion.
Ward, Geoff. Spirals. Green Magic.
Watson, James. DNA: The Secret of Life. 2003. Random House.
Wolfson, Richard. Einstein's Relativity and the Quantum Revolution. Modern Physics for Non-Scientists. 2000. Great Courses on Tape.

ABOUT THE AUTHOR

Nahu has been a professional psychic reader, teacher, writer and poet for over forty years. In addition to being an avid consumer of the latest scientific research, he has given much time and serious thought to cryptozoology, UFO phenomena, the paranormal, metaphysics and mysticism. He is also an author of three other books: *UFOs: God from Inner Space, Dolphina's World and Other Stories, Wavelets,* a volume of mystical poems. The concept of the spiral force or template is a part of Nahu's ongoing theory of the emergence of life and all order in the cosmos. A more thorough examination of this theory can be found in the February 2008 academic journal of WORLD FUTURES (Taylor & Francis) entitled: *The Revolution in the Evolution from Simple to Complex Systems.*
Nahu now resides in Eugene, Oregon with his wife Elena of 16 years. The two enjoy writing and exploring the reaches of the psyche in addition to hiking, working out, running and martial arts.

www.ingramcontent.com/pod-product-compliance
Lightning Source LLC
Chambersburg PA
CBHW070851180526
45168CB00005B/1770